Praise for Troubleshooting Life

"Think of this book as a software update for your soul. With wit, wisdom, and surprising sources, Malik shows you how to debug your mindset and upgrade your life. I love the page-a-day format – stay with it for a month, watch your life change, and you'll be hooked till the last page."

— Salvador Litvak, film director, author, influencer

"Akash Malik's Troubleshooting Life blends wisdom, practicality, and creativity into a format that speaks to professionals and dreamers alike. His one-page-a-day approach challenges readers to think differently, act decisively, and lead with clarity. It's a rare book that you can both learn from and live by. It is worth the read."

— Plinio Ayala, CEO of Per Scholas

"Troubleshooting Life is a masterclass in modern resilience—delivered one brilliant micro-lesson at a time. If you want to have a year of thinking deeply and pushing yourself to your best version of you, Troubleshooting Life is your hard truth served up with creative soul."

— Caitlyn Brazill, President, Per Scholas

"This is the kind of book you leave out on your coffee table or desk. It invites reflection."

— Irina Kensinger, Director of Enterprise Risk, CISO-NA

"Troubleshooting Life is like daily debugging for your mental codebase. With one page a day, Akash Malik helps you trace thought loops, patch outdated patterns, and refactor your mindset for long-term resilience. Whether you're stuck in an infinite loop or just due for a reboot, this book delivers practical updates for your internal architecture."

— Dustin Lehr, application security Leader, co-founder of Katilyst

"If you take seriously this adventure we call life, you need to read Troubleshooting Life. It's a truly honest and insightful book that expertly combines the old and the new, helping anyone on their life's journey."

— Richard Greenberg, CISSP, Information Systems Security Association (ISSA) Hall of Fame

TROUBLESHOOTING LIFE

366 DAILY ONE-MINUTE IDEAS TO MAKE THIS YEAR YOUR BEST EVER

Akash Malik

www.akashlinks.com

www.highpointpubs.com

Copyright © 2025 by Akash Malik

All rights reserved. Published in the United States of America. No part of this book may be reproduced or transmitted in any form or by any means, graphic, electronic or mechanical, including photocopying, recording, taping or by any information storage or retrieval system, without permission in writing from the publisher.

This edition published by Highpoint Life.

For information, write to info@highpointpubs.com.

First Edition
ISBN: 979-8-9908488-9-4

Library of Congress Cataloging-in-Publication Data
Malik, Akash
Troubleshooting Life: 366 Daily One-Minute Ideas to Make This Year Your Best Ever

Summary: "*Troubleshooting Life* provides readers with 366 one-minute life lessons, or *neetis*. The book is organized into 366 quotes, one for each day of the year, in three sections: Education, Entertainment, and Enlightenment. Readers can read one each morning as a way to set their compass for new levels of happiness and success." — Provided by publisher.

ISBN: 979-8-9908488-9-4 (paperback)
1. Self-Help: Personal Growth

Library of Congress Control Number: 2025910989

Cover and interior design by Sarah Clarehart.

Manufactured in the United States of America

EPIGRAPH from macOS Dictionary

trou·ble·shoot | ˈtrəbəlˌSHo͞ot | verb

1 solve serious problems for a company or other organization:

"When managers troubleshoot, it strengthens the whole team."
"One overworked executive flew from country to country troubleshooting problems."

2 trace and correct faults in a mechanical or electronic system:

"Follow the error messages to troubleshoot the malfunction."
"Courses dealing with PC repair and troubleshooting are proving to be heavily subscribed."

life | līf | noun (plural lives | līvz |)

1 the condition that distinguishes animals and plants from inorganic matter:

"Scientists continue to investigate the origins of life."
"The ice cream vendors were the only signs of life."

2 (In art) the depiction of a subject from a real model, rather than from an artist's imagination:

"The pose and clothing were sketched from life."
"In art class we practiced life drawings."

CONTENT HOME +

Epigraph	iii
Dedication	vii
Acknowledgements	ix
Introduction	xi

Dedication

Family and Friends

Temple University

Edison High School

Thomas Jefferson Middle School

John Marshall Elementary School

Acknowledgements

Amar Chitra Katha, the ancient thinkers/writers, and modern artists.

Per Scholas

Chanakya

Aristotle

Plato

Socrates

DISCLAIMER: This book reflects the author's personal reflections, reactions and interpretations of real-life events. Although real people and conversations inspired many entries, in many cases edits to names and identifying details have been made to protect the privacy of individuals. This book content is provided by the author for educational and reflective purposes only.

INTRODUCTION

Dec 16, 2021, 8:06 pm EST. *Troubleshooting Life* is born.

Akash, what is it that you wish to share with people of this planet? You do have a gift, you know.

Sure, sometimes you have tearful moments.

Moments you struggled to get yourself out of bed.

What's a person to do?

You start troubleshooting life.

A person remembers the words of Marcus Aurelius, translated into English by Gregory Hayes.

> "We have to sleep sometime…. Agreed. But nature set a limit on that—as it did on eating and drinking. And you're over the limit. You've had more than enough of that.
>
> But not of working. There, you're still below your quota.
>
> You don't love yourself enough.
>
> Or you'd love your nature too, and what it demands of you.
>
> People who love what they do wear themselves down doing it. They even forget to wash or eat. Do you have less respect for your own nature than the engraver does for engraving, the dancer for the dance, the miser for money, the social climber for status?
>
> When they're really possessed by what they do, they'd rather stop eating and sleeping than give up practicing their arts. Is helping others less valuable to you?"

The book this is from, *Meditations,* was never meant to be published because it is the diary of a true **philosopher-king**, such as the one Plato envisioned in *The Republic*.

Reader, what I once saw as my "curse," I now see as my "gift." I realized that whenever I was bored, I enjoyed expressing myself with any variety of implements: classic pen and paper, iCloud Notes, Google Docs, Microsoft Word, Apple Pages, Final Draft, Game Boy or PlayStation, or even Facebook media input boxes!

At this moment I realize that in my 30 years of life, I have lived through many years of media technology development, electronic or not, from birth, to puberty, to manhood.

Reader, perhaps you are five years old. Or 15. Or 85!

The world of 2026 and beyond is always on fire, and changing rapidly, especially as Big Tech companies continue swallowing Hollywood in the chess game of computing dominance.

At this point it has been many years since 2019, when I first discovered Ryan Holiday and his Stoic philosophy after the "shipwreck" of losing two part-time jobs. Holiday writes about the Stoic philosopher who had a shipwreck, Zeno, and here I was in my own shipwreck. I burned through my savings. I moved back in with my parents. I had a quarter-life crisis.

I interviewed at many different companies in New Jersey and New York in 2019. On weekends, I did oral history interviews with my grandparents and other family members about surviving the partition of India. Oral history is the best kind, an attempt to preserve history in the words of its survivors, like Spielberg, collecting testimonies of Holocaust survivors during the 1990s.

Looking back at the footage I recorded in 2019, I am happy I am not dead from COVID and still able to write and shoot more. Because I lived through a lot. I'd imagine so have you, Reader.

About the troubleshooting...

I have helped a great deal of people through my work at Per Scholas, a nationwide school that provides tuition-free tech training. I now feel this book is another great medium for me to help even more people, across multiple forms of media.

Troubleshooting Life is my attempt to give you life lessons, or *neetis*, I learned in just about 30 years of life.

I chose to organize this book into 366 quotes, one for each day of the year, in three sections:

Education, Entertainment, and Enlightenment. I suggest you read one each morning as a way to set your compass for new levels of happiness and success.

Throughout this book I have included links to source information that supports my themes and can possibly open some new windows for you! These links can all be found at www.Akashlinks.com!

I frequently quote books and people I love learning from. *Daily Stoic*, Chanakya Neeti, Dr. Radhakrishnan Pillai, or Aristotle, or cloud computing or cybersecurity … my curiosity is insatiable.

"Troubleshooting" is a word we often see in IT and do not like seeing. It is our car, computer, phone, tablet, or watch that stops working, and so our life is on hold.

We might call or chat someone to "shoot the troubles" square in the face to repair a device, like my parents calling me to help them with technology, or a Per Scholas learner-turned-alumni now troubleshooting cyberthreats at Spotify, or Barclays, or JP Morgan Chase.

We troubleshoot, then we move on with our lives or business, *ideally*.

But again, the world is anything but ideal these days.

Troubleshooters are sort of like cowboys, with a belt of tools, thoughts, feelings… like Jack Daniels, wearing a black hat or a white hat, like in old John Ford movies… or TV shows like *Gunsmoke* (1955-1975).

These terms, such as "black hat" or "white hat" from old Westerns, later became hacker terms, and since new antiracist movements have grown in prominence post-George Floyd (as they should), these are being updated along with expressions such as "master/slave" (to "authorized/nonauthorized" or "primary/secondary"). Getting the words right matters a lot.

But back to cowboys and Westerns. This is an "indigenous" American film genre, according to Martin Scorsese, a filmmaker whose work I write about a lot, as well as the work of those he inspires.

Picture a mother of two at my current age, 30, who enrolls at Per Scholas in a remote class for IT Support. Or Amazon Web Services (AWS). Or Cybersecurity, taught by me or another on the team.

She has to change diapers. Cook lunch. Answer the door, while wearing a headset or AirPods, tuning into Zoom class, as I sell and demo CompTIA or Amazon or Google training materials.

At times, she also has to work with her classmates. You can picture Coach Boone, played by Denzel Washington, in Remember the Titans (2000) as a Per Scholas "character," too.

Or me, of course—a young media professional sick of making no money as tech companies make billions, who decided to suck it up and go into tech.

When the pandemic of 2020 hit, my job became remote. Suddenly I was tasked with transforming diverse, immature technologists into troubleshooting cowboys for Per Scholas' employer partners, to unlock potential and change the face of tech and build economies.

I truly love working at Per Scholas, and I am glad I survived a 3 percent company-wide layoff in June 2023.

And hopefully, through 365 *neetis*, the blessing of my ancestors in undivided India, Chanakya, Ganesha, and Veda Vyasa, I hope that reading one page daily can help you in troubleshooting life, too.

The Indian comic book publisher Amar Chitra Katha publishes books that stick with me about the interpretation of Veda Vyasa, and Ganesh, like *Dashavatara*, the *Mahabharata, Chanakya, Bhagat Singh*, and stories about India and its partition. As a brown boy growing up in New Jersey yearning deeply for meaning, I was grateful to my family for buying me such books.

I still remember picking up my grandmother's copy of Gandhi's autobiography as a child.

Thank you to the professors and students I met through Temple University 2014-2018, which gave me a full scholarship to study film and media arts when I was in high school. It set a solid background for me to pursue a brief stint in LA, hustling, before…

Per Scholas, where I now work an academic job. I cannot thank this organization enough.

Rest in peace Cass Warner, and thank you for making an inspiring documentary about your family.

Part One:

EDUCATION

JANUARY

JANUARY 1 — Change your life.

"The life we receive is not short, but we make it so, nor do we have any lack of it, but are wasteful of it."

– On the Shortness of Life by Lucius Annaeus Seneca, translated by John W. Basore

Happy New Year, Reader!

Focus on the long term this year. Allow thoughts to move, to come and go. For example:

"What if they don't like me? What if I've done nothing so far with my life, except waste time? What if? What if? What if?"

It's a terrifying train of thought. Seneca often said the life we receive is not short, but that we waste it on thoughts like these.

I was born in 1996, so I breathe my last breath in what, 2096? Just a guess. But these corporations? They were designed to live forever.

Think of yourself as a corporation, Reader.

Me, I am no longer Akash Malik. I am now Akash Malik, Inc, CEO of Multinational Firm, Inc. I must increase my bottom line by making transactions. Not only day-to-day or quarter-to-quarter, but in deep, long-term ways.

THE TAKEAWAY: Change your life. For the long term.

JANUARY 2 — Good vibes, not digital profiles.

 In his book, *How Will You Measure Your Life?*, the late author and Harvard professor Clayton M. Christensen reminds me that when I was 10 years old, I dreamt of becoming nearly anything. An astronaut. An archaeologist. A world class athlete. An artist.

When I was in high school, I wanted to see people on TV who looked like me, or the people I saw around me in my very diverse hometown of Edison, New Jersey. For years I carried this belief that if "the plan fails" and goes horribly wrong, then my life is over.

I was absolutely wrong. You are more than your job, or your career, or the person your digital profiles portray you to be.

Perhaps you had strategies for your TikTok profile, or Facebook, Instagram, or LinkedIn. You probably had a "deliberate strategy" for posting. But then, you saw "unanticipated alternatives," such as "like my status" or the "ASL Ice Bucket Challenge," or celebrity bandwagon trends you never planned for but ended up participating in.

Did God intend for humans to curate their lives in such a way? Or did Silicon Valley want that?

I found digital profiles were useless to my writing. I am just a man with a finite amount of time, and a simple brain that is easily distracted. I cannot misspend my time scrolling through feeds of digital profiles, be it mine or yours, or corporations trying to sell me things.

THE TAKEAWAY: **Design your life with good vibes, not with digital profiles.**

JANUARY 3 — Two blades of grass.

In his satirical book *Gulliver's Travels* (1726), Jonathan Swift wrote that whoever can make two ears of corn or two blades of grass grow in a spot where only one grew, they would deserve better of mankind and be more essential to their country than all politicians put together.

I think about Swift's "blades of grass" as "words on a page." If you are a writer, you may struggle getting words on a blank page. In a sense, you are making grass grow on the blank page.

I write notes constantly in my nonprofit tech trainer role and as a manager on the Per Scholas Remote Training Team. You probably write a lot of Slack or email messages at work. This writing you do at work, in a sense, makes grass grow where it was not growing before. You wrote using computer software such as Final Draft, or Celtx, or Apple Pages, Google Docs, Microsoft Word. Sure, the writing is not perfect, but it does exist!

Find joy in your progress, not in achieving perfection.

Maybe you were interrupted by someone in your house while you were working, by your mother or father or sibling or roommate.

No need to practice hostility in those moments. Instead, practice patience.

I try to do this at work or life. To compare my work only to my work, not to others.

THE TAKEAWAY: Grow two blades of grass where only one once grew.

JANUARY 4 — Healthy media diet.

"Make the text habitable, like a rented apartment... a space borrowed for a moment by a transient."
— *The Practice of Everyday Life* – de Certeau

Time is a funny thing. We have a finite amount of it. We should spend it wisely in a way that provides us with joy, and freedom, and choices. We should earn money with our time to secure financial freedom, for ourselves and our family. Make writings, music, videos, posts, websites. In the broadest sense, we must make "media."

Media, to me, is best defined as a tool that stores and delivers information. A TV show could be called "media," but the ethernet cable delivering the show to the PC or wireless router in your apartment? This is also "media."

On HBO in 2017, in a segment titled "Trump vs. Truth," John Oliver talked about Donald Trump's media diet. Donald Trump is more than capable of standing in the rain and saying it is a beautiful, sunny day. In the words of Kellyanne Conway, Trump consumes many "alternative facts."

Reader, what media do you consume daily?

If you changed your media diet, how would it affect your leadership, your firm, your family, or your country?

To produce media that others can inhabit, you must understand that words and actions have consequences. This is especially true for a leader, who must be very wary of the media they let into their nervous system, because it influences the lives of those people they lead.

THE TAKEAWAY: **Have a healthy media diet.**

JANUARY 5 — Deep Burning Questions (DBQs).

Family interview projects are great. They are a way for people to learn their real history, not the colonizer crap you memorize to pass the AP US History test.

In fall 2019, I sat down with my grandparents and uncles and aunties with whom I am blessed and recorded some interviews. Mostly for me to answer my deep burning questions (DBQs).

My aunt (who is also my godmother) once told me and my brothers a story about her dad, my grandfather, who I only ever saw as a sweet old man. We were eating pizza in New Jersey.

AKASH: "Were my grandparents different to you as a kid than to us?"

ANJU, paraphrase: *"I needed a new uniform for school, and money came to dad's bank account the first week of the month. It was the last week of the month, but I really needed this uniform, I kept saying "now now," and my dad kept saying money comes in days, but I kept saying "now now!" Then dad took the bracelet off my mom's wrist to sell it and get the uniform that day… until I stopped him. Tears in my eyes."*

Telling that story made my aunt cry.

I asked this DBQ to troubleshoot my life! Now, here I was, regretting that I asked this question. But if I did not muster up courage to ask, I never would have seen my grandfather holistically, through the eyes of my beloved aunt.

> THE TAKEAWAY: **Work backwards from the deep burning questions (DBQs).**

JANUARY 6 — Judge by deeds, not by titles.

"Leadership is not about a title or a designation. It's about impact, influence and inspiration."

— Robin S. Sharma

I wrote on my blog about how I went from working in film to technical training.

But the title doesn't bother me. All that bothers me is whether or not my work is good.

Titles don't matter, but the work does. A title doesn't define who you are. Your actions and behavior do.

The legacy of great people is based on the actions they took in the situations they were in. A title is only an interesting name.

None of these titles matter at the end of the day. You can have a fancy title but still feel empty inside until you do what matters: bring real value to the people around you.

THE TAKEAWAY: **Judge by deeds, not by titles.**

JANUARY 7 — Bridge the gap between knowledge and skill.

"The proper work of the mind is the exercise of choice, refusal, yearning, repulsion, preparation, purpose, and assent."

— Epictetus, Discourses, 4.11.6–7

Knowledge workers are an asset, not a cost, to your firm.

A knowledge worker can work anytime, anywhere, for any firm or hospital or university that chooses to be their employer.

The firm could give that employee a laptop and a smartphone.

You know, to take whatever "knowledge" they have in their heads and make something.

Manual workers must be in onsite jobs, as Elon Musk demonstrates with SpaceX and Tesla.

But me or you? We might work "in the cloud."

I started out in film editing. I had a curiosity about movies, about not only the people in the films themselves but also those who made them.

In high school I learned Avid Media Composer. In college, I learned Adobe Premiere. Shot, reverse shot, J cuts, L cuts, keyframe. I could train a machine to learn editing. Oh wait, Adobe already did. Automated video editing with AI. Another tool I can choose to learn.

But ultimately, theories in my head must be tested by my hands to verify its usefulness.

THE TAKEAWAY: **Bridge the gap between knowledge and skill.**

8

JANUARY 8 — Separate reality from its imitations.

At an advance screening of the movie *Steve Jobs* in San Francisco, writer Aaron Sorkin and director Danny Boyle defend their fictionalized version of Jobs. (CNET)

AARON SORKIN: "This was clearly an impressionistic thing… a painting instead of a photograph."

I like Aaron Sorkin's finished work. His MasterClass, which I first binged in 2018, gave me some huge "a-ha" moments.

Sorkin is a talented writer, director, and playwright. He is no relation to financial journalist and author Andrew Ross Sorkin, by the way. (98. April 7)

Long story short, too many young people I know, myself included, saw *The Social Network* or *Steve Jobs* and believed it was real, maybe even saying, "Wow, it really happened that way?!" Sure, the characters onscreen have the same names as the people in real life. But they are just paintings. Aaron Sorkin's imitations of reality and journalism. To him, Aristotle matters most, especially Poetics, which is free to read on the MIT website.

This idea of "separating reality from imitations" is all around you.

Advertising is not reality. Neither is Goodfellas. Neither is the movie *Steve Jobs*.

THE TAKEAWAY: **Separate reality from its imitations.**

JANUARY 9 — Channel magic through the tool.

On this day in 2007, Steve Jobs of Apple unveiled a phone, an iPod, and an internet communicator, and called it… iPhone.

Reader, I truly love all my Apple devices. Not only is the hardware beautiful, but so is iOS, macOS, watchOS, iCloud. I love the entire electronic "ecosystem." I still play my old music from the 2000s and 2010s. You know, the stuff you got from LimeWire or a YouTube ripper.

I remember the blackra1n jailbreak with Cydia. I remember using the 30-pin charger, then the Lightning. Then the European Union said that Apple must be USB-C compliant by autumn 2024.

The iTunes store, which made it so we do not have to steal from artists we love. Then came Spotify, founded as a way to monetize music without piracy.

Reminder: cinema itself is a technology.

As Scorsese's Hugo depicts, early audiences were terrified at the sight of a moving train on screen. The mere presence of a movie camera was unsettling to many.

I am sure Martin Scorsese, or grandparents, are scared of Squarespace websites. At least he has his daughter to help him on the Apple computer in the 2024 commercial.

So, Reader: what magic have you made with your iPhone since 2007? Or your Windows PC. Linux. Avid. Adobe. RED. Squarespace. AWS. Many "magic" tools out there. Whatever the tool, channel magic through it.

THE TAKEAWAY: Channel magic through the tool.

10

JANUARY 10 — It's not the technology; it's what you do with it.

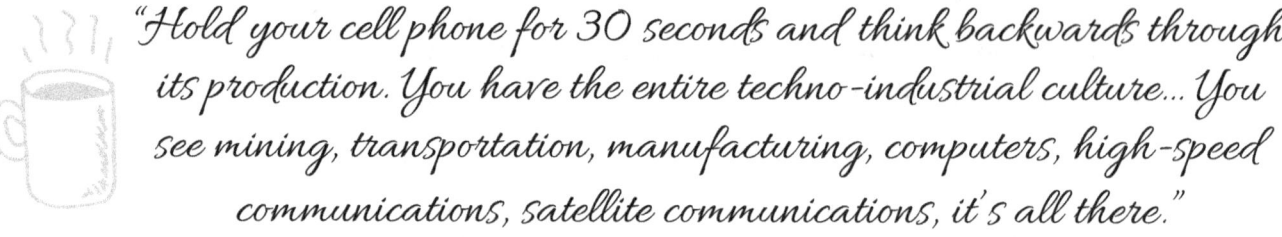

"Hold your cell phone for 30 seconds and think backwards through its production. You have the entire techno-industrial culture… You see mining, transportation, manufacturing, computers, high-speed communications, satellite communications, it's all there."

— Doug Tompkins, cofounder of The North Face, in a *2013* Guardian *article*

The Cambridge Analytica scandal taught me that Facebook (Meta) is not what I or my then-teen friends thought: free cloud storage to store the photos or videos I stored on my phone.

Here's what I have since learned: Because it is free, its users become the product. Meta takes my data to target me with annoying ads. So, no, neither Facebook nor Instagram are "free" in that sense. Silicon Valley guys like Mark Zuckerberg aren't here to save the world.

Will these guys save you from bad air, such as what many of us experienced in New York from Canadian wildfires, June 2023?

The computer is a mechanism for acceleration. Social media can create echo chambers all around you to influence your media diet.

Doug Tompkins was a friend of Steve Jobs. The two men had many arguments. Steve tried convincing Doug that computers were going to save the world. Doug kept saying the opposite: Yes, individuals use computers largely for narrow interests.

The real winners are large corporations that are able to take advantage of a person's narrow needs, on a massive worldwide scale, to become firms so powerful they are like governments.

THE TAKEAWAY: It's not the technology; it's what you do with it.

JANUARY 11 — Part quant, part qual.

Watching Netflix CEO Ted Sarandos and Marc Andreessen in conversation (edited)...

TED SARANDOS: The big fundamental difference between Silicon Valley and Hollywood, I think, is the quant and qual. There's an inability for Hollywood to wrap their head around, you know, quant.

The whole efficiency driven thing is very Silicon Valley; the whole quality driven thing is very Hollywood. Rarely do those things meet. I think why Netflix has been successful in content, it's pretty rare, is that we always kept a presence in Hollywood and a presence in Silicon Valley.

The people who work for me in LA, about a thousand people on all the aspects of content, they all think they work at the greatest entertainment company in the world, and I hope, I think they're right. I think there's about four thousand people in Silicon Valley who would think they work for the best tech company in the world. I think they're right.

We never tried to jam either culture on the other, we just respect the two cultures.

At the early days of entertainment in the internet, the tech companies would come in to Hollywood, they'd lawyer up and agent up, and have these meetings and write big checks and fly home, and nobody knew who they were.

The entertainment industry's almost all about relationships and trust, because again, there is no quant. You really have to trust your instincts on a lot of things, including people.

When your brand appeals to the entire planet, you need to embrace multiple cultures.

THE TAKEAWAY: Become part quant, part qual.

12

JANUARY 12 — Become someone helpful.

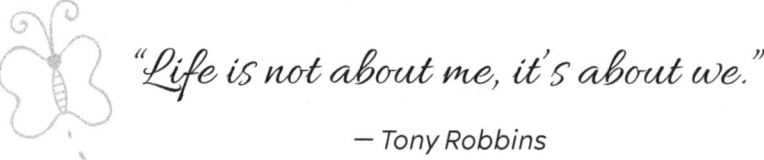

"Life is not about me, it's about we."
— Tony Robbins

"To be like your hero" implies copying and pasting your hero's actions in your own life.

"Becoming a hero" means deeper change. Acting to help a cause greater than yourself.

Live with good morals. The serenity of mind that comes from living with good morals is interest compounded from good choices and good judgment. Reflect on hardships to find ways to repeat the solution.

If you seek to "copy and paste" another's success for yourself, you live life asking *What would [insert hero] do in this situation?* instead of *What must I do in this situation?*

Reader, enable yourself to become the helpful hero you need to become. Start by walking at least 30 minutes a day. (My elders do it with physical therapists; so can you.) You are useless if you are dead. Find good emotions. Positive meaningful relationships with family, friends, and firm.

From there, spending time on your mission, or your finances, or your charity, becomes easier.

THE TAKEAWAY: **Don't be "like" anyone. Just become someone helpful.**

JANUARY 13 — You are the pilot.

Peter Drucker has described management as a liberal art. "Liberal" because it deals with basics of knowledge, self-knowledge, wisdom, and leadership. "Art" because it deals with practice and application.

I wonder what Drucker thinks of movie directors.

I remember being in high school in 2014. I woke up, opened YouTube on my iPhone 5, and *Praying with Anger,* Manoj "Night" Shyamalan's first movie, was there!

Praying With Anger was written, directed, and starred a young Night when he was still an NYU student, managing a large budget, a crew in India, and a story that was not fully cooked. Seeing the film was an educational experience!

If I had ChatGPT in 2014, I would have asked about Shyamalan, or Asian American directors I met in film school like Tanuj Chopra, or researched and learned about Justin Lin, Ang Lee, and Piyush Dinker Pandya. But the technology will not write or direct the picture! The machine can simply be trained.

The AI is more like a "copilot," as Microsoft CEO Satya Nadella told Andrew Ross Sorkin.

Praying With Anger or The Last Airbender or Lady in the Water could have benefitted from ChatGPT or **filmmaking AI tools recommended by Curious Refuge**. South Park used ChatGPT on an episode, even though the show was already funny without AI.

In the video game, MegaMan is an AI that helps the main character, Lan, make choices.

But Lan, your "avatar," not MegaMan, makes the choices.

THE TAKEAWAY: You are the pilot. Tech or AI is just your "intern" copilot.

JANUARY 14 — Leverage neuroplasticity.

"Neuro" refers to the nervous system.

This includes the body parts that send information, such as the brain, the spinal cord, and over 7 trillion nerves within you that send information throughout your brain and fingers and toes.

"Plasticity" refers to the Latin word plasticus "for molding or modeling," from Greek plastikós, which has the same definition. Perhaps you heard Keeley Jones and Jamie Tartt say the term "Pavlovian" in Ted Lasso, or heard about some famous experiment with dogs.

Like humans, dogs do not need training to make saliva when they see or smell delicious food. That is hardwired, and totally natural! Ivan Pavlov (1849-1936) demonstrated that dogs could be conditioned to salivate at the sound of a bell, if that sound was repeatedly presented at the same time that they were given food.

The saying "you can't teach an old dog new tricks" is absolutely wrong.

Like people, dogs never stop learning. Old dogs can focus for longer periods of time, whereas young dogs can be easily distracted. Older dogs are also not as hyperactive as pups. This ability to concentrate helps them learn new tricks.

This is like the "carrot and stick" metaphor in politics, or a donkey's reward and punishment.

Pain and pleasure can be re-associated in your mind and spirit. Your brain will adapt over time.

THE TAKEAWAY: Leverage neuroplasticity.

JANUARY 15 — Understand gender and communication.

On this day in 2013, I submitted an essay to my AP Language and Composition teacher, titled "Differences Between Men and Women."

I cited comedian Bill Engvall and linguistics professor Deborah Tannen. **Bill Engvall** characterizes men as being "basic," but women are "details." He tells a funny story about working out at the gym with his friend Joey, who is getting divorced. Bill tells Joey he needs to work on his abs because Joey will be dating again. But Bill's wife wants details, like "who was cheating on whom?!"

In **Gender-specific language rituals**, Tannen talks about hiring a training video company to capture three preschool boys talking about how high they can hit a ball.

The first one says, "Mine is up there."

The second says, "Mine is up to the sky."

The first one retorts, "Mine is up to heaven."

Then, a third boy in the back: "Mine is up to God."

It is the opposite of two girls talking at the same preschool.

One girl says, "Did you know that my babysitter called Amber has already contacts?"

The other girl: "My mom has already contacts, so my dad does too."

Tannen finds this interesting: the second girl repeats and mirrors the syntax, "has already contacts."

The first girl lights up and says, "the same?"

It was natural for the boys to try topping each other, and for the girls to find sameness.

THE TAKEAWAY: Understand gender and communication to leverage it.

JANUARY 16 — Free write.

 Here's an irony about freedom: Discipline gives you freedom. Like disciplined journaling.

Writing, for me, takes discipline. To freely express with words all my feelings, attitudes, thoughts, and beliefs on a new Apple Page or Google Doc as soon as I wake up.

Once I am done, I am able to finally focus my energy elsewhere.

Managers in companies, schools, or hospitals are responsible for producing results, such as
- Economic performance
- Student learning
- Patient care.

If these results are not produced, the institution will not exist much longer.

Articulate the mission of the organization, especially if the team or organization starts losing its way.

This also applies to meetings that start to lose their way: it helps if someone is taking notes!

By taking notes in a meeting, you can refer back to key questions asked during the meeting, or decisions that were made, and any relevant thoughts or feelings the participants had.

In Zoom meetings at Per Scholas, I often type the meeting notes while sharing my screen.

This practice often results in shorter meetings because everyone is literally on the same page.

I find AI note taking to be efficient too, but typing the notes myself has the added benefits of reinforcing my memory and understanding of the meeting.

THE TAKEAWAY: **Free write your way to your discipline.**

JANUARY 17 — Seek (steal) international inspiration.

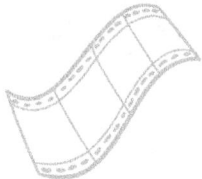

Hearing **Martin Scorsese praise Satyajit Ray** makes me deeply happy.

Scorsese saw Ray's films on TV. Scorsese is Sicilian American, but he identified with films made in India! Because the language of film is international.

Filmmakers have drawn comparisons between the lone, wandering ronin of Japan, and the lone, wandering gunslinging cowboys in America.

Both drew inspiration from European knights who were unmatched in battle prowess and were dedicated to performing good deeds in adherence to their, at times, ambiguous moral code.

Scorsese loved library books with movie stills in them. He liked them so much, sometimes he stole the library books.

I grew up in the suburbs. I stole stuff off the Internet all the time. Remember LimeWire?

I heard stories of people stealing the "6" and "9" keys off of keyboards in the Bronx, **where Per Scholas was founded.**

Tetris, the 2023 biographical thriller directed by Jon S. Baird and written by Noah Pink, centers on an international inspiration. Based on the true events around the race to license and patent the video game Tetris from 1980s Cold War Russia, I love **the bromance between Henk Rogers and Alexey Pajitnov**. Video games like Tetris are international.

No matter what language you speak, it is easy to play a visual, math-based game like Tetris.

THE TAKEAWAY: **Seek (steal) international inspiration.**

JANUARY 18 — Economics is driven by human behavior.

"How could economics not be behavioral? If it isn't behavioral, what the hell is it?"

— Charlie Munger (1924-2023)

In an article entitled "The Stripper Index," Nicole Canelakes ponders if America is in recession.

"The Stripper Index" is an unorthodox, unofficial index that says if strippers see less cash tips for long periods of time, then the economy is not doing well.

Canelakes cites a Twitter / X user with the handle @Botticellibimbo, who writes that strippers must be aware of how upper-class white men are behaving and spending their money.

Another unnamed entertainer shared her own personal story: she worked at a gentlemen's club in 2007, prior to the recession of 2008, and told a friend that "the club was way too dead for way too long" and pulled her money out of stocks.

It sounded crazy, but her friend did it, and she says her money almost doubled.

THE TAKEAWAY: Understand how economics is driven by human behavior.

JANUARY 19 — Own the rights to your work.

In spring 2009, I was in middle school English class. The assignment was to bring a song to class and talk about it like literature. I brought in Chamillionaire's "I'm So Gone." Chamillionaire raps about drinking his problems away: bills, stress, women.

Recently, Chamillionaire **appeared in a TikTok** video by @makethemovefinancial.

In the video, Chamillionaire says the music industry is "designed to rip off artists." When a check is handed to an artist, the amount is usually not right.

He heard from another rapper, Nelly, that he should do an audit, so Chamillionaire hired Jay Z's auditor. The auditor found that the label, Universal Records, was hiding $600,000 from Chamillionaire! After discovering this, he wanted to leave Universal. When Universal didn't want to let him go, he said, "If you don't, I'll teach all the guys on your label how to do an audit." They let him go.

Chamillionaire used to think a hit song magically became number 1, but in reality, he had to pay a lot of money to get his record to go number 1. He started looking at the music industry differently. Instead of chasing shows for $10,000, he focused on owning a piece of the venues that hold the shows.

THE TAKEAWAY: Learn from Chamillionaire: Own the rights to your work.

JANUARY 20 — Find meaning in life beyond work.

In *The End of Economic Man*, first published in 1939, Peter Drucker focuses on the social and political breakdown of Europe, the rise of the Nazis, and how the catastrophe of Nazism could be avoided, both in the past and in the future.

Drucker rejected the idea that people are only "economic animals," and that a person only works toward bettering their economic position, privilege, and rights.

The motivations behind human actions are complex. Especially in countries that are facing so much political and social upheaval that totalitarian leaders like Stalin or Hitler emerge.

Human beings seek more than just economic satisfaction. They seek meaning, community, and an identity beyond their jobs.

This is why the title of the book is "the end of economic man," because this model of human nature no longer works.

There are political, social, and psychological factors that also shape human behavior, not just economic factors.

THE TAKEAWAY: Find meaning in life beyond just your work.

JANUARY 21 — Gather inspiration from all sorts of artistic mediums.

In his memoir *Who Is Michael Ovitz? (2018)*, the former Hollywood super-agent writes about seeing the movie *Last of the Mohicans*. He surprised the director, Michael Mann, by correctly guessing that Mann was inspired by the 19th-century American landscape paintings of Albert Bierstadt.

It's interesting how filmmakers draw inspiration from paintings, photography, architecture, music, and many other artistic disciplines.

Stanley Kubrick's *Barry Lyndon* (1975) was directly influenced by 18th-century paintings, particularly those by William Hogarth for candlelit interiors. Kubrick even went as far as using a camera lens developed by NASA to shoot in candlelight on set and create scenes that look like period paintings.

There is a blog post featuring ten paintings those inspired scenes from movies, and it is fascinating.

Visual storytelling continues across generations of humankind, and people seeking to express themselves in new mediums can curate inspiration from traditional mediums into their new work.

THE TAKEAWAY: Gather inspiration from all sorts of artistic mediums.

JANUARY 22 — Imagine it, put it on paper, and build it.

In Chapter 6, "Good Things Can Happen," of his memoir *The Ride of a Lifetime*, Robert Iger writes about the creative and technical brilliance of Disney's Imagineers.

Who are the Imagineers? They handle everything! From Disney theme parks, resorts, attractions, cruise ships, real estate developments, live performances, light shows, and parades. The details of a cast member's costume, the architecture of the castles.

Disney Imagineers are artists, engineers, architects, and technologists, with jobs unlike any other on planet Earth.

It takes a special ability to see not only the big picture but also the granular details and consider how one affects the other.

The CEO of Disney likely uses lots of scrap paper and notebooks. Just think about all the things they have to do. Planning a growth strategy with investors. Working with Imagineers on the design of a giant new theme park attraction. Discussing new security protocols for those theme park attractions. Giving notes on the rough cut of a new Disney film.

THE TAKEAWAY: Imagine it, put it on paper, and build it.

JANUARY 23 — Become autodidactic.

In his song "Mo Money Mo Problems," Biggie Smalls raps about how money doesn't solve life's problems.

My uncle, who I love, believes money solves 95 percent of life's problems. But as the song suggests, the more money you have, the more problems you have.

People in my life talk about money a lot. Even though I'm young, I find I do as well. Earning money is necessary in a capitalist society. You cannot rebel against it. But you can surprise people regarding what you do. Especially through Information Age tech, where you can be self-taught in a creative or technical discipline.

Autodidact is a big word that means you didn't take an academic course, but through the Internet, you taught yourself how to code or edit or write a screenplay.

You can become self-taught now faster than Da Vinci ever could. Digital payments enable you to charge for your services as well. You can create work for whoever your client is.

And then you satisfy your client with your work. Your team (assuming you convince people you are someone they would be proud to work for) helps support your progress, which leads to deep happiness for you.

I like what Tony Robbins says about happiness—that it represents progress toward your goals. If you feel like you are making progress, you will feel happy. Progress is a part of happiness.

THE TAKEAWAY: Become autodidactic.

JANUARY 24 — List your strengths and develop them.

"You have power over your mind—not outside events. Realize this, and you will find strength."

–Marcus Aurelius, *Meditations*

It is so important to know one's strengths and to know what one cannot do.

If you have a hard time with this, ask your friends, parents, teachers, managers, or assistants. Start writing them down like your obituary, then live up to them, for yourself and others. Patience and confidence in the face of adversity is good.

The ability to think clearly, systematically, and creatively.

An ability to use multiple mental models.

Speed reading.

Feedback is another key to continuous learning.

Reader, get feedback on your work. Even you, a societal "misfit," can make great work.

What is best? Nobody knows. Every human being is a walking, talking contradiction. But we have figured out a strategy that works, if only we choose to apply it.

THE TAKEAWAY: **Make a list of your strengths and develop them.**

JANUARY 25 — **Always value the library. Consider remakes.**

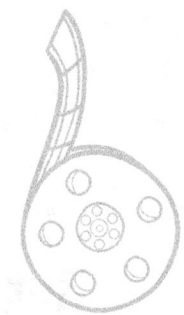

Turner Classic Movies was successful because Ted Turner bought classics and ran them on TV. It inspired kids like myself, seeing classics for the first time, to eventually find themselves in the editing rooms of Martin Scorsese, Steven Spielberg, and Paul Thomas Anderson.

As of June 28, 2023, Jennifer Maas writes for Variety, TCM will now be curated by all three of these cinephile legends.

Right in front of people who thought he lost big, Ted Turner made a huge bet on the library.

Lew Wasserman did something similar in 1958, when MCA paid $10 million for Paramount's library of pre-1948 films—about 700 titles that many people called "worthless" at the time. Within a week, MCA made $30 million for TV airing of "oldies." For decades, the library profited on this newfangled heavy device in our living rooms, and bedrooms, called a "television" or TV.

Or a tablet. Or a smartphone. Augmented and virtual reality (AR/VR).

Of course, now you can even shoot and digitize your family's home movies, to play on TVs. **(74. March 14)**

THE TAKEAWAY: **Always value the library. Consider remakes.**

JANUARY 26 — Try not to let bad news affect your mood.

Kobe Bryant died with his daughter, Gianna, in a helicopter crash on this day in 2020.

The others killed were the pilot, Ara Zobayan, Orange Coast College baseball coach John Altobelli, his wife Keri, their daughter Alyssa, assistant coach Christina Mauser, Sarah Chester, and her daughter Payton. Alyssa and Payton were Gianna's teammates.

But this was just the News app on an iPhone screen.

My job at the time was the front door manager of the Players Club from 5 to 10 pm. **The Players NYC** is a private club founded by Edwin Booth on December 31, 1888, for actors, and boasts so much American show business history.

But on this day the club is boring. My colleague, Maria, won't shut up about making a trip to Disney and showing me pictures of her kids. Glad I brought my vape stick. I can hit it discreetly if I hold it a certain way and avoid blowing clouds.

Working in hospitality, it is important to keep a positive mood. I will not bring up the news to anyone coming in today unless they mention it first.

THE TAKEAWAY: **Try not to let bad news affect your mood.**

JANUARY 27 — Make small changes that compound over time.

Teaching other human beings at Per Scholas is so much better than being the front door manager at The Players.

Now that I can afford it, I can probably even become a member of The Players if I wanted. This new job even gives me lots of writing time, which I am careful not to waste.

I consider writing to be serious work, as is reading. It may not always be "paid" work, but it is work. Philosophy, self-education, overcoming self-doubt, achieving goals that you set.

James Clear writes about how "atomic habits" can help you move toward your goal. These goals are massive, but like compound interest, habits do add up over time.

Reading as little as one page a day can make a difference. In *Chanakya Neeti*, Chanakya, an ancient Indian philosopher, jurist, and royal advisor, has similar advice:

> *"Never let any day go without some study of a written word. One should make one's day fruitful by doing good work and study."*
>
> — Chanakya Neeti

THE TAKEAWAY: Make small changes that compound over time.

JANUARY 28 — Don't put off until tomorrow what you can do today.

> *"Life is long enough, and it has been given in sufficiently generous measure to allow the accomplishment of the very greatest things if the whole of it is well invested... the life we receive is not short, nor do we have any lack of it, but are wasteful of it."*
>
> – On the Shortness of Life, by Seneca, **translated by John W. Basore**

You are in complete control over how consistent you are in sticking to your desired behaviors. People in your group chats want you to play video games or watch funny videos. But you owe it to yourself to first do what will benefit you long term.

There is a workout you are putting off. An online course you are delaying. A book you meant to read that is now gathering dust. You cannot control the mountain of snow coming this weekend to New Jersey.

Or a pandemic.

You cannot control what others say or do. You cannot control the inevitability of aging, death, or disease. Neither could The Buddha.

But you can control your smoking, your drinking, your eating, and how much you exercise. Technology, in all its forms, is designed to make you lazy. It is up to you not to become lazy.

You have a job to do.

As **Ben Franklin** put it, "Don't put off until tomorrow what you can do today."

THE TAKEAWAY: Don't put off until tomorrow what you can do today.

JANUARY 29 — Guard your reputation with your life.

Looking ahead, don't overthink your cousin's birthday party coming up like, *now*.

She is 16 today, she was 15 this day last year, she will be 17 next year, and 18 the year after. Soon she will go to college. Her brother, who you remember as a baby, is now a young man.

The subject of COVID came up. The Sweet 16 that could have been. Now everyone is looking at their phones to avoid discussing this awkward conversation topic.

Charles K. Ross was principal my freshman year at Edison High. Even he called my cousin for her birthday. I am so thankful he started managing my high school the year I started as a freshman. His reputation, as far as I care, is terrific.

A good reputation takes a lifetime to build but a moment to lose.

Consider the former Enron President and CEO, Jeffrey Skilling. BS from Southern Methodist University, Harvard Business School, McKinsey partner, 35 counts of insider trading.

For every illustrious Harvard alumni, there is a notorious one. The same can be said for any reputable school or company.

Your school or your workplace cannot protect your reputation. You have to guard it yourself.

THE TAKEAWAY: **Guard your reputation with your life.**

30
JANUARY 30 — Learn lessons from old movies.

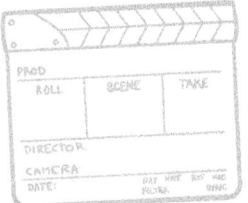

In a frame from *A Star is Born* (1937), directed by William A. Wellman from a story he wrote with Robert Carson, the English text reads: "Hollywood! … the beckoning El Dorado… Metropolis of Make-Believe in the California hills…"

This movie may be old, but the story is timeless. Bradley Cooper and Lady Gaga did a pretty good one in the fourth adaptation of this story, which Warner Bros. released in 2018.

Thousands of people come to Los Angeles from all over the world, by bus, train, or plane. A lucky few even get their names and handprints cemented into the sidewalk in front of TCL Chinese Theater.

Many wannabe movie stars move to LA as unemployed actors, which was a hard life then and is still a hard life now.

I streamed the 1937 film in my living room, and my mother watched it with me. After it ended, she said it reminded her of a movie she saw a long time ago, *Abhimaan*, from 1973.

Geeta Pandey for BBC noted on the film's fiftieth anniversary that although the director Hrishikesh Mukherjee never acknowledged it, "his film has also drawn comparisons with *A Star Is Born*."

It never ceases to amaze me that old movies inspire new movies from all over the world.

THE TAKEAWAY: Learn lessons from old movies.

JANUARY 31 — Become an optimistic leader.

On this day in 2018, I was writing to myself about the previous shitty summer.

I was living at The View on Temple University campus, interning, and making $10 an hour. I was smoking weed with a girl interning at a bank making $30 an hour. I envied this girl in private, but I was wary not to let my envy influence my interactions with her. After all, I valued the companionship.

Later in life I discovered Charlie Munger, vice chairman of Berkshire Hathaway, and his Almanack. He writes "beware of envy." Warren Buffett agrees. Envy is a silly sin with no upside. When investing, making decisions based on what others do is often risky. So what if someone is getting richer faster than you? Trying to copy that person may cause you to sabotage your own career, relationships, or investments.

This is only amplified by social media. Seeing people show off wealthy lifestyles can motivate a person to make dumb, envious, irrational decisions.

Envy exists everywhere humans exist: classrooms, boardrooms, hospitals, banks, startups.

If you are a leader in any of these places, you must be wary of envy. Even if you feel envy, as a leader it is important not to let it drive you into pessimism.

As Bob Iger notes in his autobiography *The Ride of a Lifetime*, "Even in the face of difficult choices and less than ideal outcomes, an optimistic leader does not yield to pessimism."

THE TAKEAWAY: **Become an optimistic leader.**

FEBRUARY

FEBRUARY 1 — Find a sustainable diet.

This morning in my Per Scholas Zoom class regarding a CNBC story about ending food insecurity.

"Kocho" comes from the false banana in Ethiopia. Abebe in my class is from Ethiopia and says he has been eating kocho for years. So it's new to me, and seemingly the rest of this cohort, but familiar to him. They even updated the article and linked to Kew Botanic Gardens "Foods of the Future."

As a global population, humans rely on just 15 crops for 90 percent of our energy intake.

Every few hundred years in society, there is a shift. Even if 50 years go by, society will look entirely different, with new values, new worldviews, new social and political order, arts, institutions, technology, and of course, food.

People born after the transformation can't even fathom the life or food of their grandparents or parents. Only if the food in question holds emotional significance for them will it survive.

What will the food of your future look like? How can we troubleshoot world hunger?

THE TAKEAWAY: **Find a sustainable diet.**

33 FEBRUARY 2 — Find balance like a palindrome.

The date 02/02/2020 is a palindrome.

I've had days like this before, such as 11/11/11, November 11, 2011.

I remember setting a DVR to record the 07-07-07 (July 7, 2007) promo on KidsWB.

I remember the interface of my parent's VCR: mostly whitespace, bold black text, a yellow "hover." You clicked "ok" or "select" to try and change date and/or time of your recording, and the yellow hover turned blue and the black text became white.

It was a clunky user interface by today's standards, but back then it was everything.

Palindrome dates are cool. These days are great to feel cosmic balance and throw a party.

In molecular biology, palindromic sequences are the sequence of nucleotides in the DNA double helix, where the sequence in one strand is the same as the complementary sequence of the other strand. The human genome has millions of palindromic sequences, by some counts over 13 million DNA palindromes.

THE TAKEAWAY: **Find balance like a palindrome.**

FEBRUARY 3 — Give society what it wants but doesn't yet know it needs.

Troubleshooting does not always result in solved problems.

But the process of identifying a problem, brainstorming a theory, and then testing it until it is airtight and actionable, is a process that will get you closer to a solution. Who knows? Once you solve one problem, you begin to feel confident in your ability to execute effectively in any creative, technical, or managerial scenario you might find yourself in.

You can get past that feeling of "oh shit" or "what the hell am I going to do next" by doing this for a few minutes, or days, even months or years.

Frederick Winslow Taylor analyzed mechanical engineering work to figure out industrial efficiency. That in turn improved human efficiency. (And dehumanized workers, but that's another subject.) Eric Berne analyzed transactions to explain human behavior in *Games People Play*. Hat tip to Ramon Bloomfield, who told me about Berne at The Players one night during work.

I think both Taylor and Berne embody this idea I heard from Naval Ravikant, of "giving society what it wants, but does not yet know it needs."

Nobody knew we needed to improve time and human motion to improve efficiency (Taylor), or that we need to understand psychology behind human interaction/transactions (Berne).

THE TAKEAWAY: Give society what it wants but doesn't yet know it needs.

FEBRUARY 4 — Invest in using or building helpful technology.

In 1996, **John Lasseter and Steve Jobs spoke to Charlie Rose** to promote Pixar's *Toy Story*.

They explained Big Ideas, such as how an artist at Disney, Lasseter's old workplace, would use pen and paper. But an artist at Pixar would use a computer.

STEVE JOBS [edited for clarity]: "Pixar invented all this stuff, but we don't view ourselves as a technology company. Our product is content, we're an entertainment company, and all this technology really is just in the service of the storytelling, the service of the creative people.

Computer animation is even a little bit of a misnomer. The computers don't do the animation. I've watched John and his teamwork. They're the heart and soul of the characters. They do all the acting, not the computers."

Computers, pens, and paper cannot do much without people using them.

For now. Perhaps one day we will live in a world where computers solve every problem. But if AI can one day do everything at a company like Pixar, what will the people do?

Watch the movies, of course. They may not be perfect, but with some changes they will improve.

The technology can help save time, but it cannot do everything. At least, not yet.

THE TAKEAWAY: Invest in using or building helpful technology.

FEBRUARY 5 — Search yourself on the internet and protect your privacy.

I woke up this morning remembering middle school orchestra, where I played violin.

Some of the music pieces in my head: "Eclipsys," "William Tell Overture," "Rondo Alla Turca," "Spring Breezes."

Mozart, Eine Kleine Nachtmusik.

Yo Yo Ma, Obrigado Brasil. My mind is giving me hits today! What songs are playing in your head?

Perhaps in another life, I could have been a violinist, I thought to myself. Then I Google searched my name to see if there is someone with my name who is a violinist. I did not find any, but I found one other Akash Malik who is a software engineer, another who is a bodybuilder, and a third who is an archer.

In today's digital age where you can search the Internet for classical music, or other people who share your name, it is important to see exactly what other people could learn about you. Managing your online reputation is important, but so is removing any personally identifiable information you do not want publicly available.

Embrace being you in its entirety, "holistically" as college admissions might say. Google search yourself, see what comes up, expect the unexpected.

THE TAKEAWAY: Search yourself on the internet and protect your privacy.

37

FEBRUARY 6 — Use your "weak ties" to get a new job.

Stanford University uploaded a video of Mark Granovetter discussing "weak ties."

Mark found directories for the city of Newton, Massachusetts, and chose a sample of people who recently changed jobs. He ended up with 100 men who fit that description. He interviewed those men, then he wrote a survey that he mailed out to another couple of hundred men. He received 182 responses. Mostly, they got their new job through someone they knew.

Mark would say, "So you found a job through a friend?" Those men would correct Mark: "Not a friend, just an acquaintance." If you really want new information, Mark says, go to your seventh- or eighth-best friends. These are your "weak ties."

People who stay in one job for over five years have a hard time getting a new and better job because they do not know people in other companies.

On average, people who are in a job for two to five years and who made some "weak ties" at other companies can more easily find a new job.

Employers believe the information they get through social networks of weak ties as being more objective.

Sometimes your friends are biased, or you don't want to talk about vulnerable things such as job searching with your close friends. People seem to trust the people they know, and the people they sort of know, better than LinkedIn or Internet searching.

THE TAKEAWAY: **Use your "weak ties" to get a new job.**

FEBRUARY 7 — Look through the lens of theory into the future.

In a clip on the *Harvard Business Review* YouTube channel, Professor Clayton Christensen explains what exactly disruptive innovation is.

It has a very specific definition: **To transform a product that was historically so expensive and complicated that only a few rich, highly trained people had access to it, into something affordable and accessible that a much larger population can gain access to.**

General Motors and Ford faced this problem when they tried to decide to compete against Toyota, who came in at the low-price end of the car market and started climbing higher.

And later, Toyota had the same problem from Korean manufacturers such as Hyundai and Kia.

After all, why defend the lowest-profit product when you are competing against Mercedes?

This problem extends beyond cars as well. Mainframe computers, which cost several million dollars, could only be afforded by large corporations and universities. Some people cannot afford Macs or iPhones, so they buy PCs or Androids.

Clay's theory of disruptive innovation transformed Andy Grove, the former CEO of Intel. Not by telling him what to think, but by telling him *how to think*, so he could reach his own conclusions.

Data can be used to craft a theory. Then the theory can be used to see the future more clearly.

THE TAKEAWAY: **Look through the lens of theory into the future.**

39

FEBRUARY 8 — Avoid overworking yourself.

"Work is what horses die of."

–Aleksandr Solzhenitsyn

Horses are known for their hard labor and are sometimes worked to death.

If you overwork yourself without rest, you might one day physically or mentally collapse.

Solzhenitsyn was a Russian writer and critic of the Soviet regime who may have been commenting on the harsh conditions of labor, especially in oppressive systems where people are exploited without regard for their well-being.

It is important to take care of your well-being before going back to work.

THE TAKEAWAY: Avoid overworking yourself.

FEBRUARY 9 — Persevere and innovate through any problem.

In 2019, Bob Iger released his memoir *The Ride of a Lifetime: Lessons Learned From Fifteen Years as CEO of the Walt Disney Company*.

He did podcasts, talk shows, even a MasterClass.

In episode 406 of the *Tim Ferriss Show*, Bob tells Tim a story from his memoir about when he was a low-level executive for *ABC's Wide World of Sports*. Roone Arledge, Bob's manager, asked for the rights to the World Table Tennis Championships, set to be taking place in Pyongyang, North Korea. Bob wasn't allowed to travel to North Korea directly. Instead, he arranged a meeting in Beijing to meet with the North Koreans.

After months of negotiating, when closing the deal felt close, Bob got a call from someone on the Asian desk in the US State Department. The man told Bob that he was in violation of the US sanctions against North Korea. As in… The American Broadcasting Company can go to North Korea, with their film equipment, and broadcast the games. But ABC cannot pay North Korea directly.

End of the road? No. Bob found another workaround.

He sent the money to North Korea through the World Table Tennis Federation in Wales. This way, the North Korean government was not paid directly by ABC, but by the Federation.

It worked, and it became a historic moment in sports broadcasting.

Bob cites two qualities to Tim that made this moment possible: perseverance and ingenuity.

THE TAKEAWAY: Can you persevere or innovate through any problem before you?

41
FEBRUARY 10 — Unleash the full potential of the technology you own.

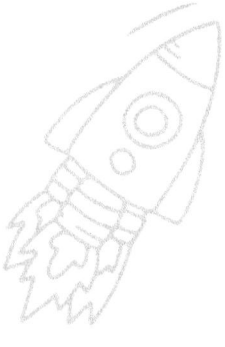

Tech training is draining. It's rewarding to do daily for sure, but still draining.

But compared to 12 hours as a production assistant or post-production assistant, this job is lit. I get to help people learn to troubleshoot, to earn and learn new technology on my work devices while I write this book on my other devices.

On this day in 2020 I was a front door manager at The Players in Manhattan. Before my shift, I went to the Starbucks on 19th and Park for a coffee. I was noting how movies are written… first, someone with a notebook or Notes app often "writes" down the initial ideas.

Like the people I saw in the Starbucks on their devices, some of whom were typing away. Their modern technology enables far more than just screenplays, though. In fact, the iPhone 6 I had at that moment with its two billion transistors **had 20 million times more power than Apollo 11.**

Of course, writing a movie about going to the moon is different from supporting a lunar mission from start to finish in terms of stakes.

But technically, it is possible.

Most importantly, it keeps me company when I am bored at work in a very interesting building **(The Players** club was founded in 1888 by Edwin Booth, 23 years after his brother shot President Abraham Lincoln).

> **THE TAKEAWAY: Unleash the full potential of the technology you own.**

FEBRUARY 11 — Bring out the best in yourself and those you manage.

A manager's goal is threefold:
1. To get team members working together.
2. Make their strengths effective.
3. Make their weaknesses irrelevant.

The goal is to create a work environment filled with open communication and individual responsibility. Everyone knows their position on the field and what they need to accomplish as individuals, but they also know what their teammates are aiming for.

Each team member understands what they owe to others. They also know what they need from others.

Everyone knows what is expected of them and what they expect from others.

As opportunities change, managers must enable the company and its individual members to grow and develop too.

Nobody should feel like they are a great actor, wasting their talents in a terrible play. But if that feeling is around, the root cause should be addressed so no more time is being wasted.

THE TAKEAWAY: **Bring out the best in yourself and those you manage.**

43   FEBRUARY 12 — Find people who encourage your desired behaviors.

On page 15 of his screenplay for *Whiplash*, Damien Chazelle writes about the Polgar sisters.

Laszlo Polgar, a Hungarian psychologist, declares in 1967 that talent is all about conditioning. He eventually finds a wife who agrees to his experiment, and they start having kids: Susan, Sofia, and Judit. Before they can even talk, these girls are playing chess. By 1984, the top female player in chess is Susan.

In 1989, 14-year-old Sofia plays the eight-straight-wins 'Sack of Rome.'

Today, the universally considered greatest female chess player of all time is Judit Polgar, the youngest of the three chess champions.

In Chapter 9 of his 2018 book, *Atomic Habits*, James Clear also cites the Polgar family. When I first heard about the Polgar sisters, I thought they hated their upbringing. But in interviews, they talk about enjoying their childhood and loving the game of chess.

Of course they would. They grew up in an environment that prioritized chess above all else, the way American parents may prioritize acting or football or studying medicine above all else. What did your parents get right...and wrong?

THE TAKEAWAY: Find people who encourage your desired behaviors.

FEBRUARY 13 — Reflect and share fond memories.

I remember in eighth grade I was sitting in Mrs. Grossman's English class, tracking James Cameron's Avatar as it became the biggest movie in the world.

Seeing Avatar on IMAX in Atlantic City with my family in 2009 when it was released was a great experience. I had just read Dashavatara as well, which features Lord Vishnu's 10 avatars.

I shared this memory with my Per Scholas class in 2020. One of my students, "Togba," actually met Stephen Lang once, from Cameron's *Avatar,* and shared a photo.

From (Toe-puh) Nathaniel Norris Jr. to Me: (Privately) (11:39 AM)

"He stayed at the hotel I was working night audit at in Manhattan Beach and I had his car brought up every morning. Sometimes we'd just sit there and chat for 15 minutes straight before he went off to set. Dude was soooooooo sweeet and a total father!! Gave me some really powerful and good life and career advice."

THE TAKEAWAY: Reflect on one, maybe two, very fond memories.

45 FEBRUARY 14 — Photos are more moving than words.

In Day 25 of his Masters of Scale course "The Mindset of Scale," Reid Hoffman talks about Scott Harrison, founder of Charity: Water.

A **former nightclub promoter,** Harrison founded the nonprofit in 2006 to help prevent deaths caused by drinking unclean water. Scott understood the hedonistic clubbing business. He had 15,000 people in his club's email list. But now, he wanted to work for humanitarian groups like the Peace Corps or United Nations.

Harrison went through many months of rejection. But eventually, Mercy Ships accepted him. Mercy Ships sends state-of-the-art hospital ships to third world countries.

Scott had an "a-ha moment" when he worked for Mercy Ships, taking over 50,000 "before" photos of patients who could not drink water because they had conditions such as cleft lips. Then, he took "after" photos of those patients drinking clean water after the clefts were treated. He emailed those before-and-after photos to the same email list of 15,000. Then he noticed people started donating to Mercy Ships and to Charity: Water.

Imagine reading a wordy email from a former club promoter about children in water crisis nations like Liberia, versus an email with photos of Liberians drinking "chocolate milk water."

Harrison learned that photos of human suffering sparks action more quickly than words can.

One hundred percent of all money to Charity: Water goes to creating clean water for over 700 million people.

THE TAKEAWAY: **Photos are more moving than words.**

FEBRUARY 15 — Use different tools to solve different types of problems.

"To the man with a hammer, every problem looks like a nail."

—Abraham Maslow

A person with the hammer pays for their ignorance because they will torture reality to fit the only model they know.

This is stupid because the world is not going to change into a nail for that person's hammer. It is instead better to be a person with a Swiss Army knife, which has different tools for different problems.

Some problems require a screwdriver, while other problems require a corkscrew, and so on.

Trying to open a can with a hammer is like using a can opener to hit a nail. You could probably do it, but it would be more effort than it is worth.

Hat tip to the Swedish Investor for a great YouTube video on Charlie Munger, where I first learned of this approach to thinking.

THE TAKEAWAY: Use different tools to solve different types of problems.

FEBRUARY 16 — Help people say your name right.

The Players is a private club founded by Edwin Booth on December 31, 1888, for actors.

Actors Equity was founded at The Players. When you walk through the club you see paintings on the wall which include people such as James Cagney, Humphrey Bogart, Lauren Bacall, Frank Sinatra, Mark Twain, Gregory Peck, Sidney Poitier, and Tony Bennett.

In 2020 at 6:03 pm, I was working as the front door manager of The Players. An older white couple walked in for their dinner reservation.

After I took their names, they asked for mine. I obliged.

> Then they asked where my name is from. I tell them it is from undivided India. I am Hindu, and my last name is "Malik" and comes from "maalik-saab," as people call "boss" in India.

They proceed to tell me things they know about India, engaging in a sort of couple's comedy routine for a solid minute or two. They remembered food they ate, places they went, in a very well-intentioned attempt to connect with me.

I talked to the doorman, Oswaldo, after they went to eat their dinner. He laughed when I told him that they asked me to repeat "Akash" a few times to make sure they said it right. I told Oswaldo I sort of appreciated it. It is good to pronounce someone's name correctly.

So what is your name? Do people ask you to repeat it or spell it when they meet you?

THE TAKEAWAY: Help people say your name right.

FEBRUARY 17 — Keep the memories even if the building disappears.

The Trump Plaza Hotel and Casino went down on this date in 2021.

My father remembers in 1988, a few years after he first came to America, he would park in that parking lot with my uncles and aunts. To me it felt like he was mourning this building going down.

He just played the implosion video on YouTube. I silently watched him play a few more videos. One building, imploding at different angles.

Trump Taj Mahal is gone now, too.

To be honest I would stay far away from POTUS 45/47. Agent Orange, as Spike Lee says. But for people from the age of my father, Trump was something of an icon for decades. Even though his buildings are gone, the memories and associated meanings of them remain.

New buildings can pop up, too. My apartment in downtown Los Angeles was once a parking lot, but now people live in it with their families and roommates, creating memories that hopefully last a lifetime.

THE TAKEAWAY: Keep the memories even if the building disappears.

49

FEBRUARY 18 — Failing to plan is planning to fail. So plan to succeed.

Do you know why Costco and Amazon Prime memberships are impossible to cancel? Because in the long term, you save so much on shipping, or food, or diapers, and more.

A lot of time, money, and energy went into designing those membership perks and pricing structure to make sure you renew yearly. If you got a membership to NJ Transit, or PATH, MTA, the LA Metro, your trains could still be delayed. Even if you planned everything, from your clothes to leaving the house to getting there to the ticket, the train could still be delayed.

Because, well, the world is imperfect.

But you should still give yourself credit: You got your Amazon Prime membership because you planned to make lots of purchases. You planned to be at the station on time, because you *intuitively* understand that failing to plan is planning to fail.

So you plan for success.

All successful enterprises plan carefully. They exercise, they eat right, they show up to work paranoid of competitors and prepared to succeed. Otherwise, their enemies will eat them. Their lives, homes, daily routines, behavior, are all designed to be actors, executives, writers, directors, athletes, and everything in between, at the top of their game.

> THE TAKEAWAY: **Failing to plan is planning to fail. So plan to succeed.**

FEBRUARY 19 — Knowledge is great, but execution is better.

I am on the PATH train approaching Harrison, NJ, and on my mind is a small talent agency I interviewed with in 2019, but still lost the job.

Later that year I interviewed at bigger agencies like Gersh and Independent Creative Management (ICM), but then I realized I would make an awful agent. Creative Artists Agency (CAA) eventually acquired ICM for $750 million.

There is no shortage of jobs in the entertainment industry but getting them takes both knowledge and skill. And with everyone having a smartphone, anyone can point and shoot a camera and tell stories.

No-budget videos can get millions of views nowadays if they are executed well and they get word-of-mouth buzz.

Perhaps I demonstrated knowledge during those interviews, but I did not execute them well. It is good to have knowledge, but it is even better to know how to use it.

THE TAKEAWAY: Knowledge is great, but execution is better.

51

FEBRUARY 20 — Raise your standards as a manager and a parent.

One hundred and forty years ago, Japan was an underdeveloped country. But it very quickly produced excellent, competent management.

Wherever we have only capital, we have not achieved development. But when we develop strong management energy, we generate rapid development. Development is therefore a matter of human energy, not economic wealth.

The task of management is to direct human energies into a well-managed project. Then and only then will rapid development occur.

An excellent example of mismanagement comes from American Senator Ted Cruz.

In February 2021, Senator Ted Cruz took a trip with his family to Cancun while Texas suffered cold and power outages. Cruz said he was trying to be a good dad to his daughters, and he thought if other parents were in his position, they would have also fled Houston and go to a luxury resort in Cancun. Meanwhile, millions of Texans had no power, no running water, and were freezing in the winter. And Per Scholas management was handling that situation in Texas for learners there.

At the time, I was working at Per Scholas as an instructor. I was amazed to see a Senator doing a worse job at managing his responsibilities than my own managers at Per Scholas, despite their not having nearly as many resources or political power.

Resources without good management are as good as useless.

THE TAKEAWAY: Raise your standards as a manager and a parent.

FEBRUARY 21 — Do what makes you happy (and make lots of mistakes).

Grandparents are a gift. While I have them, I need to appreciate them.

My grandfather's sister died recently. I know that soon my grandparents will be taken from me by old age and death. I need to spend time with them. Capture every beautiful moment while I still can.

On this day, I said goodbye to Nanima over FaceTime, and it felt ominous. To think that when I also die one day my grandkids may never have seen me over a live video feed.

There is a lot of writing about a place beyond death. Perhaps it is heaven, or hell, or reincarnation into this cycle of birth, childhood, adolescence, adulthood, old age, and death.

So there is plenty of room to make mistakes! Every child falls when learning to walk.

Good parents are managers trying to provide for their child proper training, responsibilities, and room for making mistakes. The child can breathe a sigh of relief when they feel like they can make mistakes in pursuit of their mission.

Mistakes can be beautiful. Learning from mistakes is even more beautiful. Learning from the mistakes of others without making them yourself is hard, but if you can do it, you will profit.

THE TAKEAWAY: **Do what makes you happy (and make lots of mistakes).**

53

FEBRUARY 22 — Find a meaningful name for your next venture.

On May 13, 2008, Jason Kilar **blogged** about the name he and his company are using: Hulu.

He wrote about going through a marathon of naming sessions when Eric, the Chief Technical Officer, mentioned he had actually considered the name Hulu for an online video venture that he previously founded in China.

In Mandarin, Kilar explains, Hulu has two interesting meanings.

The primary meaning referred to an ancient Chinese proverb that describes the Hulu, a literal "gourd" that was hollowed out and used to hold precious things.

The secondary meaning is "interactive recording."

THE TAKEAWAY: Find a meaningful name for your next venture.

FEBRUARY 23 — Circumstances matter more than characteristics.

In a *Harvard Business Review* article about knowing your customers' "job to be done," is the story of Bob Moesta. Bob is an innovation consultant charged with bolstering sales of new condos in Detroit.

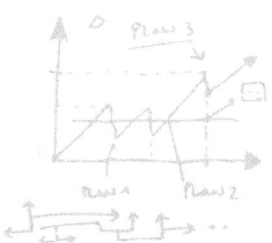

He was targeting retirees who were downsizing out of big family homes, ideally to those at a $120,000 to $200,000 price.

In Moesta's conversations with potential buyers, the "dining room table" came up repeatedly. People kept saying, "As soon as I figure out what to do with my dining room table, then I was free to move." He and his colleagues couldn't understand why. But when Moesta sat at his own dining room table with his family at Christmas, he understood. Every birthday was spent around that table. Every holiday. Homework was spread out on it. The table represented family.

Moesta suddenly realized he was not in the business of new-home construction. He was in the business of moving lives.

This "job to be done" theory could apply to streaming media as well. I often "hire" a video to do a job. I stream Professor Messer videos to train my learners in technology, for example.

That is a different from my personal viewing routine, when I search and stream comedy clips or music for fast laughs or energy boost before I resume working. Characteristics like my name or age or gender or level of education had less effect on my streams as opposed my circumstances.

THE TAKEAWAY: **Circumstances matter more than characteristics.**

FEBRUARY 24 — Find a productive way to navigate your boredom.

When I see learners fully engaged in the training, troubleshooting their way to the solution or finishing the project, I see something like a "learning flow."

I observe this when the student's heart, mind, and muscles synchronize, along with many other faces from all over the country signing into this Per Scholas "Zoom store" with me.

I do not control my past; all I control is the ability to make reasoned choices and small progress toward goals each day.

After work one day, I got bored, went for a walk, read, and worked on myself and my creative projects. Then I got distracted by Hogwarts legacy. I stopped playing Legacy to call my dad and mom. Both calls were a bit short, as they were on their way to a medical appointment.

I do have the Per Scholas library to learn new cool tech, but I could also dust off the screenplays I started and never finished. Or do I do GMAT? Go to B-school? My dad said, book a date and study for that. I joked OK, September 1, 2094, I will be ready. He meant a date about six months away. I said I would think about it.

8:10 am. Yeah, I really found myself needing *Bhagavad Gita*.

From page 77 of my copy (Swami Prabhupada, founder of ISKCON and Hare Krishna Movement): *The person who is not disturbed by happiness and distress and steady in both is certainly eligible for liberation.*

THE TAKEAWAY: Find a productive way to navigate your boredom.

FEBRUARY 25 — Find a sacred cow from which you can get milk and burgers.

Abbie Hoffman, from Aaron Sorkin's film, The Trial of the Chicago 7, *said* "sacred cows make the tastiest hamburgers."

The earliest strong match located by Quote Investigator for this statement appeared in October 1965, *The Daily Collegian*, a student newspaper at Pennsylvania State University.

An article discussed the revivification of a student publication called *Bottom of the Birdcage* which took inspiration from another periodical, *Aardvark* magazine: "Sacred cows make the best hamburger."

Anyway, I am also hopelessly obsessed with Harry Potter, ever since childhood. To me and many fans, the books and original movies could be considered "sacred cows." But Warner Bros Discovery will never stop milking the sacred cow of Harry Potter. In fact, they would make hamburgers out of that cow in a heartbeat if the fans paid for them.

At this writing, *Hogwarts Legacy* is rumored to become an HBO show after over 267 million hours played. The first seven books are being redone into TV as well, with further development planned well into the future.

THE TAKEAWAY: Find a sacred cow from which you can get milk and burgers.

57

FEBRUARY 26 — Prime yourself with the right images at the right time.

Attention is the greatest currency in the world.

Have you ever heard someone say, "I am a visual person?"

According to James Clear's Atomic Habits, the human body has approximately 10 million sensory receptors dedicated to sight.

This is why lots of time and money goes into planning movies, TV, and advertising campaigns.

In 2005, Duke University once had a team do an experiment in which 341 university students were flashed either the Apple or IBM logo so quickly that they were unaware they saw them. Then, they were assigned the task of listing all of the uses for a brick that they could imagine, beyond building a wall. The researchers were testing how creative the participants could be. The researchers found that people who were exposed to the Apple logo generated far more unusual, creative uses for the brick, compared with those who were primed with the IBM logo.

The team did a follow-up experiment testing honesty with logos for the Disney Channel, and E! Channel. Those primed with the Disney Channel logo behaved much more honestly than those who saw the E! Channel logos.

If you are exercising or doing sports today, prime yourself with images of Nike to help you perform better. If you use Disney images, perhaps you will do better creatively.

THE TAKEAWAY: Prime yourself with the right images at the right time.

FEBRUARY 27 — Understand the different attitudes toward money.

My Monday meeting with the Per Scholas Remote Training AWS team was canceled. So now I have free time I was not expecting.

A friend mentioned *The Romantics* on Netflix, which explores in four episodes the life and legacy of Bollywood filmmaker Yash Chopra with archival footage and celebrity interviews.

In Episode 1, "The Boy from Jalandhar," I learned that Yash Chopra did not like shooting retakes, but Aditya Chopra did. Aditya's work depicted a far more youthful sensibility, whereas his father's work depicted a more traditional Indian sensibility.

Yash Chopra came from a village in Jalandhar. He had little money to shoot and had to be more conservative, frugal, and efficient with his movie budgets. Every roll of film was expensive. A director in such a position must make quick decisions to stay on budget. On the other hand, Aditya grew up the son of a rich filmmaker. He did lots of retakes. Yash Raj Films was able to afford much bigger budget movies when he took over for his dad because it by then it was a well-established company.

People who earn their wealth through disciplined effort may be more cautious when spending their hard-earned money.

On the other hand, people who inherit their wealth, or are gifted a lot of money without having to work for it, may be more excited and less cautious about spending it.

THE TAKEAWAY: Understand the different attitudes toward money.

59

FEBRUARY 28 — Think of one product that billions could possibly use.

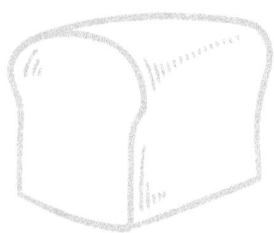

The first and most crucial question any business starts with is, "Who is the customer?" When someone meets you for the first time, they ask a similar question, "What do you do?"

These are not easy questions with obvious answers. There are many different kinds of answers you could give about your business, or your profession, depending on who is asking. Most businesses have at least two customers, both of which need to buy product for there to be a sale: the homemaker, and the grocer.

Say you are a baker, and your business is selling bread. You need the grocer to buy your bread, and for the homemaker to buy your bread from the grocer.

It does you no good for the homemaker to be eager to buy your bread if their grocer does not sell it. Or for the grocer to display your bread when no homemaker wants to buy it. Satisfying the homemaker without satisfying the grocer, or vice versa, means no bread gets sold.

For the baker, it is therefore important to start first with creating a satisfying product that billions of people could possibly use. Once that is done, then the baker can focus on at least two customers for the product.

THE TAKEAWAY: **Think of one product that billions could possibly use.**

FEBRUARY 29 — Celebrate your local libraries, bookstores, and cinemas.

For Leap Year, here's a bonus *neeti*.

There is an interview that The Script Lab does with Brian Selznick on transitioning from an author into a screenwriter with guidance from senior screenwriter John Logan.

You can argue that book adaptations keep the Hollywood storytelling engine running. Many books become movies. Both mediums market one another after a book becomes a big-screen adaptation. Some books, such as *American Prometheus*, join an elite list of memorable adaptations like *Oppenheimer* (2023). Others, such as *Percy Jackson & The Olympians: The Lightning Thief* (2010) or *Artemis Fowl* (2020), join a long list of forgettable adaptations.

Selznick talks about how natural it is for people to turn to books for inspiration. He also gives credit to John Logan, who did the *Hugo* screenplay based on the book.

Logan figured out how to make a book that celebrates the history of films and movies, but ultimately is about books. He adapted it into a screenplay that celebrates books, writing, libraries, and bookstores, but is ultimately about the importance of films and cinemas.

Without changing much of the plot, he changed the entire intention of the story.

A lot of people write books. A lot of writers write stories. Some writers like Selznick also enjoy drawing, and some of his stories are also told visually.

Stories in all their forms, and original storytellers, matter a great deal to humankind.

THE TAKEAWAY: Celebrate your local libraries, bookstores, and cinemas.

MARCH

MARCH 1 — Become aware of your mental strengths and weaknesses.

As Epictetus writes in his *Discourses*, in the 2008 edition translated by Robert Dobbin, the beginning of philosophy is "an awareness of one's own mental fitness."

When you become aware of your ability to analyze your own mind, you become a philosopher.

Not every person is a philosopher. Usually, a philosopher is a deep thinker who is trying to troubleshoot problems within themselves or problems they see in the world around them. This is good. It means you are training your senses to anticipate strengths, weaknesses, opportunities, or threats.

Every great manager, in my humble view, has some kind of philosophy.

Perhaps their philosophy is constantly changing. That is expected, because people are constantly changing; therefore, their philosophy is too.

My mind often yearns for 2014, the year I graduated high school. High school graduation is a time of great change, when old philosophies are challenged and new ones are developed over decades of adulthood. Since March 2020, I have been through multiple graduations at Per Scholas, in person and remotely. As a Technical Trainer for over four years, I trained 249 adults in technology across multiple cycles and discovered an average graduation rate of 81 percent, and certification rate of 82 percent.

Every time, graduation is bittersweet. You say goodbye to people you knew for months, sometimes years, but you hope for the best. After the parties and cheering, you hope for positive changes for your classmates or students-turned-alumni.

THE TAKEAWAY: Become aware of your mental strengths and weaknesses.

MARCH 2 — Stop overthinking the problem and find a simple solution.

> **Akash Malik updated his status.**
> Stop thinking, and put an end to your problems.
> Mar 2, 2017, 10:33 AM
>
> **Akash Malik updated his status.**
> Artists are eternally self-absorbed. I know this because I am an artist.
> Mar 1, 2017, 8:20 PM

Lao Tzu wrote the *Tao Te Ching*.

I have seen people online quote "Stop thinking and end your problems." I liked it, and I shared it on Facebook. It might be something you shared or saw on social media too.

It is catchy to say, but as a knowledge worker, you can't not think. Thinking is how you solve problems, but ironically, thinking also creates problems that action could probably solve.

I recall an HBO documentary on billionaire Warren Buffett. It depicts him living simply; eating whatever whenever; and reading. His simple living is not necessarily penance living. Maybe he overthinks, but he doesn't show it in the documentary.

It shows a kid who sells items like Coca Cola® or Wrigley's® gum. The kid understands you do not spend the principle, you invest it. Then, you use the profits to fund growth. He sells soda and gum, two items that are hard to resist. The strategy is deceptively simple because it requires no thought. In fact, overthinking would destroy this simple strategy.

The simplest strategy is often the best strategy, but it is easy to screw up with overthinking.

THE TAKEAWAY: Stop overthinking the problem and find a simple solution.

MARCH 3 — Find disruptive technology outside your industry.

Can you imagine your jeans or jackets without a zipper?

Katia Moskvitch writes for BBC that this invention was first patented in 1851 by Elias Howe, the inventor of the sewing machine, but was made significantly better over 40 years later by Whitcomb Judson in 1893, and then again by Gideon Sundback in 1913.

It took decades before the fashion industry used zippers on garments, especially after Esquire magazine applauded the zipper on trousers and called it the "Newest Tailoring Idea for Men."

Hollywood movies often have biker jackets with multiple zippers, like Marlon Brando in *The Wild One.*

Over hundreds of years, zippers were reinvented and modified several times across multiple industries. This device is so widespread now it is basically invisible.

It started in one industry, then began taking over other seemingly unrelated industries, causing everyone in those industries to adapt. Imagine making pants with buttons and then having to remake them with zippers because zippers are so popular in completely unrelated industries such as shoes and tobacco pouches.

THE TAKEAWAY: Find potentially disruptive technology outside your industry.

64

MARCH 4 — Discover new heroes to share with others.

Princeton was beating UPenn in overtime college basketball. UPenn was down 42-25 when the second half started, but then it looked like they would win (and they did). Games like this one are where new heroes are born, specifically in the world of basketball.

Sometimes, when you see heroic moments in a game like this, you want to tell others about it, whether they are basketball fans or not!

I felt that way again later the same day when I went to see *CREED III* at Alamo Drafthouse in Downtown Los Angeles. A preview for another movie came onscreen from Searchlight Pictures: prodigy, lover, revolutionary, *Chevalier.*

I was kind of excited to learn about a man who people were calling "Black Mozart." Mozart was 10 years younger than Chevalier. It was interesting to learn that Amadeus was inspired by Chevalier, particularly the character Monostatos in Mozart's opera *The Magic Flute*, according to a BBC show with musician Chi-chi Nwanoku.

New heroes are being born during basketball games in March Madness, and another who has long been dead is being rediscovered because of this movie.

Life is a constant discovery of heroes, ones who are living and ones long gone. Stories of such heroes, when shared well, can energize both individuals and large groups of people.

THE TAKEAWAY: **Discover new heroes to share with others.**

MARCH 5 — Understand primal reactions to colors, such as red.

Hinduism is an "open source" religion. That's a good metaphor to describe it, as Josh Schrei did for *The Huffington Post*. It is very inclusive by its nature, as opposed to Western religions which are monotheistic and more "closed source."

The color red is common to many religions because red is a primal color. The color red often means fire, or blood.

Fire is a living being of sorts, requiring fuel, oxygen, and heat. People thought fire came from the gods. Westerners have stories of Prometheus, who stole fire from the gods to give to humans. He matches a similar character, Mātariśvan in the Rigveda of India, who stole fire (Agni) to give to humans as a gift.

In *The Wizard of Oz*, Dorothy has red slippers. They were not red originally, they were silver, but with Technicolor technology featured in the film, MGM had to make the slippers red to show it off.

Snow White gets a red apple in the Walt Disney film. Martin Scorsese often uses the color red, as in *Mean Streets*, where the titles are red. Red could mean danger, or anger, or lust.

Kurukshetra, the battlefield of Mahabharata, was *soaked* with blood. The sand is red now from all the blood spilled over 18 days of battles.

And stop signs are red. Why? To make you STOP!

THE TAKEAWAY: Understand primal reactions to colors such as red.

MARCH 6 — Identify ideas that are low risk but high opportunity.

Many successful entrepreneurs are not "risk focused" but "opportunity focused."

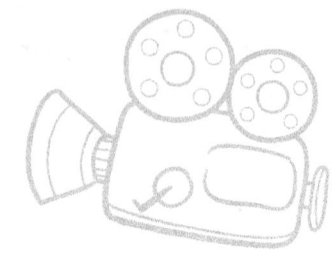

Enrolling in Per Scholas for me was very low in risk because I had already been out of work for months, interviewing at various entertainment companies in 2019, and constantly falling short.

Eventually, I figured I could enroll in a free technical training course. And guess what? This low-risk idea was absolutely transformational for me.

I have so many more tech skills now through Per Scholas, and many wonderful colleagues. I get to help so many people. I hope to continue helping more people with my writing, too.

Drucker might nod and say yes, Per Scholas is a low-risk, high-opportunity pursuit.

But for someone who cannot be out of work for 15 weeks, the risks would be higher.

So was going to Temple University over NYU Tisch School of the Arts for me.

I got into both schools. Temple gave me the full scholarship. NYU, on the other hand, wanted me to get a $70,000-per-year loan. It was an easy choice for me to go to Temple because the risk was significantly lower.

Film and Media Arts is an inherently risky major already.

THE TAKEAWAY: **Identify the ideas low in risk but high in opportunity.**

MARCH 7 — Create a whole greater than the sum of its parts.

Did you know John G. Avildsen, who directed 3 *Karate Kid* movies and *Rocky*, has a YouTube channel?

Or that Martin Scorsese was an assistant on Avildsen's short film *Smiles* in 1964?

A documentary about Avildsen, *King of the Underdogs (2017)*, opens on the steps of the Philadelphia Art Museum, also known as the "Rocky steps." The movie begins with an interviewer asking people if they knew who directed *Rocky*. But nobody could guess this forgotten director of Oscar-winning movies.

The director has a very important job as the "manager" of a movie. The director's effort, vision, and leadership is what unites a team, creating a whole greater than the sum of its parts.

Of course, nobody can expect an average person to know the names of directors behind the camera. People mostly know the actors they see in movies. Actors are important, but they are just the tip of the iceberg!

Actors are important in a movie, but so is the script, the music, the costumes, the camera moves, sets, and so on. A lot of work goes into movies behind the scenes to create memorable movie experiences.

THE TAKEAWAY: Create a whole greater than the sum of its parts.

68   MARCH 8 — Support your definition of "cinema" or "art."

In November 2019, Martin Scorsese sparked a debate in *The New York Times* by saying Marvel movies are more like Disney theme park rides, not "cinema" as he experienced it. He sees a difference between the "worldwide audiovisual entertainment" of Marvel and "cinema."

James Gunn responded **on Instagram**, "Superheroes are simply today's gangsters/cowboys/outer space adventurers… not everyone will be able to appreciate them, even some geniuses."

In an effort to say that Marvel Studios commits to many different types of films, President Kevin Feige responded to Scorsese in *The Hollywood Reporter* saying 2015's *Ant-Man* was a heist movie. 2014's *Captain America* was a political thriller. Then in 2018, the studio took a huge risk by snapping away half of the cast in *Infinity War*.

Alex Abad-Santos for Vox writes, "It's possible to love Marvel movies and also be terrified of a future where no one makes anything but Marvel movies."

I find myself agreeing with Abad-Santos. I do enjoy superhero movies, but they should not become the only kinds of movies getting made.

Of course, I am just one person. Ultimately, customers decide with their dollars and their streams what art they are interested in, and as a result, more of *that* sort of art will be created.

THE TAKEAWAY: Support your definition of "cinema" or "art."

MARCH 9 — Identify the qualities you admire and desire for yourself.

My older brother was on **Wheel of Fortune**. He won a trip to Egypt. I was lucky to be chosen to go with him in October 2021.

There was one night we were resting in our Nile River Movenpick cruise ship room, after a long day of exploring. I started asking Aman about his experience at UVA Darden School of Business. He told me about doing a semester in India and an exercise his teacher gave.

"Think of your heroes. Real or fictional. Up to five. Then start describing what qualities you admire in them." Once my brother and his class made their lists, his teacher said:

"The qualities you admire in heroes are the qualities you desire in yourself."

What you admire is what you desire.

That day in October 2021 I listed my inspirational heroes: Martin Scorsese, Tony Stark, Jeff Bezos, Steve Jobs, and Ryan Coogler. The first and last were easy, Scorsese and Coogler both make terrific movies, and I want to make terrific movies one day too.

I admire Tony Stark because he built his own super suit and Tom Holland's Spider Man suit.

Then came the list of qualities I desire:
- Creativity
- Intelligence
- Financial Literacy
- Leadership
- Technical Aptitude

Not everyone will have the same list, and that is a good thing. Different people have different interests.

THE TAKEAWAY: Identify the qualities you admire and desire for yourself

70   MARCH 10 — Treat your creative job like a real "nine-to-five."

In a *Daily Stoic* titled "Find Yourself a Cato," Ryan Holiday and Stephen Hanselman write that the influential ancient Roman, Cato the Younger, never wrote anything down.

Cato taught no classes. He gave no interviews, and he certainly never uploaded a video to the Internet. But others write about how Cato was one of the most principled men in Rome.

Seneca says we should all have our own Cato, a person whom we can measure ourselves against in our souls.

The lesson here is to ignore fads and find yourself good role models.

This day in 2020, I got off work as a TA at Per Scholas Newark. Then I had a few hours until later that day around 9 pm, when I worked as front door manager at The Players.

I got to meet Michael Riedel, a writer at the *New York Post*. I showed him *Meditations* Book 5 on my iPhone, and it resonated with him. He thinks he heard of Ryan Holiday before too.

I asked him about his writing schedule. He said, "Well, a bank teller starts at 9, ends at 5, and writers should too!" I agreed with him on that, then pointed out that I had two jobs, but if I ever had the chance to make a living as a writer, I would treat it like a real job.

> THE TAKEAWAY: **Treat your creative job like a real "nine-to-five."**

MARCH 11 — Jump into and out of research rabbit holes.

A Wikipedia rabbit hole led me to the historian Erika Lee, *The Making of Asian America*, where she writes, "Mrs. Swinton, a captain's wife who accompanied her husband on the coolie ship Salsette as it sailed from Calcutta to Trinidad in 1858, likened the journey to the African slave trade."

It was a desire for more Asian history knowledge that led me to finding Erika Lee. Then I bought the book on Apple Books and am now exploring this footnote.

"E. Swinton and Jane Swinton, *The Other Middle Passage: Journal of a Voyage from Calcutta to Trinidad, 1858* (London: Alfred Bennett, 1859), 3. Mortality rates between 1857 and 1862 from Mangru, *Indenture and Abolition*, 25. 1870s mortality rates from Tinker, *A New System of Slavery*, 165."

Sometimes, a rabbit hole takes you into another rabbit hole. You do have to come up for air eventually, but once that is done, you jump back into your journey.

THE TAKEAWAY: **Jump into and out of research rabbit holes.**

72
MARCH 12 — Focus on marketing and innovation to win customers.

A business has only one purpose: to create a customer.

To create a customer and become what Peter Drucker calls "an organ of society," a business needs two things: marketing, and innovation.

To me, NBA basketball is an organ of society. Say the Lakers are playing the Knicks. During the game you have professional sports commentary, ad breaks for new movies, fast food, cars, beverages, beer, and much more, all of which NBA fans sit through while watching the game.

Companies making these products spend a lot of time and money to market them. These companies also have competitors to innovate or market against to get customers.

The goal is to turn a potential individual customer watching the game into a paying customer.

In a society with so many organs, which businesses survive? It's the ones that do well in marketing, or innovation.

THE TAKEAWAY: **Focus on marketing and innovation to win customers.**

MARCH 13 — Measure your life with positive impact numbers.

On March 10, 2023, Silicon Valley Bank (SVB) failed after a bank run, marking the third-largest bank failure in US history, and the largest since the 2007-2008 financial crisis.

A lot of startups and tech companies had money in SVB. The Fed only guarantees deposits up to $250,000 through the FDIC, but most depositors had accounts far bigger than that. So, a bank failure means layoffs. A person who gets laid off might respond by switching careers.

A person switching careers might choose a training company like Per Scholas for a fresh start. Per Scholas has completely changed my own life. The leadership team, led by Plinio Ayala, recently shared an awesome slide with us in the town hall, which I had to save.

It feels good to work for a nonprofit that is trying to help people.

THE TAKEAWAY: Measure your life with positive impact numbers.

74

MARCH 14 — See your life through the eyes of others, not just yours.

Earlier today I digitized my parents' baby tapes of myself. It is a rather remarkable experience to connect a VCR to my MacBook with an adapter, digitize VHS tapes, then share clips, or entire movies, via iMessage or iCloud or Google Drive. I suppose I could have also used Amazon S3, but that would have taken a bit more effort.

It was one of multiple long tapes, but digitizing all these home movies was deeply rewarding.

Did your mom or dad record you growing up?

> **If you are blessed with a big family of aunts, uncles, parents, cousins, and so on who love you, some of whom may not be with us anymore, you understand that your life is not truly "your own life."** (359. December 24)

It is very easy for me to shoot new video on an iPhone of new babies, but digitizing old tapes is a humbling experience that reminds me it was not always so easy to shoot and store video.

> **THE TAKEAWAY: See your life through the eyes of others, not only yours.**

MARCH 15 — Five-year plans suck. Have compounding habits instead.

I downloaded *The Mandalorian* on Disney+ for the bus ride from downtown LA to West Hollywood, where I am meeting my old boss, Sal Litvak. We chatted for 40 minutes.

I told Sal about living in DTLA and how it has been almost five years since I worked as his assistant, doing things such as managing his calendar, booking podcast guests, helping him schedule shoots, finding cool locations where we could record him, all for his Accidental Talmudist nonprofit. He even showed me clips he was editing of his upcoming feature film, *Guns & Moses*.

I told him how I now laugh at the idea of a five-year plan. Imagine all the five-year plans in 2019 that went completely out the window during COVID-19. It is a bit sad, honestly.

But then I told him about my study habits. I earned a lot of tech certifications during the pandemic. I earned promotions at Per Scholas during the pandemic.

I did not have a five-year plan, but I did have a diary.

Keeping the diary helped me stay focused on learning new things. It helped me get better at managing my mental health, and it now helps me manage other people remotely.

Every day, I studied philosophy, read business books, and religious wisdom and saved as much money as possible. These daily practices compounded.

Then one day I looked up, and five years had passed.

THE TAKEAWAY: Five-year plans suck. Have compounding habits instead.

76   MARCH 16 — Win the war, not the battles.

"The stock market is designed to transfer money from the active to the patient."

–Warren Buffett

At any given moment, there are a thousand things you could be studying or investing your money in. The only way you lose money is if you swing and miss.

As long as you are careful to pick the ball you want to hit and wait for the right time to swing for it, you should be in great shape.

People will try to distract you, there will be dramatic headlines and market volatility, but as long as you keep your cool and are not overreacting, you are good.

Sometimes, you need to practice *strategic patience*. There are people who will try to convince you to do risky things with your time, money, or energy, but you need to pick what you engage with.

Emphasizing cheap and quick wins can often cost you in the long run

THE TAKEAWAY: **Win the war, not the battles.**

MARCH 17 —It is better to earn compound interest instead of paying it.

"Compound interest is the eighth wonder of the world. He who understands it, earns it; he who doesn't, pays it."

–Albert Einstein

Ideally, you want compound interest for your money. On a chart, you want stock to build up and to the right. The growth spirals out of control because you stay invested for the long term, reinvest dividends, and add money consistently.

The same is with knowledge.

If you grow your knowledge consistently, eventually it also yields compound interest.

Continuous learning of new concepts builds a stronger knowledge base you can consult. Studying with a strong existing knowledge base can lead to deeper insights. Some of these insights may even be innovative.

Otherwise, worst case, your chart ends up going down and to the left. Failing to understand compound interest means debts can also grow. You start making mistakes on mistakes that compound in a not-so-pretty way, like death or jail or crippling debt.

THE TAKEAWAY: It is better to earn compound interest instead of paying it.

78

MARCH 18 — Make sufficient profit to cover the costs of innovation.

Joseph Schumpeter, former Finance Minister of Austria and later a professor at Harvard, had this concept of "creative destruction."

Innovation leads to the destruction of old industries. New technology, products, or business processes create new markets that grow fast but make old technologies or products obsolete.

Capitalism is dynamic, and the proof is everywhere. Old structures are replaced by newer, more efficient ones. Digital media versus legacy media. E-commerce versus brick-and-mortar. Netflix versus Blockbuster.

To build a company that withstands the test of time, there have to be enough profits so teams can "creatively destroy" their way to a new, unexplored growth area.

This cascades down to what education we need for new jobs or careers.

The question becomes, is there sufficient profits, or enough capital, to provide for the future costs of staying in business, the costs of "creative destruction"?

THE TAKEAWAY: Make sufficient profit to cover the costs of innovation.

MARCH 19 — *Facta, non verba* **(Deeds, not words).**

Spike Lee told *Vanity Fair* that his motto is "Deeds, not words."

Spike Lee also **shared** something surprising with *GQ*: that his father hated films.

It is surprising because, as Spike Lee fans know, his father Bill did the score for *She's Gotta Have It (1986)*, *School Daze (1988)*, *Do the Right Thing (1989)*, and *Mo' Better Blues (1990)*.

But he hated films when Spike was growing up. Why? Because he hated how movies portrayed Black people at that time.

So instead, Spike's mother would take Spike to the movies. Spike said his mother was responsible for Spike becoming a fan of Martin Scorsese when she took him to see *Mean Streets* in theaters in 1973. At that time, he didn't want to be a filmmaker. He didn't know people made films. You just, you know, went to the movie theater. That really had an impact on Spike, who was 16 years old.

He remembers the first time he met Scorsese, at a screening of *After Hours* (1985) at NYU.

Afterwards, Spike went up to him and told the story of seeing *Mean Streets* with his mother. Spike knew he made an impact on Marty by telling him he liked the film.

It is one thing to say, in your own words, how you feel about a piece of art. But it is a deed to go up to an artist and say how you honestly feel about their work.

THE TAKEAWAY: *Facta, non verba* **(Deeds, not words).**

80

MARCH 20 — Choose to be rich and anonymous, or poor and famous.

In episode 1309 of the podcast, *The Joe Rogan Experience,* Rogan interviewed Naval Ravikant, who at that point was well known for a series of tweets titled "How to Get Rich Without Getting Lucky." I enjoyed the whole podcast a great deal and found it inspiring.

One thing that Ravikant said to Rogan that stuck with me was, "Social media is making celebrities of all of us, and celebrities are the most miserable people in the world."

Rogan, a well-known celebrity, says there are benefits to being famous, but he also says it comes with unusual problems. He describes being out in public with his wife and daughter, and then some guy comes over to take a picture of Rogan for social media, and he does not care about interrupting the Rogan family. Such is the price of being famous: no privacy in public.

It might be hard for someone who isn't famous to understand how valuable anonymity can be. The ability to leave your house and do errands or have lunch with your family in public without people coming up to bother you is a privilege.

THE TAKEAWAY: Choose to be rich and anonymous, or poor and famous.

MARCH 21 — Take some time to imagine and build the future.

"Imagination is everything. It is the preview of life's coming attractions."

– Albert Einstein

E-commerce companies such as Amazon or Google have become worldwide digital distributors of information, advertising, goods, services, and much more. The people who work at these companies spend a great deal of time building their vision of the future so they can stay ahead of changes.

It is a good idea to take some time to imagine what could come next. By thinking ahead, you are preparing for possible future challenges.

So what could emerge beyond the year 2045?

Here are three ideas I have that may already exist:

1. Freemium, highly advanced AI companions that can interact with humans the way the "NetNavis" in beloved games like MegaMan do. These companions can be customized in their settings and do things such as healthcare reminders, Internet search, transcribe dictation, wait on hold for you, read messages and email, and even destroy viruses they encounter.

2. AR/VR Experience Centers for games with huge fanbases like American football, basketball, Pokemon Go, Star Wars, or Harry Potter.

3. Autonomous Delivery and Services: self-driving fleets of vehicles and drones, robots that cook or clean or do laundry, fix plumbing, or electrical maintenance

THE TAKEAWAY: Take some time to imagine and build the future.

82   MARCH 22 — Learn about historical figures who are new to you.

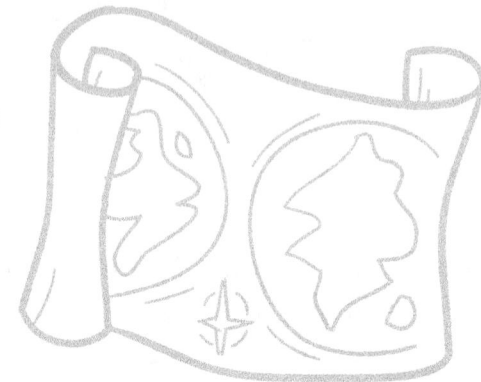

Aaron Burr Jr. was an American founding father who had an Indian-American son, according to Princeton University. An author named Susan Holloway Scott wrote a historical fiction novel about this, titled *The Secret Wife of Aaron Burr*.

Mary Eugénie Beauharnais Emmons was born in Kolkata (Calcutta), India, around 1760. She migrated to Haiti, where her original Indian name was abandoned to become Eugénie Beauharnais. Then, in the United States, her name was changed again to Mary Emmons.

She became Aaron Burr's slave and had two children with Burr: Louisa Charlotte, born in 1788, and a son, the abolitionist John Pierre Burr, born in 1792.

I wish I got to learn about figures like this in school, but it is never too late to learn new history.

THE TAKEAWAY: Learn about historical figures who are new to you.

MARCH 23 — Every job is important, big or small.

"There are no small roles, only small actors."

–Konstantin Stanislavski

If you ever see theater shows, live or on TV, you might see that the supporting actors are just as dedicated to the production as the leading actors.

In fact, those leading actors might have started in the ensemble, or as understudies. Then after they put in the time doing small parts faithfully, they get entrusted with bigger parts to play.

The same can be said for a company: there is no job too small, and if a person does their job well, they might be offered a bigger, more important job to do in the future.

No director wants to deal with a cast member who is ungrateful for the job they have. Such a member might even be at risk of losing their "small job" because they might not perform well with the rest of the team. It doesn't do much good to have a bad attitude at work or in rehearsal.

THE TAKEAWAY: Every job is important, big or small.

84   MARCH 24 — Research ways to make e-commerce better.

In my job at Per Scholas, remote training has completely transformed product delivery. Classes are on Zoom, course content is all in the learning management system Canvas, and communication is all done in Slack and email. I have trained hundreds of people across the US, without ever having to physically meet them!

This goes beyond the classroom too. Amazon sells almost everything you could imagine. You could list your products there, but you could also list them on your website and sell direct to your customer, giving you control over your brand, price, and customer relationship.

You may not even need storage space because of third-party logistics (3PL) providers who can do warehousing, packaging, and shipping for your company, enabling you to scale your business without investing in physical infrastructure.

Robots and AI can also make more efficient processes such as managing inventory, forecasting future demand, and automating delivery, powered by reusable energy and electric vehicles.

All these trends will make e-commerce faster, more flexible, and sustainable than it is currently

THE TAKEAWAY: Research ways to make e-commerce better.

MARCH 25 — Ask for help when you need it.

"What plan you have thought of in your mind should not come on your tongue. Contemplate and rethink over it, keeping it guarded. Put the idea or plan into action without voicing it."

–Chanakya

It is a struggle to keep a secret, especially if it is an exciting secret like "I am writing a book."

But if you ever had a big plan like this and then announced it to your friends or family or on social media, and ultimately fail, you could end up getting laughed at. Or perhaps even worse, someone steals your idea and executes it before you do.

It is better to be walking the walk instead of talking the talk. Actions speak far louder than words.

THE TAKEAWAY: Ask for help when you need it.

86
MARCH 26 — It doesn't matter where you came from.

"A great dynasty is not great if it is bereft of educated members. If a person is of low birth gains learning and wisdom, he would be honorable for nobles even."
—Chanakya

"I see now that the circumstances of one's birth are irrelevant. It is what you do with the gift of life that determines who you are."
— Mewtwo in *Pokemon: The First Movie*

There are royal, influential, and ultra-wealthy families in the world with terrible, stupid, selfish children.

The world also has poor families who have educated their children and acquired enough money to rise above poverty and into the heights of prestige.

Take it from Chanakya, or Mewtwo, it does not matter where you came from. What matters is what you do with the gift of life.

THE TAKEAWAY: It doesn't matter where you came from.

MARCH 27 — Use consistent language to cut through the noise.

A brand makes you feel a certain way. It is not a slogan or a logo, it is a feeling you give to people about you and your company when it comes to mind.

The world is a noisy place, full of digital notifications, cars, buses, trains, planes, and so on.

David Axelrod and Karl Rove, in their MasterClass on campaign strategy and messaging, say it helps to have a phrase said throughout a politician's campaign, such as "Build Back Better" for Biden, "Yes, We Can" for Obama, or "Make American Great Again" for Trump.

Cycling through too many slogans can cause confusion within the campaign operations on what message the staff needs to send, and it is hard for potential voters to remember among all the other noises they have in their life.

Taking control of the narrative indicates offense, because the campaign can talk about what it wants, *when* it wants. Losing control of the narrative means the opponent forced a campaign to talk about things it does not want to talk about.

To win this chess match of messaging, against direct opponents and indirect opponents, you need to have consistent messaging and branding across your entire organization.

THE TAKEAWAY: Use consistent language to cut through the noise.

MARCH 28 — Treat AI like a child, not like your overlord.

James Stanger, Chief Technology Evangelist of CompTIA, did a presentation titled "All I really need to know I learned from ChatGPT" that had some amazing insights.

Stanger started by listing various industrial revolution generations:
1. Steam, waterpower, mechanization
2. Mass production, assembly lines, electricity
3. Information age, automation, space age IT systems
4. Cloud, cyber systems intelligence

Over the past 300 years, there have also been some growing trends in emerging technology:
1. Democratization — Only governments used to have tech, now everybody has tech.
2. Miniaturization — From powerful, giant computers, to powerful *small* smartphones.
3. Virtualization — Companies can use virtual servers in the cloud instead of building servers.
4. Automation — Tasks can be done efficiently and error free, without human intervention.

Artificial intelligence is now capable of doing some work for you, but it only works as well as the training data the large language model (LLM) learned from.

Bad data can mean that AI hallucinates.

This is a problem for humans, who tend to trust technology too much. "Well, I found it on the Internet, so it must be true," or "Well, ChatGPT said it, so it must be true." These assumptions can cause big problems.

Like trusting the assumptions of a child. Sometimes they are right, sometimes they are not.

THE TAKEAWAY: **Treat AI like a child, not like your overlord.**

MARCH 29 — Comfort is the enemy of achievement.

"Comfort is the enemy of achievement."
—Farrah Gray

On the common application for college, they might ask you about an accomplishment that transitioned you from childhood into adulthood. I wrote about my experience in my high school marching band.

I spent fall of my sophomore year in the front ensemble, or "pit." I left in my junior year because, in all frankness, I was bored. I didn't have a lot to do besides hit cymbals together, but I did have a really cool djembe intro in our show, Box-Six's **Fusion.**

Nevertheless, I perceived that the drumline had more fun, and so I joined the line the next year as a bass drummer.

When we started going over technique and fundamentals, and then picked up our drums and did warmups, that really drilled into me how valuable hard work was toward creating a great performance as a team.

Our instructor had this mantra, "Comfort is the enemy of achievement," and it sticks to my head even now. Later on, I found this phrase is attributed to the businessman and author Farrah Gray.

THE TAKEAWAY: Comfort is the enemy of achievement.

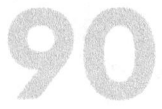

MARCH 30 — Be curious, ask good questions, remember to have fun.

At State Social House in West Hollywood, I spoke to a film student who drove into LA from a community college in California.

I told them that at some point in their future career, the tools will change. After all, the film industry had switched from Avid Media Composer to Adobe Premiere, but some movies used Final Cut Pro. All those people had to learn new tools in order to survive and grow in their filmmaking careers.

I even mentioned how the cloud was involved during the pandemic, making it possible to create and edit content worldwide. All you need is a good Internet connection for cloud video editing.

The guy I was talking to kept asking more questions. It is fun to find someone who is curious and asks you questions that you can answer.

THE TAKEAWAY: Be curious, ask good questions, remember to have fun.

MARCH 31 — Keep your supporting players in focus.

The Rainmaker is a good movie with a lot of heart. After finishing it last night, I looked up Roger Ebert's review of the film and learned some interesting backstory about this movie from 1997.

Francis Ford Coppola bought the Grisham book in an airport. Ebert thinks Coppola got interested in the supporting characters, such as Miss Birdie, Deck, Bruiser or Kelly, and the scorned woman from the insurance company.

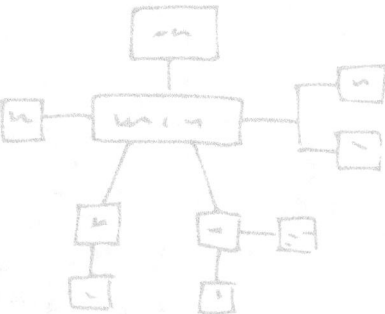

By keeping all these supporting players in focus, Coppola shows the variety of Rudy Baylor's life, where every client is necessary and most of them need a lot more than a lawyer.

I feel this advice, to "keep all of the supporting players in focus," applies to classrooms at Per Scholas as well. Even if one learner in the class is smart and does a lot of talking, it is the job of a trainer to keep those people in the back of the class, or muted people on Zoom, in focus, too.

THE TAKEAWAY: **Keep your supporting players in focus.**

APRIL

APRIL 1 — Don't let fear or anxiety rule your choices.

I got a ticket at noon for Alamo Drafthouse in Downtown LA for the *Midsommar* director's cut. The event description says there will be snacks, a livestream Q&A with the director Ari Aster, and a 10-minute preview of *Beau Is Afraid* with Joaquin Phoenix, Aster's latest movie.

The lights went dim and the voice said, "This theater is now a quiet zone." I come to find out that the movie wasn't *Midsommar* at all, but a surprise screening of *Beau Is Afraid*!

Then, after the *three-hour long* movie, Emma Stone interviewed the director on livestream. I agreed with Emma that the movie is funny, but also miserable. Aster said it was special for him.

I stayed a few more minutes and then left for the bathroom, expecting an article to be written about this eventually. By 5:30 pm Pacific time, I was reading Brent Lang's **Variety article** about this experience of seeing this film 20 days before release as an April Fool's Day joke.

For me, seeing Beau's ambivalence and anxiety around traveling and figuring out what to eat for lunch, was *excruciating*. It was honestly a very divisive movie, with critics loving it and fans not loving it. *TheWrap* reported the movie lost **$35 million**. I'd watch it once, but not again.

Beau is afraid, but you don't have to be.

THE TAKEAWAY: Don't let fear or anxiety rule your choices.

APRIL 2 — Find your quiet time.

An enterprise is a social organization, made up of individuals. Every enterprise exists for a different reason. The people doing their job, in various enterprises, achieve and measure success differently.

For a business, managers exist to create profits. For a hospital, managers exist to create care for the patients. For a university, managers exist to create teaching, learning, and research.

No matter your workplace, they are all noisy in their own way.

In the book *Arthashastra* by Chanakya, which is cited by Dr. Radhakrishnan Pillai in the book *Chanakya in Daily Life*, Chanakya writes:

In conformity with the place, time, and work to be done, he should deliberate with one or two [persons], or alone by himself.

You probably need your "silent time," either by yourself or with a couple of trusted people, before you go to work. Try to find that silence before you troubleshoot your life and work.

THE TAKEAWAY: **Find your quiet time.**

APRIL 3 — Divide your day into 16 parts.

In his book *Chanakya in Daily Life*, Dr. Radhakrishnan Pillai cites from the book *Arthashastra* to illustrate how its author, Chanakya, schedules a king's day:

He should divide the day and night into eight parts, as also the night by means of nalikas *(time measurements).*

Owls, bats, hedgehogs, and rodents tend to be nocturnal, meaning they are active at night and resting during the day. In contrast, humans, lions, and eagles are diurnal, active during the day and resting at night.

It is important to find a schedule that works for you.

A 24-hour day is 1,440 minutes. The first 12 hours could be written as eight blocks of 90 minutes. The night is another eight parts. Like this table:

Block	Start Time	End Time
1	00:00	01:30
2	01:30	03:00
3	03:00	04:30
4	04:30	06:00
5	06:00	07:30
6	07:30	09:00
7	09:00	10:30
8	10:30	12:00

Block	Start Time	End Time
9	12:00	13:30
10	13:30	15:00
11	15:00	16:30
12	16:30	18:00
13	18:00	19:30
14	19:30	21:00
15	21:00	22:30
16	22:30	00:00 (next day)

The human attention span tends to falter after 90 minutes of focused work and needs a break. This also applies to the science of sleeping. Normally, a person does not enter rapid eye movement (REM) sleep until after 90 minutes.

THE TAKEAWAY: Divide your day into 16 parts.

95

APRIL 4 — Don't take this time for granted.

In his blog post *"History of Memento Mori,"* Ryan Holiday writes about the Roman origin of the phrase.

After a Roman victory, most of the public would look to the victorious general up in the front. But only a few would notice, behind the general, an aide whispering into the general's ear that "thou art mortal."

Even at the peak of a victory, to be reminded you are mortal is a very sobering reality.

When you graduate from school, you feel victorious, but a small part of you still knows the work has only just begun.

- Sticking to a work schedule.
- Having time with family and friends.
- Good learning habits.

You do your best, and you have wins and fails along the way. What is most important is you use this time you have as best as you can.

THE TAKEAWAY: Don't take this time for granted.

APRIL 5 — Conduct a pre-mortem.

"All I want to know is where I'm going to die, so I'll never go there."

—Charlie Munger

With this funny quote, Munger emphasizes the importance of avoiding errors and bad decisions through inversion.

Others call this a pre-mortem, where the team lists every potential obstacle, the likelihood of those obstacles coming up, and how big or small the impact could be in preventing success.

It is a good exercise if you are concerned about how a project might turn out, or when you need to align your team on what strategy to use.

THE TAKEAWAY: Conduct a pre-mortem.

97
APRIL 6 — Practice your imitation.

"The instinct of imitation is implanted in man from childhood, one difference between him and other animals being that he is the most imitative of living creatures, and through imitation learns his earliest lessons."

—Aristotle's Poetics

Aaron Sorkin adapted Ben Mezrich's book *Accidental Billionaires* into a script titled *The Social Network* (2010). The film won three Oscars for Adapted Screenplay, Original Score, and Film Editing.

In his MasterClass, Sorkin cites Aristotle's *Poetics* as his rulebook for drama, and drama is all about imitation. In fact, learning anything new requires imitation, or *mimesis* in Ancient Greek.

What do you wish to get better at? Are you imitating those who are better than you to improve?

THE TAKEAWAY: **Practice your imitation.**

APRIL 7 — Cultivate strategic relationships.

I think you tell the story that has to be told. You tell the story that's the truth. You tell the story that readers will be interested in and should know about.

—Andrew Ross Sorkin

Why would Hank Paulson or Jamie Dimon pick up the phone and talk to Andrew Ross Sorkin? They want to hear what everyone else on Wall Street is saying.

Gabriel Sherman, in a *New York Magazine* piece titled "The Information Broker," writes that it also helps that Sorkin is only looking for a story, he does not have "an ax to grind." Sherman also quotes Graydon Carter, former editor of *Vanity Fair* magazine: "There's something about his boyish, Jimmy Stewart charm that older men he deals with find incredibly winning."

I start almost every morning by reading *DealBook*, a digital newsletter that Sorkin founded and is an informative source of crucial business and policy news. I find his work ethic incredible.

What can we learn from Sorkin? Well, in fields where information is critical, building trust and your network is very important. It takes a strong work ethic, but it will pay off big time if you do it right and provide value wherever you go.

When you can provide something with value consistently, others eventually return the favor.

THE TAKEAWAY: Cultivate strategic relationships.

APRIL 8 — There are some things you can't delegate.

"The more books we read, the clearer it becomes that the true function of a writer is to produce a masterpiece and that no other task is of any consequence."

— Cyril Connolly

To say that a writer's only true purpose is to create a masterpiece, dismissing all other efforts as a distraction or a compromise, is honestly a bit ruthless.

Then again, some things require a personal dedication that cannot be outsourced or done half-heartedly. If a writer claims they wish to create a masterpiece, something that withstands the test of time, then they will have to do the hard work themselves, with complete devotion to the craft.

True greatness in writing, or sport, demands a level of focus and sacrifice that not everyone is willing to make.

THE TAKEAWAY: There are some things you can't delegate.

APRIL 9 — Human beings are meant to help each other.

In the Manoj Publications edition of *Chanakya Neeti*, Chanakya writes:

> *"Female fish, tortoise, and hen birds care for their offspring by looking adoringly, by caressing and by pecking gently. Similarly noble saints look after the spiritual needs of the common man through discourses."*

In the Hayes translation of *Meditations* by Marcus Aurelius, he similarly writes:

"Don't you see the plants, the birds, the ants and spiders and bees going about their individual tasks, putting the world in order, as best they can? And you're not willing to do your job as a human being? Why aren't you running to do what your nature demands?"

I find it amazing that two brilliant minds, in Greek or Sanskrit, captured a similar idea. That humans are animals that help, or "create value," for one another.

We may not want to help ourselves, but we are built to help others. The way that the animals also help one other.

Help your family, your business, community, country, or planet.

THE TAKEAWAY: **Like all animals, human beings are meant to help each other.**

101

APRIL 10 — Reading builds character, but writing completes it.

In his TEDx talk **How to Get Richie Rich Quickly,** Dr. Radhakrishnan Pillai, explains that "Arthashastra" is a Sanskrit word that combines two words: "Artha" and "Shastra."

Artha is Wealth; Shastra is scripture.

Unfortunately, in India, when you talk about wealth, money, or finance, there is a feeling of guilt. Indians do not like to openly discuss money, because Indian philosophy is about the opposite.

But here is Chanakya, Dr. Radhakrishnan Pillai says, a man who believes we have to talk about wealth. He cites the opening verse of Chanakya's book *Arthashastra*:

"This single treatise on the science of politics (Kautilya's Arthashastra) has been prepared mostly by bringing together the teachings of as many treatises on the science of politics (previous Arthashastras) as have been composed by ancient teachers for the acquisition and protection of the earth."

Even Chanakya learned from somebody. His "habit of documentation," writes Dr. Pillai, was to share what he learned to protect the earth and teach others how to effectively run a kingdom.

Writing should become your daily habit.

Bob Iger reads and writes his learnings from his staff about "The Magic Kingdom" of Disney, or perhaps from visits to the Disney archives.

The same likely goes for teachers or doctors or anyone in any sort of management position.

THE TAKEAWAY: **Reading builds character, but writing completes it.**

APRIL 11 — **Listen, communicate, re-create mistakes, subordinate ego.**

A leader can grade themself weekly on four leadership skills:
1. Listening.
2. Communicating.
3. Re-creating mistakes
4. Subordinating their ego to the task.

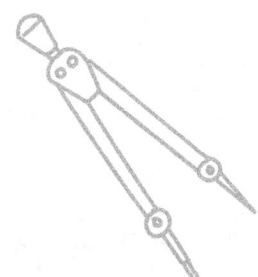

When troubleshooting a technical issue, being able to re-create the issue can be crucial to solving the issue.

This is also why athletes go back to the locker room and rewatch tape of their game. They can reengineer the mistakes and see where they can improve in the next game.

Subordinating the ego is also very important. A leader must indeed subordinate themselves to the task of solving a problem and not only be thinking about themselves.

THE TAKEAWAY: **Listen, communicate, re-create mistakes, subordinate ego.**

103 APRIL 12 — Beware the threats to your business.

"At the end of the day, Disney is a storytelling machine. We used short-form video on YouTube as a promotional device for our content. But I don't think that we at Disney, nor have any other traditional media companies, leaned into YouTube as an original storytelling device the way they probably should have."

– Kevin A. Mayer, co-founder and co-CEO of Candle Media, former CEO of TikTok, former head of Walt Disney Direct-to-Consumer & International.

I remember as a kid, my attention was on Disney Channel, Nickelodeon, and Cartoon Network.

August 2007 specifically, I remember setting my TiVo recorder to record *High School Musical 2* and *Drake & Josh Really Big Shrimp*, because I had a family vacation, and on-demand streaming wasn't a big thing yet.

Out of these three networks, we might say Disney is the winner because of its undeniably successful shows, original movies, and long-lasting impact on the entertainment industry.

In the decades since 2007, the real winner that emerged seems to be YouTube, which is now over 10 percent of all connected TV viewing in the US, according to Nielsen.

Throughout the 2000s and 2010s, YouTube forced media companies to adapt. They started on laptops and mobile phones, but soon took over the TV, the biggest screen in the house.

As a consumer looking for something to watch, none of this matters. But as a producer looking to get people to consume your content, this absolutely matters.

THE TAKEAWAY: **Beware the threats to your business.**

APRIL 13 — Everyone can relate to violence and loss.

"Tears are the silent language of grief."
– Voltaire.

In 1919, the European population in Punjab feared that local Indians would overthrow British rule. Mahatma Gandhi had called a nationwide strike, followed by the arrest of two of the protest's leaders.

On April 13 of that year demonstrators headed for the residence of Miles Irving, the Deputy Commissioner of Amritsar. British Brigadier General Reginald Dyer lead about 90 soldiers on foot to the Jallianwala Bagh garden at around 4:30 p.m. local time to take position at the main entry and exit point. They then fired upon the protesters, who had nowhere to run in the closed-off area. The shooting lasted around 11 minutes. British figures estimate the dead around 300, the Indian National Congress claimed around 1,500 people. My family members said it was closer to 2,000.

The first time I heard about this massacre, I was shocked that I didn't learn about it in school.

Later on I started learning about more massacres, like the Katyn massacre in Poland, carried out by the Soviet Union between April and May 1940. When you learn about massacres like Jallianwala Bagh, and see that a Polish person can relate to it because their family lived through a similar event, you begin to see that violence and loss are languages that everyone can understand.

THE TAKEAWAY: Everyone can relate to violence and loss.

105   APRIL 14 — Build your personal brand.

"Your personal brand is what people say about you when you're not in the room."

— Jeff Bezos, Founder of Amazon

In an episode of the *Masters of Scale* podcast, Tyra Banks talks about leveraging her personal brand to make the reality TV show, *America's Next Top Model,* and her ice cream company.

She says the easiest personal brand is the one that you don't have to act. No act, just a real person, walking into the office in the morning and fully transparent and authentic with others.

There is only so much time in a day. To get anything done, you have to say no to things. Tyra said no to wearing furs. She said no to advertising campaigns focused on alcohol, cigarettes, and tobacco. These are high-paying campaigns, and Tyra says her agent was pissed that she had declined the offers.

For her, the goal is to expand the definition of beauty. At first it was about showing empathy for Black models in the industry, but it expanded from there when Tyra heard from red-headed girls about freckles holding them back in fashion.

This experience became a microcosm for what the show *America's Next Top Model* became. Casting for the show was very intentional about empowering beautiful girls who were told throughout their careers they weren't beautiful for some reason or another.

THE TAKEAWAY: Build your personal brand.

APRIL 15 — Do not forget to pay your taxes.

106

"The hardest thing in the world to understand is the income tax."

—Albert Einstein

They say two things are guaranteed in life: death and taxes.

The filing date is April 15 in the US, but virtually every country, sovereign state, or territory has its own income tax structure and deadlines.

However, income tax is not the only tax we pay. Getting to the airport early and waiting at the gate is a tax. If you suddenly become famous, you pay the tax of people making rumors and gossiping about you. For me, the tax for getting the CompTIA Security+ certification was studying for it outside of working at Per Scholas. Studying is a tax on acquiring knowledge to the point you can pass a test.

Basically, everything we do in life has its form of taxes.

THE TAKEAWAY: Do not forget to pay your taxes.

107 APRIL 16 — Leave the crown in the garage.

On the *Masters of Scale* podcast, Indra Nooyi told Reid Hoffman about getting a call from Pepsi's then CEO, Steve Reinemund.

She was working on the Pepsi acquisition of Quaker Oats the night Steve called to say that the Pepsi board had decided Indra was going to become president and join the board of directors. She hangs ups, wraps up her work, and goes home. Her husband's car is already there. She opens the door and sees her mother waiting at the top of the stairs in the kitchen.

Before Indra can share her big news, her mother says, "Go get milk." Indra still has big news *swirling!* But she goes and gets milk. Then, she shares the big news. Her mother did not care at all. When Indra walks into the house, she is a wife, a mother, a daughter, and daughter-in-law.

To Indra's mother, those are the most important roles she can play. According to her, Indra can "leave the crown in the garage."

In a **post** on LinkedIn, Indra says her mother was "right, of course. No matter who we are, or what we do, nobody can take our place in our families. Now, I'll admit, I've found it's rarely possible to be the kind of mother, wife, employee, and person you want to be—all at the same time. Often, you need to make a choice, and that's especially true if you want to be CEO. There's no way around it."

THE TAKEAWAY: **Leave the crown in the garage.**

APRIL 17 — Sit on your ass and work.

In *The Devil's Guide to Hollywood*, writer Joe Eszterhas says the key to being a successful screenwriter is "*sitzfleisch*—a German term that means the ability and the strength to sit on your ass."

It is deceptively simple, but it works. You sit, and you work, and you keep going until the work is done.

It can be hard to sit for long periods of time, but a standing desk can help with this. According to the Stand Up Desk Store website, which sells standing desks, Leonardo Da Vinci had a standing desk where he created the Mona Lisa, and the University of Cambridge records the use of standing desks as early as 1626.

The brain is a part of the body, but it can only create and deliver amazing code, books, scripts, music, games, or videos through dedicated hours of *sitzfleisch*.

Standing or sitting, it is about having the perseverance to work. This is a very commendable quality. Wouldn't you want to work with someone who can stay focused on doing the job well for long periods of time?

THE TAKEAWAY: Sit on your ass and work.

APRIL 18 — Train people for jobs that play to their strengths.

"Cultivate a deep understanding of yourself—not only what your strengths and weaknesses are but also how you learn, how you work with others, what your values are, and where you can make the greatest contribution. Because only when operate from strengths can you achieve true excellence."

–Peter F. Drucker

You cannot judge a fish by how fast it climbs a tree.

People who can use their natural talents in an environment that suits their strengths are more efficient and effective. They learn new skills faster, and they are more satisfied with their work.

Customers will also be happier to engage with employees who are engaged with their jobs.

As someone with years of experience at Per Scholas, a technical training organization, I see it all the time. Learners like having an instructor who seems to enjoy their job, as opposed to having an instructor who does not want to be there. This is the same in any school—we would rather have a teacher who likes their job and wants to help students, as opposed to a teacher who hates going to work every day and would be happier somewhere else.

When people are in roles that fit their strengths, surrounded by competent teammates who have complementary skills, that team is going to perform with more confidence, experience less burnout, and maybe even solve problems nobody else could figure out.

THE TAKEAWAY: Train people for jobs that play to their strengths.

APRIL 19 — Misery makes strange bedfellows.

Last night I was watching *Barry* on HBO, season 4, episode 2—an episode that involved the characters making some strange bedfellows. Upon further investigation, I discovered that the expression *strange bedfellows* comes from the Shakespeare play *The Tempest* (Act 2, scene 2): "Misery acquaints a man with strange bedfellows."

In a Zoom breakout room, my Amazon Web Services class was working on labs, and I witnessed some great teamwork. It took a bit of effort on my part to get them talking to each other, but once I reminded the learners that one day at work their boss will need AWS skills, and they had the chance to build them here at Per Scholas, then they started troubleshooting with more courage and confidence.

It is crazy how a pandemic forced so many people to change careers, from young people who finished high school in 2020, to new mothers, ex-veterans, to people with PhDs. They all had their reasons to apply to Per Scholas.

And somehow, I ended up being the guy doing the training, watching people on Zoom do AWS lab 267 in the Management Console, now renamed Console Home.

At Per Scholas, or in troubleshooting life, you never know who you will be "bedfellows" with.

Misery acquaints us all with strange bedfellows. Make the best of the cards you are dealt.

THE TAKEAWAY: Misery makes strange bedfellows.

111   APRIL 20 — Find an audience that wants to support your work.

"When I'm making a film, I'm the audience."

— Martin Scorsese

In his book *Who Is Michael Ovitz?* by Michael Ovitz, the author writes about fixing the finances of one of his star clients, Martin Scorsese. Apparently, Marty's business manager had not paid the filmmaker's taxes. Two of his last features, *New York, New York (1977)* and *The King of Comedy (1982)*, were inspired works that never found an audience.

Ovitz says he did not sign Scorsese for the commission. After all, Marty hardly cared if his movies made money. For a long time, my idol *was* Martin Scorsese.

I was in college in 2017, but I was fascinated by how different the world was in 1967, when Scorsese released his debut feature *Who's That Knocking at My Door*. I watched it on DVD on a PS4 in my apartment bedroom at Temple University.

I was very quickly beginning to realize that I do need to care about money after college ended and not just care about watching movies and figuring out what movie I want to make.

Artists, especially those who are young, are often deeply passionate about their art, but at some point they have to put up a shingle and sell their services. It is a tricky balance between finding creative expression and doing business as an artist.

THE TAKEAWAY: Find an audience that wants to support your work.

APRIL 21 — Either run from the past or learn from it.

> *"The past can hurt. But the way I see it, you can either run from it, or learn from it."*
> — Walt Disney

Is it possible to be free from error? Not by any means.

Walt Disney's first animation studio, Laugh-O-Gram, went bankrupt in 1923. He lost the rights to *Oswald the Lucky Rabbit* to Universal because he did not retain ownership of the character. When he proposed creating Disneyland, he faced skeptics and struggled to get funding because he was going into a new industry without prior experience.

He learned a few things.
- Balance creativity with financial discipline to grow sustainably.
- Retain ownership of intellectual property.
- Produce a TV show for ABC so the network would fund the park, which doubled as a park ad.

These failures became opportunities for Disney to grow, pivot, and refine the approach he and his company took.

When a person learns to walk, they fall along the way. But eventually they figure out how to run, ride a bike, drive a car, or even fly a plane. You make mistakes and get better through study, reflection, and meaningful practice.

THE TAKEAWAY: Either run from the past or learn from it.

113
APRIL 22 — Recommit to protecting the environment on Earth Day.

"Our future is being gambled away, and our leaders, those whom we entrust to protect us and set the example, are either failing to stop these dangerous trends or in some cases denying the very science of this climate catastrophe."

– Leonardo DiCaprio at Global Citizens Festival, 2019

It makes sense to start small and work your way up. Going up from one push-up a day is easier to do than starting with a hundred right away.

The same goes for the environment.

In 2019, **Jeff Bezos** spoke at Blue Origin that it is "just arithmetic" that Earth will run out of energy. "What happens when unlimited demand meets finite resources? The answer is incredibly simple: Rationing," he says. Or colonies in space.

Today is Earth Day, and all the troubleshooting you did so far is for nothing if the planet is no longer here. Even small changes can add up.

THE TAKEAWAY: Recommit to protecting the environment on Earth Day.

APRIL 23 — Study Peter Drucker to improve your management chops.

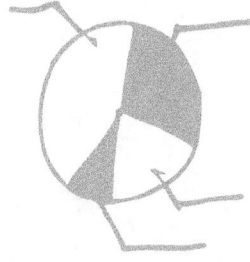

"There is nothing so useless as doing efficiently that which should not be done at all."

— Peter Drucker

Peter Drucker was an Austrian-American management consultant, educator, and author, widely regarded as one of the most influential thinkers in the field of management. He is often referred to as the "father of modern management."

Born in Austria in 1909, Drucker also worked as a journalist in Germany before moving to the United States in 1937, similar to the film director Shmuel Vildr/Billy Wilder. **(347. December 12)**

In the 1940s, Drucker began writing about management. He later became a professor at the New York University Graduate School of Business Administration.

He wrote more than 30 books on management, economics, and society, including *The Practice of Management, Innovation and Entrepreneurship,* and *The Effective Executive.*

THE TAKEAWAY: Study Peter Drucker to improve your management chops.

APRIL 24 — Experience the magic of taking notes.

"Keepers of private notebooks are a different breed altogether, lonely and resistant rearranger of things, anxious malcontents, children afflicted apparently at birth with some presentment of loss."

— Joan Didion, "On Keeping a Notebook," from Slouching Towards Bethlehem (1968)

In his newsletter, author Ryan Holiday writes about how he experienced something close to time travel. He writes about sitting at his desk, pulling out his notecards, and finding an old, worn notecard mentioning something that Joan Didion had written in chapter in her book, *Slouching Towards Bethlehem*. He walked over to his shelf and found the book, and a specific essay titled "On Keeping a Notebook," written in 1966.

He says he happened to be sitting in Joan Didion's chair, which he had bought at a charity auction after her death, when he found this notecard, and it gave him goosebumps because it was like the space-time continuum was helping him exactly when he needed it!

As an obsessive note taker myself, I sometimes write things down and read it again years later.

Sometimes I remember writing it down, and other times I have no memory of why I wrote something down, but there it is, a blast from the past.

There is something powerful about writing something down, then finding it years later, only to find a warm memory, or perhaps your past self giving your present self exactly what you need for something you are working on.

THE TAKEAWAY: Experience the magic of taking notes.

APRIL 25 — Balance artistic integrity with what the client wants.

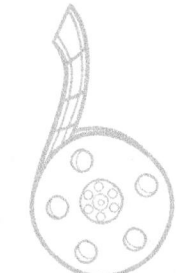

As former agent Michael Ovitz wrote in his memoir *Who Is Michael Ovitz?*, film is not a "creative medium" but a commercially creative medium. He says his clients often gloss over that distinction so they can see themselves as "artists" rather than "talent for hire," but he always kept the latter in mind.

This is a bit of a mindset shift regarding creativity and commercial work.

Creativity can exist in a commercial context, but the goal is not purely artistic expression; it is also fulfilling a client's needs.

Whether you are an author, an artist, a designer, or in any field where creativity is involved, it is important to understand the commercial aspects of your work so you can do the following:
1. Manage expectations.
2. Navigate client relationships.
3. Make decisions that balance artistic integrity with market or client demands.

Creativity often exists beyond personal expression. Having awareness of this can guide both professional and artistic decisions.

THE TAKEAWAY: Balance artistic integrity with what the client wants.

117   APRIL 26 — Recharge yourself by learning something new.

"Learning never exhausts the mind, it only ignites it."

– Leonardo da Vinci

The archetypal Renaissance man, Leonardo da Vinci demonstrated brilliance in multiple fields—painting, engineering, sculpting, anatomy, and much more. At his core was a curiosity about the world and an ability to connect fields that seem completely unrelated.

When we challenge ourselves to learn something outside our comfort zone, such as a skill or a new subject or game, it stimulates our curiosity and creativity by opening our minds to new possibilities, ideas, or ways of thinking.

Learning is a dynamic force, and it can be used to recharge yourself in moments you need it. You go on this path of exploration and discovery, making sketches and writing down observations, patiently embracing the mistakes along the way.

What we call "genius" is a commitment to seeking knowledge and a desire to listen to new ideas.

In a world that is quickly changing, we cannot stop being curious. Feeding an insatiable curiosity is the highway to growth.

THE TAKEAWAY: Recharge yourself by learning something new.

APRIL 27 — Do good while doing good business.

Howard Schultz explains on the podcast *Masters of Scale* that *"parents in China, especially given the one child rule, are deeply involved in the lives and aspirations of their children."*

At Starbucks, innovation doesn't just mean new drinks. It also means new programs for employees to keep them loyal to the company.

When Howard Schultz took over Starbucks, he was aware that most of the staff was young, while college was very expensive. So he had this wild idea: free college tuition for every employee, in addition to health insurance.

Although this could be seen as financially impractical, to Schultz it made sense. The US government, already deeply in debt, wasn't going to do it, so the responsibility falls on citizens or companies to pay tuition.

Eventually, Starbucks figured out a partnership with Arizona State University to provide online degree programs for Starbucks staff working 20 or more hours a week. Starbucks and ASU split the costs 60/40, and now a parent in America might feel better about their child working at Starbucks if their child can also get a degree.

> **A parent in China might also feel good about their child working at Starbucks because Starbucks has learned to focus on extending benefits for parents of employees.**

They soon extended health insurance to parents of employees, then invited parents to the Starbucks China annual company meetings, to celebrate their kids.

Who knew? Being a good human can also be good for business.

THE TAKEAWAY: Do good while doing good business.

119   APRIL 28 — It is never too late to start over.

"It's only after you've lost everything, that you're free to do anything."

—Chuck Palahniuk, Fight Club

This quote captures a poignant truth: that liberation can be found in detachment. Stripped of material possessions, societal expectations, and any other burdens, a person discovers a blank slate to redefine one's purpose or identity.

I started 2019 with no job in film or media, and barely any money.

I was lucky to have gotten IT training at Per Scholas at a time when I needed a fresh start. I even got a job at Per Scholas just before the worldwide COVID-19 pandemic.

Around this time I also discovered Stoic philosophy through **Ryan Holiday**, and business wisdom through Peter Drucker.

Long story short, it is never too late to start over.

THE TAKEAWAY: **It is never too late to start over.**

APRIL 29 — Pursue visual literacy.

As a teenager, I saw the Martin Scorsese movie *Hugo* for free on iTunes. The movie was a **box office bomb**, but I enjoyed seeing Ben Kingsley play Georges Méliès and explore movie history.

I later researched the director, and found a video on YouTube of Martin Scorsese explaining **visual literacy**. He said the rules of cinema would apply to digital video, and that both forms share a "grammar."

The grammar would be
- Panning left and right.
- Tracking in or out.
- Booming up and down.
- Intercutting a certain way.
- Use of a close-up as opposed to a medium or long shot.

All these decisions about the camera, different kinds of lighting, sound design are some of the tools that storytellers use to make emotional and psychological points for an audience.

Young people need to know how to use these very powerful tools, Scorsese says. He mentions World War II, when the great director from Germany Leni Riefenstahl did *Triumph of the Will (1935)*, a film that helped shape the Third Reich. Walt Disney used these tools for his country, the United States, during WWII as well.

Artificial intelligence is yet another tool in an already large arsenal of tools. These tools need to be understood so they can be used effectively.

THE TAKEAWAY: **Pursue visual literacy.**

121   APRIL 30 — Protect your blindspot.

"We all have a blind spot and it's shaped exactly like us."

—Junot Diaz

The blind spot is what is outside your own lived experience. The best way to cover your blind spot is to build a team with diverse viewpoints on a given problem.

Imagine a person who attends an all-girls school in South Carolina. She has glasses, braces, and is very awkward. Yet somehow, she steels herself and ultimately goes to work on Wall Street.

This is how the executive **Sallie Krawcheck** describes her past before joining the hyper-masculine culture of Salomon Brothers in the 1980s. On the *Masters of Scale* podcast, she talks about getting Xerox copies of penises on her desk, calling it "outrageous" and "humiliating."

Sallie, and her network, saw a huge opportunity in Wall Street's blind spot. They started building Ellevest, a company that provided wealth management services for women.

The "Elle" in Ellevest is the client. Elle could be age 18 all the way up to 82. It is less about age and more about a mindset.

Elle earned her own money. She is confident in all areas of her life, *except* her money. Elle is either married or single, but she has agency over her money. She wants to make the world a better place, and she sees that a way to make the world a better place is for her to do better.

No one on Wall Street except Sallie could have built Ellevest because of all the blind spots they had.

THE TAKEAWAY: **Protect your blindspot.**

Part Two:
ENTERTAINMENT

MAY

MAY 1 — Embrace the power of gamification.

In case you don't know, gamification is when a company integrates game-like elements into nongaming environments to motivate and engage users.

Like when you buy from Starbucks, you get "stars" that you can redeem toward your next purchase. You get points, badges, challenges, and rewards to encourage their desired behavior of buying Starbucks products.

Or, on LinkedIn there is a "profile completeness bar" so you upload as many details as possible to earn an "All-Star" profile status.

In 2017, the McDonald's app targeted Philadelphia residents with its Money Monopoly campaign, offering cash prizes, free public transportation, and the ability to participate in a life-size Monopoly board game.

Robinhood discontinued animated confetti celebrations for trades because the feature was accused of gamifying investing for young people and vulnerable populations. This controversial feature had been a part of the Robinhood app since 2016, to celebrate actions like making trades or opening accounts. But critics say it could also encourage making risky investments.

Gamification is a powerful way to engage users, especially younger users who grew up playing games.

It can be used or misused, depending on what behavior you wish to encourage and the outcomes you are aiming for.

Regardless, using gamification thoughtfully can make your product or service addicting for potential customers.

THE TAKEAWAY: **Embrace the power of gamification.**

123   MAY 2 — Understand the limitations of artificial intelligence.

"You don't have to burn books to destroy a culture. Just get people to stop reading them."

–Ray Bradbury

Bradbury's quote is striking because nobody seems to have time to read. We have people across the country using laptops running Zoom, a web browser, Slack, Discord, a word processor, and so on. Millions of people generate *so much data* to train different AI models to further distract them from getting quality information from the source.

Right now, I use ChatGPT while delivering the AWS re/Start curriculum at Per Scholas. Instead of answering questions people ask me, I can quickly type them into ChatGPT and not have to talk or type out long technical explanations.

On April 14, 2023, Nintendo released Mega Man Battle Network Legacy Collection for Switch to capitalize on the nostalgia of guys like me who loved this game, but I think it is also because AI hype is high, and the game heavily features AI.

AI can only take you so far. At some point you do have to get back to work. And keep reading books.

THE TAKEAWAY: Understand the limitations of artificial intelligence.

MAY 3 — Do your best work without worrying about rewards.

"Forty-hour work weeks are a relic of the Industrial Age. Knowledge workers function like athletes—train and sprint, then rest and reassess."

–Naval Ravikant

If you grew up in India and read the *Bhagawad Gita*, or heard the song **"Yeh Hai Geeta Ka Gyan"** from the 1975 hit film *Sanyasi*, you know the meaning of the philosophy *Karm kiyeja, phal ki icha maht kar*.

In English: Put in your best work today, without worrying about results.

As the quote from writer Naval Ravikant suggests, it is unlikely you need a full 40 hours to do some of your best work. You probably need a sprint, then a rest, reassess, and restart.

You can deal with the results after you do your best.

THE TAKEAWAY: Do your best work without worrying about rewards.

MAY 4 — Smaller teams are better than big teams.

In *AWS Executive Insights*, Jeff Bezos famously calls a small team a "two pizza team," as in two pizzas is enough to feed everyone.

Naval Ravikant, on the Joe Rogan podcast (Episode JRE 1309), says we can educate people very quickly. One of these myths we have is that adults can't be re-educated, when in fact they can.

There are great boot camps and coding schools, there is a wealth of information on the Internet if you know what to look for.

You don't even need a lot of people to get a lot of work done. Naval refers to Ronald Coase's article, "The Nature of the Firm," and how companies tend to be happier when they are smaller.

Coase believes that firms should assess and balance the costs and benefits of internal "transactions" versus external "transactions."

Smaller teams mean less transactions internally. Study groups does better when they are smaller. Work groups might do better too.

THE TAKEAWAY: Smaller teams are better than big teams.

MAY 5 — Be nimble and open to new ideas.

There is still much to learn, no matter your age. To quote Barry Diller, "Nobody knows anything about anything, including me."

In the spring of 2018, I was a student at Temple University doing the LA Study Away Program.

While in LA, I got to meet many Temple alumni. They talked about their entertainment careers, and their experiences were helpful to students like me navigating their own career. I learned things like
- The difference between agents and managers
- Advertising
- The music industry
- Independent filmmaking,
- Post-production
- Line producing
- Script coordination
- Production assisting (PA'ing)
- Hollywood assistants (Lloyd from *Entourage*)

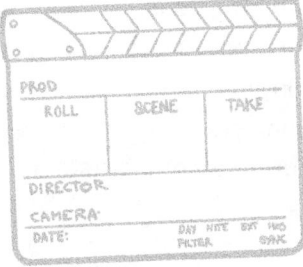

One executive in Tanuj Chopra's class in particular was very inspiring. From ICM to Salma Hayek's production company Ventanazul to 20th Century Fox to UTA, Gina Reyes has an inspiring career. She introduced me to the *Masters of Scale* podcast, an episode with Barry Diller.

Barry Diller tells Reid Hoffman he spent three years in the William Morris file room, learning everything about the American entertainment business from like 1898 to modern day.

Michael Ovitz, before building CAA, also read everything he could in that same file room. In his memoir, he writes that William Morris had a file room the length of a basketball court lined with steel cabinets, the hard drives of that era.

THE TAKEAWAY: **Be nimble and open to new ideas.**

127   MAY 6 — Learn as much as possible before making your next move.

The William Morris file room has knowledge on the entertainment business from 1898 to the modern day. Before they were able to question everything about the business and work on building their own, Michael Ovitz and Barry Diller learned everything they possibly could.

Taking the time to read and absorb knowledge sets the foundation for doing great in your field.

The people who work at talent agencies are as much "knowledge workers" as they are "manual workers." The same goes for a large number of fields:
- Computer technicians
- Software designers
- Software engineers
- Security analysts
- Manufacturing technologists
- Paralegals
- Movie directors
- Performing artists

Their knowledge is the foundation for their skills, and it is critical to have as much information as possible before making your next strategic move.

Before a surgeon makes their first cut, the surgeon has to know the patient. Diagnosis might take a while, but it is important to have the proper diagnosis before proceeding with surgery, otherwise a patient can die.

The same goes for music performance: setting up for the sound tests may take a while, but it is necessary to know the venue and set up the area before the big show begins. Otherwise, a performance can fall flat.

> **THE TAKEAWAY: Learn as much as possible before making your next move.**

MAY 7 — Specific detail gives more room for interpretation.

In this 2014 Showrunner roundtable with *The Hollywood Reporter*, about 13 minutes in, Jenji Kohan talked about how there is something universal about the specifics.

Kohan is best known as the creator and showrunner for American TV shows such as *Weeds* and *Orange Is the New Black*.

Weeds is about a widowed mother of two boys who begins selling marijuana to support her family.

Not everyone in the audience knows about selling weed.

But there are likely some parents in the audience who work to support their families. And so the tone and the characters are still relatable.

Maybe you never sold weed or went to a women's prison before.

Yet somehow, you can relate the specific details about a show's characters to yourself

THE TAKEAWAY: Specific detail gives more room for interpretation.

129   MAY 8 — Read to lead.

"Not all readers are leaders, but all leaders are readers."
—President Harry S. Truman

The 33rd President of the United States is a remarkable example of an autodidact, or self-taught person. Born in Missouri on May 8, 1884, Harry Truman attended public schools but was unable to afford college, making him the only twentieth-century President without a college degree.

The Truman Library credits his early exposure to books such as Plutarch's *Lives* and Benjamin Franklin's *Autobiography* as important to shaping his worldview.

Before politics, Truman worked as a newspaper wrapper, a bank clerk, and a farmer, and served in World War I as a US Army captain. There he got to demonstrate some of the leadership skills he had been reading about.

In the 1920s, after World War I and a brief stint running a men's clothing store in Kansas City, Missouri, Truman entered politics, where he earned a reputation for independence and fighting corruption. Even if people around Truman were corrupt, he stayed honest.

Truman's lifelong commitment to reading and learning helped him navigate his life before the Oval Office and the decisions he made during his presidency. By his desk was a sign that read "the buck stops here" because *he* took responsibility for all those pivotal decisions, from authorizing the atomic bomb, post-war reconstruction efforts, the Cold War, the Marshall Plan, and the Korean War.

Today, make a point of cultivating a reading habit. You never know where it could lead.

THE TAKEAWAY: Read to lead.

MAY 9 — Consider whether living too long is in our best interest.

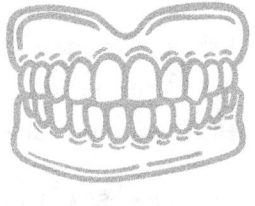

"Of the three brothers, Rahm is the most famous, Ari is the richest, and Zeke, over time, will probably be the most important. Zeke is also, according to his brothers, the smartest."

–"The Brothers Emanuel," *The New York Times*

Dr. Ezekiel Emanuel, brother of the talent agent Ari Emanuel and former White House chief of staff Rahm Emanuel, is a nationally recognized oncologist and medical ethicist. He makes a point in the *Atlantic* about how old our Congress is. I even learned the word "gerontocracy," which is a society run by old people.

At a certain point, working in politics over the age of 75 is either
1. self-inflicted elder abuse
2. not in the long-term interest of a national median age of 39.

I think differently at 27 than I did at 17. I'll probably think differently at 37 or 87. I'll probably walk differently, and talk differently, and have dentures instead of adult teeth.

The human psyche is governed by flaws, not laws.

What do you think, Reader?

How has aging and life experience affected the way you live your life?

THE TAKEAWAY: Consider whether living too long is in our best interest.

131 MAY 10 — Avoid deeply flawed assumptions.

Franklin Leonard, founder of the storytelling platform *The Black List*, spoke to Reid Hoffman on the podcast *Masters of Scale* about how conventional wisdom in Hollywood is more often just "convention" and not "wisdom."

The success of the scripts on *The Black List* was Franklin realizing that.

Now, Franklin Leonard is just suspicious of all "conventional wisdom" in Hollywood.

He recalls being pitched *Slumdog Millionaire* by its eventual producer and saying: "Good luck with that. I'll probably see it, but I don't know."

After Slumdog Millionaire was complete, it was meant to be released by Warner Bros. But that studio did not think the movie would profit in theaters. Fox Searchlight bought in. Then took the film to $270 million worldwide and seven Oscar wins.

This is a clear example of Hollywood having deeply flawed assumptions about what audiences want.

There are many more examples like this, including *Juno, The King's Speech, Argo,* and many others.

So ignore what Hollywood (or any other industry leader) tells you. They listen to balance sheets and Wall Street. (Not their fault; it's how they got the job.)

Then they take bets on artists like you until one home run pays off all the other misses.

You are an artist. Listen to your gut. Keep your fans happy, but most importantly, keep yourself happy. Have fun.

THE TAKEAWAY: **Avoid deeply flawed assumptions.**

MAY 11 — Do not fear the "gray areas."

"When I was young and rich, all I thought about was art and music. Now I'm 36, all I think about is money."

— Wallace Shawn, *My Dinner With Andre (1981)*

In this movie about a dinner between two friends, Wally is a man who enjoys simple comforts such as writing plays, paying his bills, and sipping a hot cup of coffee in the morning. Meanwhile, his friend Andre has been traveling to places such as Tibet, the Sahara, England, Poland, and more, doing outlandish things like moonlight theater rituals or briefly getting buried alive.

A lot of thoughts might hit you when you first see this movie. Andre does most of the talking, and your mind cannot help but try to picture what he says in the story.

Like Wally, I was only concerned with art and music when I was younger. Now that I am older, I seem to only think about money.

I sometimes even blamed myself for majoring in filmmaking and working in Hollywood. Once I pictured my doppelgänger in another universe who studied medicine, or computer science, who is doing much better in life than this version of me.

But of course, that is not reality, it is a story my mind made up in the gray area.

THE TAKEAWAY: Do not fear the "gray areas."

133

MAY 12 — Don't get hooked on porn.

"From cave painting to photography to the internet, pornography has always been at the cutting edge in adopting and exploiting new developments in mass communication."

— Patchen Barss, author of *The Erotic Engine*

The Atlantic has an article about how porn inspires people to upgrade their tech.

For years the Consumer Electronics Show (CES) in Las Vegas coincided with the AVN Adult Entertainment Expo. The porn expo emerged from the adult-video section of CES in the 1990s, when the fans grew tired of being relegated to a dark basement of the convention center.

There is an endless appetite for obscene or lascivious content. There is also an endless supply of porn on the Internet, not to mention online communities.

Barss writes about how porn has been about two things: people finding new ways to connect to other people, and people finding more private ways to consume pornography.

Terry Crews admitted to struggling with porn addiction. So did Billie Eilish. In a world of digital abundance, resisting porn is a test of willpower and restraint.

THE TAKEAWAY: **Don't get hooked on porn.**

MAY 13 — Advertising is inevitable, even if you hate ads.

On March 10, 2017, Netflix tweeted "Love is sharing a password." It took **about five years** before the company went from that philosophy to charging account holders an additional fee for users outside their households.

Ironically, many people signed up for Netflix *because* it was cheaper than cable, ad-free, and on demand. People loved sharing their passwords with friends and family in other places.

But when the company reported losing subscribers in 2022, Netflix turned their back on this philosophy of sharing passwords. They forced people to sit through ads, pay more money for users outside a household, or create a new Netflix account, which they did. Subscriber numbers did rise after this crackdown, and some people did go to ad-supported Netflix.

In May 2024, the company even signed a three-year **deal with the NFL** to show Christmas Day football games! Which means more ad revenue for Netflix, a company that is starting to look and sound more like the TV networks they were trying to compete against initially.

The higher a country's ad spend, the unhappier its people become, according to *Harvard Business Review.* The tragedy is this: advertising is inevitable and will never die, even if technology such as ad-blockers and mute buttons help.

You will likely need to embrace advertising on some level to grow your business. It might cost a lot, and make both you and your potential fans unhappy, but it is a necessary evil.

THE TAKEAWAY: Advertising is inevitable, even if you hate ads.

135   MAY 14 — Done is better than perfect.

"Done is better than perfect."

This is a phrase that floats around. Sheryl Sandberg, former COO of Meta Platforms, used it in her book *Lean In: Women, Work, and the Will to Lead*.

Perfect is an idea that only exists in the imagination. "Done" is something that is not perfect, but it actually exists, and it does a decent job at what it was made to do.

I know from personal experience that there is a feeling of relief when you are done with something. The sense of making progress toward a goal feels good.

The excuse that something is not perfect is often another way of procrastinating. People delay or postpone taking any action at all because they are afraid they have already failed. Then they get stuck in this cycle of thinking too much and not taking any action at all.

Striving for the unattainable is not helping you or the team move forward. Striving for some tangible result, to just be done with the task, is often enough.

This is especially important in a fast-paced environment where progress is more important than being perfect. Perfect is subjective, and chasing it sometimes leads to wasting time and resources on something minor that doesn't really matter at the end of the day.

Start that project or task you've been putting off. It is better than never starting it at all.

THE TAKEAWAY: Done is better than perfect.

MAY 15 — Don't be afraid to change the model.

"Don't be afraid to change the model."

— Reed Hastings, former CEO of Netflix

Netflix is a company that went from DVD rental-by-mail in 1997 with no late fees, to streaming video in 2007, to a producer of original programming like *House of Cards* in 2013. Over time, its service got good at serving up movies and TV with personalized algorithms, and binge watching became mainstream.

The company was famously ad-free for a long time, but when they started facing stiff competition from other streaming services in what the press calls "the streaming wars," they started offering tiered pricing with cheaper ad-supported options.

Starting on December 25, 2024, **Netflix started broadcasting live NFL Games**. Because what better way to try and boost a new ad business than with live football?

Changing the model is hard. Blockbuster did not want to change its model and stop charging late fees, and look what happened to them.

THE TAKEAWAY: Don't be afraid to change the model.

137 MAY 16 — Prepare for life after graduation with confidence.

"Go confidently in the direction of your dreams. Live the life you have imagined."

— Henry David Thoreau

My big brother graduated from University of Virginia Darden School of Business today!

I still remember when he was graduating from high school. And I remember when I was graduating from high school. Then college. I remember countless cycles of students graduating from Per Scholas as well. Maybe it is just me, but every time I am at a graduation, I feel like I remember every graduation I ever went to.

A graduate has so many dreams, so many problems they want to troubleshoot in the world.

But before any of that high-minded ambition can be achieved, more mundane things need to be figured out after graduating.

Where will you live after graduating from school? Do you have a job lined up? Will you still get to see your friends, or will you have to make new ones? What about student loan payments? Do you take time off to travel somewhere new?

Depending on who you are, and where you are in life, you will likely make choices that are different from other people, and that is completely natural. As long as you proceed with confidence, you will probably do fine.

THE TAKEAWAY: Prepare for life after graduation with confidence.

MAY 17 — Tell a great story again and again.

"It takes a great deal of courage to stand alone, even if you believe in something very strongly."

— Juror 9, Sidney Lumet's *12 Angry Men*

When I watched Sidney Lumet's *12 Angry Men* for the first time with my father, I felt so inspired. This movie is incredible, a masterclass in storytelling packed with powerful acting and life lessons.

When it ended, my dad told me about the 1986 remake he saw in India, *Ek Ruka Hua Faisla*.

He also remembered the movie **Ghajini (2008)**, inspired by Christopher Nolan's *Memento* from 2000.

A good writer can take a story, or characters or plots, and weave them into a new story. It can happen all over the world too.

People often do not like repeating themselves, but when the story is too good, or a jury needs to decide a verdict, sometimes it gets told again and again, with new and different ideas emerging from the story with each retelling.

It takes courage to tell a story, especially a personal story.

THE TAKEAWAY: Tell a great story again and again.

139   MAY 18 — Enjoy the ad without buying the product.

"Spending your life trying to dupe innocent people out of hard-won earnings to buy useless, low-quality, misrepresented items and services, is an excellent use of your energy."

–Jerry Seinfeld

At the 55th annual Clio awards for advertising, Jerry Seinfeld joked that he loves advertising because he loves lying.

In an advertisement, everything is how you wish it was. It doesn't matter that the product in the commercial doesn't look like it does in real life. Jerry already knows the product is going to stink because in the real world, *everything stinks*.

But humans are a hopeful, stupid species. Even though everything stinks, humans see a commercial and optimistically think, "Maybe this won't stink."

To Seinfeld, the brief moment of happiness between seeing the commercial and making the purchase is a pretty good moment. Making money and buying nice things is a good way of life, and materialism gets a bad rap when it shouldn't. He jokes that this will all be explained in his new book, *Soulful Materialism*, which is not a real book, though I sort of wish it was.

I find that people love buying things that could make them happy, but even if they buy something good, it does not take long before they see another commercial, triggering another desire, and now they are unhappy until they buy the new thing.

Or, they could just enjoy the commercial *without* having to buy anything.

THE TAKEAWAY: Enjoy the ad without buying the product.

MAY 19 — Misery makes strange bedfellows.

"The most valuable of all talents is that of never using two words when one will do."

— Thomas Jefferson

Journal every day. Even one word or sentence a day is a start.

For me, writing always came easily. What came hard was *sharing* my writing so others could read it. I can be very shy sometimes.

This book basically emerged from a diary I kept during the COVID-19 pandemic, while working at Per Scholas. Writing was important for me.

Having gone from a teaching assistant to a manager at Per Scholas, I found that writing out the problems helps a team think through the solutions more clearly.

First one, then two, then more words start flowing. Eventually, some solutions become visible.

As John Steinbeck says, "Ideas are like rabbits. You get a couple and learn how to handle them, and pretty soon you have a dozen."

THE TAKEAWAY: **Misery makes strange bedfellows.**

141   MAY 20 — The world is a machine. You are an essential part of it.

Originally a book written by **Brian Selznick**, *Hugo* was turned into a screenplay by John Logan. One of my favorite quotes from the movie comes from the title character, Hugo.

HUGO: *"Machines never have any extra parts, you know. They always have the exact number they need. So I figured if the entire world was a big machine, I couldn't be an extra part, I had to be here for some reason…"*

Today I saw two people post about getting laid off in my LinkedIn feed. One was a recruiter at AWS I was talking to about a potential job at AWS as a trainer. Another was a manager for the Masters of Scale LinkedIn Community who I got to connect with over two years remotely. It sucks to scroll and see good people write about getting laid off.

The next day, my team was impacted by layoffs, and one of my teammates was let go. I was reminded of the moment I got laid off in 2019. In fact, every person I talked to about getting laid off remembers that moment in their life incredibly clearly. One moment you are a part of a work family, and suddenly you are not, and it stings.

But the world is a big machine with lots of moving parts in it. You are here for bigger reasons beyond working, or not working, a job.

THE TAKEAWAY: The world is a machine. You are an essential part of it.

MAY 21 — Stick to your strengths and adapt your strategy.

"The real benefit has been the number of incoming calls from talent to us saying, 'We want to be doing business with you because we know you're a theatrical distributor and producer.' That has actually worked very well for us."

— Sony Pictures CEO Tony Vinciquerra (*The Verge*)

In May 2020, Sony Pictures CEO Tony Vinciquerra spoke to CNBC about selling the Tom Hanks movie *Greyhound* to Apple for $70 million during the coronavirus pandemic.

Streaming is not a profitable business. Unlike companies such as Disney or Warner Bros, which focused on building Disney+ and Max at a loss to compete with Netflix, Sony has avoided a dedicated service for its movies and TV shows with the exception of Crunchyroll, a niche anime streaming service that Sony bought from AT&T's WarnerMedia in 2021.

In May 2023, Mr. Vinciquerra said to an investor briefing that this decision to stay out of the crowded streaming space, and instead stay a content supplier, was clearly the right choice. Sony shows like *The Boys* on Amazon Prime, *The Last of Us* on Max, and *Cobra Kai* on Netflix have done well with this "streaming arms dealer" approach.

My takeaway here is that it is easy to think you should follow what everybody else is doing in your industry. But sometimes, it can be good to stick to your strengths, double down on what makes you unique, and adapt your strategy to suit market dynamics.

THE TAKEAWAY: Stick to your strengths and adapt your strategy.

MAY 22 — Make your mailroom an attractive proposition.

"No job is beneath you. You ought to be thrilled you got a job in the mailroom. And when you get there, here's what you do: Be really great at sorting mail."

— Randy Pausch, The Last Lecture

To become someone in show business, they say, you have to start in "the mailroom." Or perhaps as a production assistant, like Disney CEO Bob Iger did at ABC. When you say, "I started in the mailroom, now I'm an agent," or "I was a PA, now I'm a director," that resonates deeply with the people you work with.

For me at Per Scholas, it resonates with people I work with that I was once a teaching assistant in March 2020, then an instructor, and then a manager of technical instruction. (Then, an *author!*) Working your way up means you know the job well, and you could probably show someone else how to do it as well as, if not better, than you did, before you go do your new job.

Michael Ovitz sorted mail before running CAA. Jeff Bezos sorted mail for Amazon before recruiting B-school students like Jason Kilar or Andy Jassy. Mark Zuckerberg sorted mail for Facebook.

These were all startups that became powerhouses, run by people who understand that sorting mail is just as important as closing huge deals.

Now, these companies get LOTS of mail. Their mailrooms went from being terrible career moves to "an attractive proposition" for the right candidate.

THE TAKEAWAY: Make your mailroom an attractive proposition.

MAY 23 — Leave a good legacy for your successor.

144

In Chanakya in Daily Life, *Dr. Radhakrishnan Pillai writes, "When a person is born, there is one thing that is certain—death."*

This applies to a job or a career as well: the first day you join a company, you are metaphorically "born," and the day you retire from the company, you metaphorically "die."

It is a bit morbid to think this way, but it is true! I have been working over four years at Per Scholas, but I know *somewhere* inside me that I won't be here forever, and I will need to leave a professional legacy for my eventual replacement.

Dr. Radhakrishnan Pillai says Chanakya had a similar view when he wrote:

"He (king) should strive to give training to the prince."

Bob Iger was the literal king of the magic kingdom at The Walt Disney Company. In his 15 years as chief executive, he postponed his retirement four times, and basically set his successor, Bob Chapek, up to fail.

Do not get me wrong, he did a great job as Disney CEO, but he royally screwed up succession, causing a lot of pain to Disney employees, shareholders, and fans of their products. The *Financial Times* even put out a short film saying Chapek's time was so bad, there were conspiracy theories Iger purposely chose Chapek to fail and make himself look better.

THE TAKEAWAY: Leave a good legacy for your successor.

145   MAY 24 — Just stand up and go.

"I believe that if you'll just stand up and go, life will open up for you."

—Tina Turner

On this day in 2023, news broke that Tina Turner died. She was 83.

I was supporting my teammate at Per Scholas, James Miao, who started an Amazon Web Services training session today talking about her. He said he has been a fan of Tina Turner's music for decades.

He tells our class to do what makes you happy today. That way if you were to die tomorrow, you would die happy. Ask that cute girl or guy out. Ask for a raise. It won't kill you, but it will demonstrate courage.

Eventually we got to work on the next AWS lab, "Troubleshoot a VPC," but James had more to say about courage.

He said whether or not you get a date, or a raise, you can die happy because you mustered up the courage to ask. I transcribed that in the Zoom chat—"Do not be afraid to ask"—and the learners reacted positively.

THE TAKEAWAY: **Just stand up and go.**

MAY 25 — Remember George Floyd.

Exactly 8 minutes and 46 seconds is how long Derek Chauvin knelt on George Floyd's neck on this date in 2020. A learner in my IT class that day, Togba, tearfully shared that he knew Floyd personally.

George Floyd's murder had a big impact on society, sparking Black Lives Matter protests, police reform, corporate DEI initiatives, and many deep, burning questions within many people, including myself.

Asking document-based questions (DBQs) is how I found Tim Wise on YouTube. Wise talks about "the history of whiteness" in a very engaging way, saying in the mid-1600s, there was no such thing as "white people."

He said English people hated Irish people in the 1600s. Northern Italians didn't think Southern Italians were even Italians. The Germans hated everybody, and everybody hated the Germans.

So how did "whiteness" become a thing?

Well, rich European landowners in the American colonies did the math and realized they were outnumbered by African slaves and European peasants who were indentured servants. They eventually decided to recruit the poor Europeans, who looked like them and shared some customs and culture, and create this thing called "whiteness."

The rich Europeans got rid of indentured servitude and told the "white men" they can testify in court, enter into contracts, vote, and own land.

By the time of the Civil War, Southern white men announced that the reason they wanted to break away from the Union and go to war with the North was to maintain "white supremacy."

THE TAKEAWAY: **Remember George Floyd.**

147 MAY 26 — Learn something from YouTube.

"It's crazy… without the Internet I would never be in this place… without YouTube and stuff."

— Justin Bieber

On February 1, 2004, in Houston, Texas, over 150 million people across the US were watching the annual Super Bowl halftime show featuring Janet Jackson and Justin Timberlake. During the show, Justin ripped off a piece of Janet's top as planned, but it went famously wrong.

"Nipplegate" soon became a big news story, the same year in which a devastating earthquake in the Indian Ocean created a massive tsunami that affected 14 countries.

These incidents are unrelated, but they shared one thing in common: it was hard to find videos of these events online in 2005.

Around this time, three young men, Chad Hurley, Jawed Karim, and Steve Chen, were quite rich and comfortable after their company, PayPal, was acquired by eBay in 2002. They were in good shape financially. They, too, were annoyed these videos were not online.

Allegedly, later that year, there was a dinner party in Chen's San Francisco apartment, which Karim and Hurley also attended. The three guys started showing each other videos of their cats, then remembered how hard it was to find videos of Janet Jackson or the tsunami.

That was when they had a revelation:

What if we created a website where people didn't have to search all around the internet for a specific video?

That is how YouTube was born. Ironically, I learned all this from a NationSquid YouTube video from July 2023.

THE TAKEAWAY: Learn something from YouTube.

MAY 27 — Prepare for some troubleshooting to get what you enjoy.

"I have nothing but respect for HBO."
— James Gandolfini

In *Tinderbox*, a book about the history of HBO, author James Andrew Miller quotes Joe Collins, who explained that "HBO needed cooperation" for a customer to get it. A customer first needs to order HBO from their cable company. Then, somebody from the company has to run RG 59 cable into the customer's house and send them a monthly bill.

In the digital age, HBO still required cooperation for me to get it. On May 27, 2020, AT&T launched HBO Max. I pulled out my iPhone immediately, only to discover the app didn't work!

I couldn't get the app on my Roku TV either, because WarnerMedia didn't finish negotiating with Roku until December 2020.

This is how my family and I ended up rewatching *Harry Potter* on HBO Max that day in May:
1. Sign into HBO on my MacBook Pro via my cable provider.
2. Physically connect the Mac's HDMI port to my living room TV.
3. Mirror the laptop and TV screens.
4. Change the audio output to the TV speakers.

Later that week, once the HBO Max app was actually working on the iPhone, I bought an Apple Lightning Digital AV Adapter so I could connect my iPhone to the TV via HDMI.

Did you ever have to troubleshoot to watch HBO? When HBO Max became Max, I remembered having to cooperate by uninstalling HBO Max to install Max.

THE TAKEAWAY: Prepare for some troubleshooting to get what you enjoy.

149

MAY 28 — Talk your way out of writer's block.

"No one ever gets 'talker's block.' No one wakes up in the morning, discovers he has nothing to say and sits quietly, for days or weeks, until the muse hits, until the moment is right, until all the craziness in his life has died down. Why then, is writer's block endemic?"

— Seth Godin's blog

I love this quote from Seth Godin because when I talk to people, especially my friends or family, I usually speak freely and respond naturally to the conversation. It is much more fluid because the stakes of "saying it right" are not high.

When I am writing, on the other hand, it requires reflection, organization, and immense self-pressure to make each word count. It's not just about me *saying* something but *creating* something that stands on its own and communicates ideas in a polished way.

Writers, myself included, are often overwhelmed by the need to be perfect and fear that their ideas won't come across as intended. This leads to self-doubt and the dreaded "writer's block."

But as Godin points out, talker's block does not exist, so why is writer's block a thing?

Talker's block, if it existed, would probably be caused by someone or some external thing shutting you up, whereas writer's block is an internal struggle to express oneself.

So if you ever get writer's block, imagine you are talking freely to your friend, then type it, and the writer's block will most likely go away.

THE TAKEAWAY: Talk your way out of writer's block.

MAY 29 — **Sometimes you have to suffer for the things you want.**

"We are the men in the arena. With our dust, sweat, and blood on our faces. I think a lot of people can relate to this team, because sometimes you have to suffer for the things that you really want."

—Miami Heat coach Erik Spoelstra to TNT Sports, after leading the team to making the NBA finals this day in 2023

This was an absolutely awful night for the Boston Celtics, who became the first team to lose Game 7 of the NBA Eastern Conference finals to a number-eight seed—on their *home court!*

No wonder Erik Spoelstra was quoting Theodore Roosevelt's "Man in the Arena" speech, with the "dust, sweat, and blood" and all.

Seeing this post-game speech reminded me of February 6, when I wrote in my diary about going to The Players club in New York City an hour before my front door manager shift.

The club is half a mile away from 28 E 20th St, the Roosevelt Birthplace Museum, so I walked over and asked the man in the lobby about President Roosevelt.

Spoelstra's reference to Roosevelt's famous speech captured the Heat's emotional journey of almost squandering a 3-0 lead to ultimately win Game 7 of the Eastern Conference finals and face the Denver Nuggets in the NBA finals that year.

THE TAKEAWAY: Sometimes you have to suffer for the things you want.

151 MAY 30 — Use image search to identify birds.

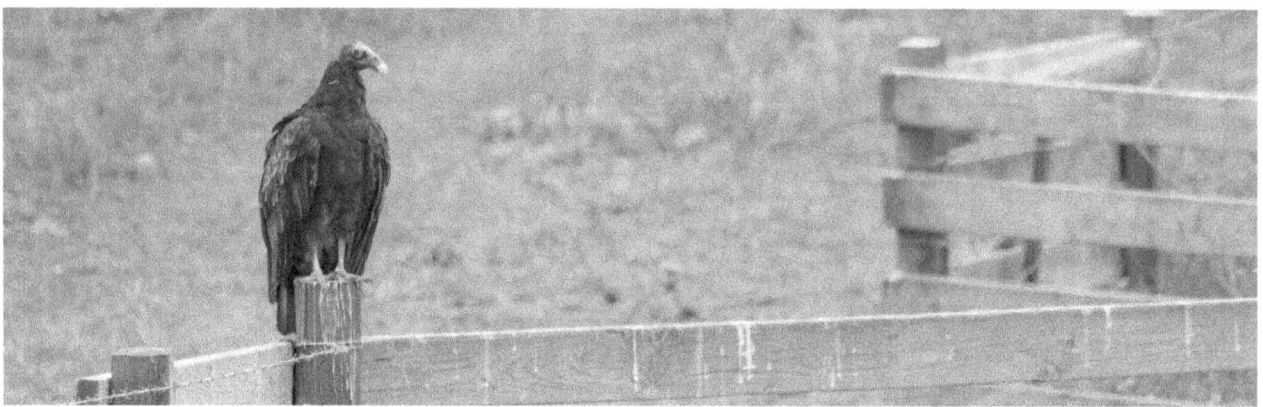

On this day in 2020, my dad saw a bird outside when we went for a walk in New Jersey.

I took a photo of the bird with my iPhone, then I gave access to that photo via iOS settings to the Google app so that I could run an image search to identify this unknown bird.

I ultimately learned that the bird in the photo is a **turkey vulture**.

This technology can be applied to plants or animals all over the planet. Even if you take a picture and you don't have data at the spot, you can run the image search later on.

Step-by-Step:
1. See a bird.
2. Get close enough for a photo.
3. Take a photo.
4. Allow your favorite ID app to run an image search.

THE TAKEAWAY: **Use image search to identify birds.**

MAY 31 — Start local, then national, then international.

"A network was really a tenant pretending to be a landlord... It was an odd business."

—Ken Auletta, Three Blind Mice

After Jason Kilar became CEO of WarnerMedia, I researched him. I write about his **TEDxYouth talk** on Day **352, December 17**. I bought a book he mentioned titled Three Blind Mice by Ken Auletta.

Since government regulations did not allow networks such as CBS, NBC, or ABC to own more than a handful of the stations that distribute their TV programs, these networks are at the mercy of the 600+ TV stations across the US that agree to call themselves "affiliates."

Then, after stitching together a national network of local stations that want to show TV shows from Hollywood, or independent producers, these networks then go to advertisers and sell them expensive ad slots based on mass audiences they rent from local stations.

A television network is, in fact, nothing more than a broker.

After learning this, I became a fan of Ken Auletta. I even found interviews he did on **C-SPAN** and the **GaryVee** podcast.

One takeaway is that content should first spread locally. A rapper in Atlanta, for example, can start making waves in Atlanta, then radio or TV networks in the state of Georgia, and from there the music can spread through national affiliates.

Basically, this rapper can start locally, then go national, then go international, spreading across the world. Even coronavirus started in Wuhan, China, before spreading worldwide.

THE TAKEAWAY: Start local, then national, then international.

JUNE

JUNE 1 — Be careful what you pretend to be.

> *"We are what we pretend to be, so we must be careful about what we pretend to be."*
>
> — Kurt Vonnegut, Mother Night

Our actions and choices can shape our reality and influence our sense of self. Maybe we copy someone else because it is convenient or amusing. Pretty soon, these things we "pretend" to be have a way of becoming core to who we are.

And so, we must tread carefully when adopting roles or projecting images, as they might bind us more tightly than we expect.

We must be careful to be true to who we are and mindful of the stories we tell to ourselves about ourselves. Those stories have the power to define who we become throughout a lifetime.

THE TAKEAWAY: Be careful what you pretend to be.

154

JUNE 2 — Learn something from the pandemic.

Adonis Goris came from an IT Support cohort I led in 2020. I was overjoyed to see his picture and story featured in the *Wall Street Journal!*

In an article entitled "Tech Jobs Lead the Way in New York City's Covid-19 Pandemic Hiring" they write about Adonis. He had no college degree and was laid off during a pandemic. He was 25 years old, and he decided to learn something new.

With me as his instructor, Adonis got certified in CompTIA A+ and Google IT Support training, and now has a career troubleshooting life and tech.

He fixes machines. He helps human beings. The habits he formed at Per Scholas turned into strong work habits.

Former Per Scholas alumni like Adonis walk the halls of JP Morgan, Barclays, Google, and all sorts of companies that use computers, tablets, mobile devices, and cloud computing.

History repeats itself until we choose to learn from our mistakes and the mistakes of others. During the pandemic, people had nothing but time to learn new things.

THE TAKEAWAY: Learn something from the pandemic.

JUNE 3 — Anticipate and shape the future instead of reacting to it.

On this day in 2002, the influential Hollywood executive Lew Wasserman died.

That same day, Jack Valenti, former Special Assistant to US President Lyndon B. Johnson and president of the Motion Picture Association of America, wrote a guest column for *Variety* about Wasserman.

His life has been covered extensively in media, such as Connie Bruck's biography *When Hollywood Had a King*, and the Barry Avrich documentary *The Last Mogul*.

I learned a few lessons on business, life, and leadership from studying him, such as building strong relationships with clients, colleagues, and political figures. In *The Last Mogul,* Avrich brings up 1966, when Wasserman helped Reagan become Governor of California. He would later bail Reagan out of financial trouble by brokering a deal to sell 236 acres of Reagan's Malibu ranch to 20th Century Fox for $2 million, when the county appraised the land at $115,000.

He was also masterful at working behind the scenes.

Wasserman shunned the spotlight, wielding influence quietly and effectively in an industry full of glamorous stars. Leadership can be impactful from the shadows without being overly visible.

In the *Variety* article, Valenti quotes Winston Churchill, who said Lew Wasserman had:

"[T]he seeing eye, the ability to see beneath the surface of things, to know what is on the other side of the brick wall, to follow the hunt three fields before the throng."

THE TAKEAWAY: Anticipate and shape the future instead of reacting to it.

156   JUNE 4 — Be responsible for studying the information you deliver.

"The advancement and diffusion of knowledge is the only true guardian of liberty."

— James Madison

The members of an orchestra are responsible for playing the right "information," or music notes. Doctors and paramedics are responsible for using elaborate information systems for their work of healing patients. A technical instructor at Per Scholas, or a university professor, or a movie director, all are responsible for their information.

All these professionals have superiors who depend on them for some information. They also have subordinates who they depend on for some information. And so, each party is also responsible for studying the information they must deliver.

The actress, the director in charge of the set, the movie producer, and a movie marketing specialist— all of these professionals must take full responsibility for their information. Learning their lines, or planning camera moves, or staying on budget, or designing the poster.

Dr. Radhakrishnan Pillai writes about study time in *Chanakya in Daily Life*, citing *Arthashastra*:

> **"The duties of a king (leader) are — studying, performing sacrifices for self, making gifts and protecting beings."**

It is important to study whatever it is you must study. That way, when the time comes and you must act, you can take full information responsibility.

THE TAKEAWAY: Be responsible for studying the information you deliver.

176

JUNE 5 — You have no idea how many people want to say "yes."

On this day in 2021, my friend and comedian Coleman Cosby opened for the comic Josh Johnson at a show in Philadelphia.

I was standing right next to Cole as Josh gave him this advice:

"You have no idea how many people want to say yes to you."

Josh Johnson says he is a Black man "from Louisiana by way of Chicago," and what he said is absolutely right. People are out there who want to say yes to you and buy your work.

Many people hesitate to ask for help out of self-doubt or a fear of rejection. But the truth is, there are *lots* of people out there who are willing, even *eager*, to say yes to offering their time, expertise, even their financial support of you and your work.

There is something you are hesitating to ask for: some advice, an introduction, a helping hand with a task you are stuck on.

By overcoming your hesitation and making a confident request, you increase the chance of opening doors that were once closed.

> **THE TAKEAWAY:** You have no idea how many people want to say "yes."

JUNE 6 — A successful meeting needs a clear agenda.

"You should never go to a meeting or make a telephone call without a clear idea of what you are trying to achieve."

— Steve Jobs

My friend is filling me in on a Zoom screenwriters group meeting she went to today. She was looking forward to this writing group all week, but the dynamic did not work out as expected.

So what did they do in the meeting? Apparently, they just chatted for about 30 minutes, and they did not workshop or read any scripts.

I feel a great deal of sympathy for my friend. Her job at Sony is soul sucking, and she was really looking forward to working with other screenwriters on making her screenplay better.

My friend knows about my job leading IT classes on Zoom four days a week at Per Scholas, and she asks me how I run my Zoom meetings.

I tell her that every successful meeting needs to have an agenda, and end with action points.

Every individual needs to accept responsibility for their goals, their priorities, their working relationships, and their communications. Otherwise, nothing ever gets done.

Ideally, this screenwriting group should have a cadence of reading scripts, giving notes, and following up, until every writer in the group has a script they have a chance to improve upon by the time the meeting ends or the class graduates. Otherwise, what's the point?

THE TAKEAWAY: **A successful meeting needs a clear agenda.**

JUNE 7 — Examine how antiheroes make you feel.

"I know there are women, like my best friends, who would have gotten out of there the minute their boyfriend gave them a gun to hide. But I didn't. I got to admit the truth. It turned me on."

—Karen Hill, Goodfellas (1990)

In his memoir *Who Is Michael Ovitz?*, the author writes about the movie *Goodfellas*, adapted by client Martin Scorsese, from the bestselling book by another client, Nicholas Pileggi. Henry Hill is a cocaine-addicted gangster who beats his wife, pistol-whips an unarmed man, and hangs out with mobsters who casually shoot people in the head.

Universal passed on *Goodfellas*, but Bob Daly and Terry Semel at Warner Bros. approved it.

The first problem was casting. *Goodfellas*'s only star was Robert De Niro in a supporting role. Martin Scorsese decided that Ray Liotta should be Henry Hill. The studio tossed out bigger names, from Tom Cruise to Eddie Murphy, but Marty wanted Ray. Today, nobody can picture anyone but Ray Liotta as Henry Hill.

He had to play four distinct characters: the wannabe wise guy, the mature wise guy, the cocaine addict wise guy, and the "schmuck" in the witness protection program.

After this movie, America had over 30 years of antihero movies and TV shows, such as: *Pulp Fiction, The Usual Suspects, Casino, The Sopranos, Mad Men,* and *Breaking Bad*.

As it turns out, people are rarely "pure good" or "pure evil."

THE TAKEAWAY: Examine how antiheroes make you feel.

160   JUNE 8 — Recognize brilliant manipulation when you see it.

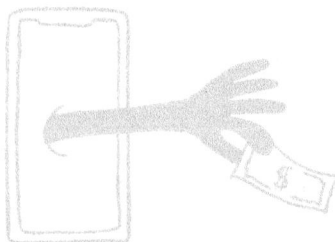

"Advertising is the art of convincing people to spend money they don't have for something they don't need."

— Will Rogers

At its best, advertising simply informs and connects us with solutions to real problems or desires we have. But at its worst, it is convincing us to spend money we don't have on things we don't need but are compelled to buy because the advertiser told such a good story.

Advertising is an art form, using all the tools available to manipulate us to buy things. There's text, audio, images, moving images. There are a lot of tools available to use for individuals or companies trying to sell products.

As a kid I would go crazy for ads, but as an adult I realize how ads can be used to manipulate our buying habits.

Many ads in public places and restaurant menus now include QR codes to scan with mobile phones for a digital copy or more information about the ad, or a link to the online store. It makes advertisers happy when you do this because, like all people, they want to be remembered for doing effective work that helps them make sales and solve problems for the consumer community.

As a potential product creator yourself, take note of these effective manipulations and use them to sell your own products or those of your clients.

THE TAKEAWAY: Recognize brilliant manipulation when you see it.

JUNE 9 — Design a great user experience for your products.

"Design is not just what it looks like and feels like. Design is how it works."
— Steve Jobs

The term "user experience" was first coined by the cognitive psychologist Don Norman. When he worked for Apple in the mid-90s in the User Experience Office, he was the first person to hold a position that had the term "User Experience" (UX) in the title, a term that is now commonplace in tech.

His 1988 book *The Design of Everyday Things* remains a sort of UX bible, discussing how design serves as the communication between object and user, and how to optimize that communication so that the experience of using the object is more pleasurable.

In ancient China, there is a concept of *feng shui*, rooted in the idea that life energy (*qi*) flows through everything. To apply *feng shui* to your physical or digital space, you can do things such as:
- Clean up clutter.
- Arrange elements in a natural flow of action.
- Incorporate natural colors.
- Add organic shapes and nature-inspired visuals.

The important thing is to prioritize clarity, balance, and purposeful design to create an experience that "feels right" for your product as your users use them.

When it is done right, the products can become incredibly addicting, like the iPhone or YouTube.

THE TAKEAWAY: **Design a great user experience for your products.**

162   JUNE 10 — Start by relaxing your mind.

In *Chanakya in Daily Life,* Dr. Radhakrishnan Pillai cites Chanakya, who wrote in *Arthashastra*:

"Anvikshiki keeps the mind steady in adversity and prosperity and brings about proficiency in thought, speech, and action."

On **Wikipedia**, it says Ānvīkṣikī is a Sanskrit term that roughly means the "science of inquiry," and that over the centuries, its meaning has changed.

Chanakya presents *anvikshiki* as a foundational discipline, important to maintaining mental balance so that one's thought, speech, and action are aligned in life's challenging moments.

A meditative person is able to see things as they are, not as their emotions dictate. They use speech to build understanding instead of creating more conflict.

When things are going completely wrong and nobody knows what to do, it is important to stay calm. When things are going completely right and everyone knows what to do, it is *still* important to stay calm. This is made possible by sitting quietly and observing your mind, until eventually you are so calm you could fall asleep. But then you don't go to sleep. Instead, you get ready to work, with a fully alert mind.

THE TAKEAWAY: **Start by relaxing your mind.**

JUNE 11 — Embrace weird hobbies like Charles Darwin did.

In *The Secret Power of Middle Children*, Catherine Salmon, Ph.D., and Katrin Schumann write about Charles Darwin.

His father, Doctor Robert Darwin, said Charles would disgrace himself and his family.

Charles dropped out of university after two years. No matter how badly his father wanted it, Charles was not becoming a doctor.

Instead, Charles pursued weird hobbies like collecting beetles or preserving dead animals. His father, out of desperation, sent Charles off to Cambridge to become a priest in 1828. But even that did not work! At age 22, Charles begged to accompany a team of researchers on a mission halfway across the world. His father refused, but his uncle Josiah intervened, and Charles went on the *HMS Beagle* in 1831. He sailed around South America, across the Pacific Ocean, and to the Galápagos Islands.

While on the islands, Charles Darwin studied the native animals. In particular, he studied 13 species of birds, now known as "Darwin's finches." This study led Charles Darwin to develop his theories of natural selection and evolution.

Could you imagine if Charles Darwin became a doctor? Modern biology would not exist today. Darwin was an unpretentious, mild-mannered middle child, wrote Salmon and Schumann. He displayed average intelligence in school but an above-average drive and passion for those things he did find interesting.

This drive and passion led him to becoming a trailblazer in the scientific community. Almost 200 years later, the theories he developed still remain relevant.

THE TAKEAWAY: Embrace weird hobbies like Charles Darwin did.

164

JUNE 12 — Support nonprofits with missions that help society.

"Only a life lived for others is a life worthwhile."

— Albert Einstein

Neither can the government nor any single business provide everything that a citizen needs.

Consider Microsoft, which in 2021, announced Windows 11. To get the world on 11, Microsoft must release documentation, software, and security updates, but it will come down to nonprofits like Per Scholas to actually deliver accessible training and know-how to help people become proficient at using Windows 11. New Per Scholas graduates can fix machines and stop cyber attacks wherever Microsoft products are used, from churches to professional associations to homeless shelters and so on.

Do you have any favorite nonprofit organizations?

Aside from Per Scholas, another nonprofit I like is the Information Systems Security Association of Los Angeles, or ISSA-LA.

ISSA-LA provides educational forums and peer interaction opportunities that enhance the knowledge, skills, and professional growth of the cybersecurity and IT communities.

The Los Angeles chapter is also the founding chapter of ISSA International, which has members and chapters all over the world, all of whom network to learn and share problems and solutions to secure the digital world.

How can your favorite nonprofits create new communities in US cities or all over the world?

THE TAKEAWAY: Support nonprofits with missions that help society.

JUNE 13 — View history from multiple perspectives.

"History is the version of past events that people have decided to agree upon."

— Napoleon Bonaparte

The greatest sin of education around the world is failure to engage its staff and stakeholders.

In America, and in India, the history being taught is biased, and boring

All the history taught to my grandmother in Indian schools was written by the British. Only outside of school did she learn about freedom fighters such as Guru Gobind Singh, Bhagat Singh, Mangal Pandey, and others.

The Jallianwala Bagh massacre took place in 1919 in India during a protest against the Rowlatt Act and the arrest of pro-Indian independence activists. Wikipedia states that it resulted in between 379 and 1,000 deaths, but my grandma and dad said the number was closer to 2,000, and I believe them. It would have been in the interests of the British at the time to cite a number that was far lower than the actual amount in order to avoid further rebellion.

History is not just a fixed set of events but a dynamic process that can be understood in different ways depending on who you ask. Or as Friedrich Nietzsche says, "There are no facts, only interpretations."

THE TAKEAWAY: View history from multiple perspectives.

JUNE 14 — Do not neglect your body.

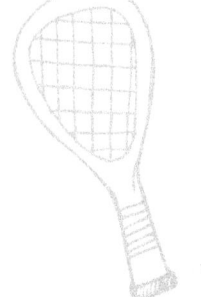

"Take care of your body. It's the only place you have to live."

— Jim Rohn

Your health is your most valuable possession. Without good health, what can you do?

I will be the first to admit that I sometimes spend too much time studying and not enough time exercising, but whenever I do go exercise, I never regret it.

People usually get fit to look good in spring and summer clothes, but it is important to take care of the body all year. Exercise is a great way to relieve stress. It sharpens your mind and brain, and it helps you sleep better at night. In the long term, exercise even increases your life span so you can do more cool stuff on planet Earth.

It might even inspire others in your life to exercise, people who want you to live longer and who you would like to see live longer as well.

THE TAKEAWAY: Do not neglect your body.

JUNE 15 — Make sure your work is formatted correctly.

AP exams from the College Board require essays. Students can either type their response or upload a photo of handwritten work as a JPG, JPEG, or PNG file.

But when Apple released iOS11 and macOS High Sierra in 2017, HEIC files became the new standard image format for billions of Apple devices. In May 2020, an article in *The Verge* discussed the problems this update caused, when students were failing AP tests because the College Board couldn't handle the new HEIC file format. This was devastating to the stressed-out students, who had to then study for three more weeks until they could do a retake.

The College Board *did* tweet about the formats and directions on how to save photos as JPEG, but many tests had already begun by that time, and it was too late for students to get information from Twitter.

There are a few takeaways from this:
- The College Board should have been up to date in accepting the HEIC file format when Apple released it, or it should have had a system in place to automatically convert the files to acceptable formats.
- The students should have been explicitly informed about acceptable file formats well in advance.

When you are about to turn in an important deliverable, making sure everything is formatted correctly can save you, big time.

THE TAKEAWAY: **Make sure your work is formatted correctly.**

168

JUNE 16 — Use social media carefully.

"Social networks do best when they tap into one of the seven deadly sins. Facebook *is ego.* Zynga *is sloth.* LinkedIn *is greed."*

—Reid Hoffman, co-founder of LinkedIn

ShootingReels has a full **timeline** of how Facebook has changed over the years.

- 2003: "Hot or not": A way for boys to rate girls, made by hacking Harvard's student face book.
- 2004: "The Facebook" is born, a directory for Harvard students, and soon other elite universities.
- 2005: High school users. Mark Zuckerberg was sure about monetizing with ads, but unsure how to execute.
- 2006: "The News Feed" is available to anyone over the age of 13.
- 2008: 100 million worldwide users. Mark Zuckerberg said "we learned… exactly how important privacy is."
- 2009: 200 million users. The "Like" button.
- 2010: *The Social Network* movie is released, written by Aaron Sorkin **(Day 97. April 6)**
- 2011: Facebook's "wall" is now a "timeline" in chronological order of updates.
- 2012: Facebook acquires Instagram for $1 billion.
- 2014: Facebook buys WhatsApp for $19 billion.
- 2017: Two billion monthly users.
- 2018: Facebook changes its news feed algorithm. Problems with misinformation and untrustworthy news begin to mount.
- 2019: Netflix documentary *The Great Hack* explores the Facebook-Cambridge Analytica scandal.
- 2021: Facebook becomes Meta.

Meta platforms are incredibly big. It is good to know how to use them, but it is also good to avoid getting consumed by them to the point you do nothing with your day. *How* you use social media is key.

THE TAKEAWAY: Use social media carefully.

JUNE 17 — Adopt an empowered state of mind.

"The difference between peak performance and poor performance is not intelligence or ability; most often it's the state that your mind and body is in."

— Tony Robbins

Tony Robbins has joked about how smoking a joint is a way to "change your state," like exercise or alcohol or chocolate.

All of these things can affect your emotions as a human being. It is easy to think emotions are beyond our control, but they aren't!

On his website, he writes how you can always retrain your mind to look for good things in life, as opposed to looking for bad things and triggering "fight or flight" response.

Accept every moment as it comes, and avoid setting expectations that are unmeetable, otherwise you will just be upset and taking it out on others.

Instead, it is better to smile and empower yourself to set a positive tone for the day.

THE TAKEAWAY: Adopt an empowered state of mind.

170 JUNE 18 — Embrace your quirks, struggles, and vulnerabilities.

"Imperfection is beauty, madness is genius, and it's better to be absolutely ridiculous than absolutely boring."

— Marilyn Monroe

People like to say that Marilyn Monroe was the most perfect, beautiful woman in the world, but even she knew that perfection doesn't exist.

This woman was regarded as the epitome of beauty and perfection, which makes it fascinating that she was deeply aware of the imperfection that is inherent in human nature. Monroe recognized that perfection is an illusion and that real beauty lies in embracing one's uniqueness and flaws.

Our quirks, struggles, and vulnerabilities, those things we try to hide, are what make us relatable and authentic.

Even those who are admired for being "a blonde bombshell" can struggle with the pressures of perfection.

THE TAKEAWAY: Embrace your quirks, struggles, and vulnerabilities.

JUNE 19 — Do the right thing on Juneteenth.

"Facta, non verba."

—Latin phrase

Spike Lee's motto is *Deeds, not words (facta, nonverba)*. **(79. March 19)**

Spending the start of Juneteenth 2023 watching NBA basketball.

Jazz and Clippers in the fourth, Clippers up by seven right now, let's see if Utah comes back to win this game six. Was watching Philly beat Atlanta before this to force a game seven.

Focus on the present moment. It will not return.

I am watching Spike Lee's *Do the Right Thing* at Alamo Drafthouse in downtown LA. The film is an asset that he can leverage infinitely to get financing for more projects that a Spike Lee fan like me hopes for.

Ryan Coogler shared how he saw his film on Malcolm X at eight years old.

AI Spike Lee would not make *Do the Right Thing* the way it will play at Alamo tonight. Would Lee, or the kid in *Clockers*, have used ChatGPT or AI if they had it? I would! **(321. November 16)**

But I'd also expect the machine to compensate the copyright owners of that material—as well as the filmmakers, the creative teams who create these assets, and of course, the "suits."

Educate, entertain, and enlighten, Reader.

As this book illustrates, even one page a day can make a huge difference.

THE TAKEAWAY: Do the right thing on Juneteenth.

JUNE 20 — A calm leader must study their empire daily.

Bestselling author Dr. Radhakrishnan Pillai, in *Chanakya in Daily Life*, writes that a person should not study only to pass exams. Instead, a person must develop a thirst for knowledge, no matter what walk of life you are from. He cites the *Arthashastra*:

"The duties of a king (leader) are—studying, performing sacrifices for self, making gifts, and protecting beings."

Kings have to study the ins and outs of their kingdom. Yes, they have advisors, and are often surrounded by boardrooms of experts. Even then, they need to study the kingdom themselves.

Kids or adults may have excuses like "I have no time to study" or "I am too busy." But as Dr. Radhakrishnan Pillai points out, who is busier than a king or a CEO?

The leader has to recognize that studying is the most important duty for a strong kingdom. Just imagine what a wise and knowledgeable business leader, or teacher, can do. Or imagine a leader who knows absolutely nothing and the chaos that could ensue.

In *Arthashastra*, the Sanskrit word for study is *swa-adhyaya (self-study)*. Another word I like is "autodidact."

THE TAKEAWAY: A calm leader must study their empire daily.

JUNE 21 — Ignore the trash talk.

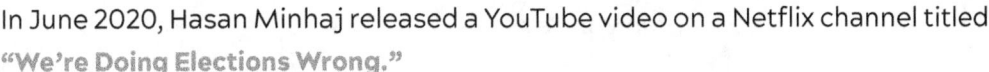

"People throw rocks at things that shine."
— Taylor Swift, "Ours"

In June 2020, Hasan Minhaj released a YouTube video on a Netflix channel titled **"We're Doing Elections Wrong."**

I learned that plurality is American democracy, not "majority rules" as we like to say.

A "plurality" of votes is when a candidate or proposition gets more votes than any other. That does not mean 51 percent of all votes; it just means more than all others.

Hasan also points out the negative partisanship of modern politics, or how everything is "trash talk" about who we hate, instead of who we like. He made me laugh when he said that "politics is more like baseball" because a lot of the cheating is done by out-of-shape white people.

Whether you are in politics, or sports, or any field, remember to ignore the trash talk.

THE TAKEAWAY: Ignore the trash talk.

174   JUNE 22 — Sometimes, a leader must embrace change.

"The greatest discovery of all time is that a person can change their future by merely changing their attitude."

— Oprah Winfrey

It has been said that the definition of insanity is doing the same thing repeatedly but expecting a different result.

But that is exactly what most people do.

Today in 2020, I was scheduled to teach at Per Scholas. Specifically, Chapter 14 of the Mike Meyers CompTIA A+ book, "Maintaining and Optimizing Operating Systems." The slideshow provided with the textbook was very heavy on Microsoft Windows. There were 12 slides just on Windows Patch Management. Like going to Control Panel in Windows 7 or 8 to check for updates, or going to Settings in Windows 10 and finding "Windows Update."

But we had Apple and Mac users in this remote Zoom class as well, *including myself.* So I decided to schedule into class time a livestream of that year's Apple's Worldwide Developer conference (WWDC 20). Apple showed off a new Apple TV+ show called *Foundation,* based on an Isaac Asimov science fiction novel, with the actor who played Lane Pryce on *Mad Men,* real name Jared Harris.

Perhaps people thought it was insane for Apple to make their own M1 chip, or iOS 14 widgets.

My class on Zoom loved that I shared my screen for this and live chatting during the video. It was a nice change of pace to talk about brand new Apple stuff instead of the usual CompTIA A+ Microsoft.

THE TAKEAWAY: **Sometimes, a leader must embrace change.**

JUNE 23 — Learn Nodder's four levels of persuasion.

"Happiness rarely triggers commerce. Unhappiness often does."
—Chris Nodder

My cousin graduating from high school on this date was a very happy moment. He plans on going to medical school and becoming a doctor, which is awesome. When I went home that night, I could not sleep. Instead, I started studying Chris Nodder's user experience course and reading his book, *Evil by Design*.

Deception isn't always bad. In fact, while I was reading the book, I remember being a teenager eating dinner with my uncle and aunt and this same cousin, who was then a kid.

He had a hard time eating his vegetables. Then he saw me, his older cousin, make a big show of how much I enjoyed them. Then suddenly, the kid started eating more vegetables, to the joy of his parents, who had been trying to get him to eat them.

Not all deception is "evil."

Perhaps you told a white lie earlier today to your parents, kids, manager, or your subordinates.

Nodder might describe this vegetable incident as motivational or charitable persuasion. In his book, and on his website, he describes **four levels** of persuasion.
1. Commercial design persuades people for equal benefit to the user and designer.
2. Motivational design persuades people to do something that benefits them in different scenarios.
3. Charitable design is a designer persuading people for the good of society.
4. Evil design persuades people for the benefit of the designer, often at the expense of the user.

THE TAKEAWAY: Learn Nodder's four levels of persuasion.

176

JUNE 24 — Understand how to use numbers as well as their limits.

"Not everything that can be counted counts, and not everything that counts can be counted."

— William Bruce Cameron

Peter Drucker believed that management education is only good for people who are already succeeding in some way, and that management courses for people without experience are a waste of time.

He also believed this education should be for people in all sectors, private, public, and nonprofit. While at school, students should also be doing real work at real organizations, like how doctors do residency at real hospitals during medical school.

Outside of just management, there should be classes on government, society, history, and politics, from seasoned teachers with real experience, possibly their own consulting practices.

All that is great to have, but the hardest part is measuring that which cannot be measured. Relying solely on numbers and quantitative data gives a limited picture. There are a number of intangible aspects, things such as love, happiness, and personal growth, that do matter but cannot always be easily quantified in numbers.

It is easy to find people who know how to crunch the numbers that are available. It is much harder to find people who also understand that numbers have limits to them.

THE TAKEAWAY: Understand how to use numbers as well as their limits.

JUNE 25 — Push creative boundaries and take risks.

> *"I'm starting with the man in the mirror.*
> *I'm asking him to change his ways."*
>
> — Michael Jackson, *"Man in the Mirror"*

Pun intended, Michael Jackson's music rocks my world. Truth be told, I only started searching this man's name after he died on this day in 2009. I remember I was at my neighborhood pool with my friends, about a week before I was going to turn 13, and my little brother was home watching the news. That October, MJ's *This Is It* tour was cancelled.

A movie was going to be released in the AMC theater on Route 1 for one show only of *This Is It*. My heroic dad somehow got tickets for the whole family, who by that point *had* to see it. Michael Jackson fandom was at an all-time high by that point.

We all sat down in the theater. Previews played. Then, weirdly, Where the Wild Things Are (2009) played, for something like 10 minutes.

The crowd, who had been waiting in line to buy tickets for this single exhibition, started chanting "Mi-chael Jack-son!" until *This Is It* started playing. It was insane!

About 10 years later, I talked to my friends about this. The consensus was, we were toddlers when 9/11 happened, and we sort of remember it.

But we were teens in 2009, and we *definitely* remember when Michael Jackson died. This artist constantly reinvented himself. As I got to know his work post-mortem, I found him inspiring.

THE TAKEAWAY: **Push creative boundaries and take risks.**

178   JUNE 26 — Understand math is how God wrote the universe.

"Mathematics is the alphabet with which God has written the universe."

— Galileo Galilei

Today in 1959, Walt Disney released *Donald in Mathmagic Land.*

I remember this short film was something my Calculus 1 teacher showed our class in high school, when we were about to graduate.

Walt Disney and his team on this film connected math to music, starting with Pythagoreans and Pythagoras, who met "in secret" because science was persecuted at that time. We see harp strings divided into octaves, a series of eight notes between (and including) two notes, one with either twice or half the frequency of vibration of the other.

The film eventually leaves animations for real life jazz music, almost as if to say, "this is not just cartoons, this is real life."

The golden rectangle, jasmine flowers, starfish, sports … math magic is everywhere.

The film ends with a quote from Galileo Galilei:

"Mathematics is the alphabet with which God has written the universe".

No wonder Walt Disney's life and career inspired founders such as Steve Jobs, Jason Kilar of Hulu, and Brian Chesky of Airbnb, and likely many others.

THE TAKEAWAY: Understand math is how God wrote the universe.

JUNE 27 — Embrace the region from which you come.

"Know from whence you came. If you know whence you came, there are absolutely no limitations to where you can go."
—James Baldwin

Took some videos with my iPhone in my New Jersey hometown. I thought my camerawork was good. Now I'm reading Steven Soderbergh's advice to filmmakers in the Los Angeles Times.

Soderbergh talks about this Andrew Patterson movie he saw, The Vast of Night, and says there are three components to directing that a filmmaker should grasp:

   1. Narrative   2. Performance   3. The camera

Soderbergh says people have created successful careers knowing one or two of those things, but it is rare to see somebody have a grasp of all three, such as Andrew Patterson showed in this film, especially for somebody who'd never made a feature before.

Soderbergh talks about how one of the first things he did after *Sex, Lies, and Videotape* emerged was to move back to Charlottesville, Virginia, to get married.

He felt that hanging out and becoming a social Hollywood person was not going to help his artistry.

So he stepped away from Hollywood and embraced being a "regional filmmaker" who lives outside of the film business, though he does reside in New York.

If a filmmaker makes their movies where they grew up, it increases the chances the film will turn out well. Here are a few examples: Martin Scorsese, New York. Ryan Coogler, Bay Area. Robert Rodriguez, San Antonio. Kevin Smith, New Jersey. Rajkumar Hirani, Nagpur.

THE TAKEAWAY: Embrace the region from which you come.

180   JUNE 28 — Write someone a letter of recommendation.

> *"The best way to find yourself is to lose yourself in the service of others."*
> — Mahatma Gandhi

Today in 2023, I wrote this letter:

Back on April 17, 2023, I was supporting James Miao in training 2023-RTT-14 AWS re/Start, and was very impressed by this message in Zoom class from this learner:

From Anthony Oleska to Me (Direct Message) 10:52 AM

Hey Akash, you think later I can get into a breakout room with you or James to ask a few questions about AWS. ive been playing around more with it and im still trying to understand gateways, routing tables, and how interconnected subnets/networks all function within AWS.

And I did talk to Anthony about those things.

Later that month, I remember Ant had questions about my website, and I enjoyed answering his questions as we continued the AWS Certified Cloud Practitioner training.

This past Monday started week 15 of 15. With his graduation this Friday, Anthony (now a Certified Cloud Practitioner) was showing me he had been making HIS cool new website (antoleska.net). Reflecting on it, I truly enjoyed training and managing Anthony in the AWS re/Start class. It is truly a joy to meet a fellow human being who is curious, self-driven, energetic, and most importantly, helpful to others in class.

Ant, I look forward to seeing what you do in the cloud and beyond.

THE TAKEAWAY: Write someone a letter of recommendation.

JUNE 29 — Appreciate life every day, and practice kindness.

"Grief is like the ocean; it comes on waves ebbing and flowing. Sometimes the water is calm, and sometimes it is overwhelming. All we can do is learn to swim."

— William Shakespeare, *Much Ado About Nothing*

Thirty minutes ago, I found out that my aunt's mother passed away. It's making my mother cry very hard. It's making everyone cry, actually.

The departed was still only in her 50s. She was in chemotherapy two or three times, and at one point she even requested death because she was in so much pain.

It is sad, but at the very least I am glad her suffering has ended.

Reader, remember to mourn your lost loved ones, but continue living. Practice kindness in everything that you do.

THE TAKEAWAY: Appreciate life every day, and practice kindness.

182
JUNE 30 — Understand primordial images and archetypes.

"The primordial image, or archetype, is a figure—be it a daemon, a human being, or a process—that constantly recurs in the course of history and appears wherever creative fantasy is freely expressed."

— Carl Jung

When I went to Temple University, I got to take class with the documentarian and professor Lou Pepe, who guided the class in what I think he called a primordial image exercise. He asked everyone in the class to stand with our feet shoulder-width apart and look down. Then, he asked us to sway back and forth like a pendulum. Soon, images and sounds will flood the imagination, and you end up in a meditative place. I can still clearly remember the classroom, and hear Lou's voice, when I first did this.

You might see your parents, past lovers, these phantoms from the past who are deeply rooted in your psyche, come up from within.

Entering and leaving this dreamy state can enrich your personal life and your creative work. The hero's journey archetype, for example, has been the basis for countless movies from *Star Wars* to *The Dark Knight* and beyond.

By better understanding your own psyche, you better understand the motivations, fears, and desires that drive you and, possibly, what drives others in your family or workplace.

THE TAKEAWAY: **Understand primordial images and archetypes.**

JULY

JULY 1 — Monitor "the seven windows of opportunity."

> *"Efficiency is doing things right; effectiveness is doing the right things."*
> — Peter Drucker

Successful entrepreneurs do not wait until the "the Muse kisses them" with a bright idea; they go to work.

It means monitoring seven sources of innovative opportunity. The first four sources are within the business, industry, or service sector.
- The unexpected success, failure, or outside "force majeure" event (like a pandemic)
- The difference between reality as it is versus how reality "should be"
- Innovation, based on business process need
- Changes in industry or market structure

The second set of sources for innovative opportunity involves changes outside those mentioned above.
- Demographics (population changes)
- Changes in perception, mood, and meaning
- New knowledge, both scientific and nonscientific

The lines between these seven sources are blurred and overlapping like "seven windows" on a different side of the same building. Each window shows some things that can also be seen from other windows, but the view from the center of each window is distinct and different.

THE TAKEAWAY: Monitor "the seven windows of opportunity."

184   JULY 2 — Write your obituary and try to live up to it.

"In many ways, women are death's natural companions. Every time a woman gives birth, she is creating not only a life, but a death. Mother Nature is indeed a real mother, creating and destroying in a constant loop."

— Caitlin Doughty

Today was the funeral for my aunt, the grandmother of my wonderful cousins. The following day I turned 25. My family and I drove to Atlantic City after the funeral to celebrate my birthday.

The funeral was very emotional. On the drive to Atlantic City, my mom noted that funeral homes operate on emotional blackmail. Here is an industry that preys on grief, using guilt and fear to convince families to spend money on things like a casket. You could get a $3,000 casket, or a $10,000 casket in oak or cherry or sandalwood.

I joked, "Get my casket from Costco." My brother adds, "Get me the cheapest casket. Spend the rest on booze and girls."

It is nice to hear my mom laugh at these jokes about funerals after attending one, on the way to celebrate my birthday.

I wondered about my own funeral. What will my obituary say? Someone else will likely write it for me, but what if I try writing a draft?

I would want to die a person whom others call hardworking, smart, creative, and driven. A brother, a son, a wholesome guy who helped people and was a faithful and loving husband to his wife and kids.

THE TAKEAWAY: **Write your obituary and try to live up to it.**

JULY 3 — Make a positive impact on your birthday.

"There are two great days in a person's life—the day we are born and the day we discover why."
—Unknown

It took a while for me to realize I take way more notes than the average person. It took me a while longer to realize I should try and publish my notes in a book or other media.

Today is my birthday, but I know I will not live forever.

If I look at how I spend my time, I spend it alone.

Sometimes I feel lonely. I sometimes feel despair, because I perceive I am not as successful as I hoped. I feel envy when I scroll through social media.

It's not like these feelings are unique to me. They are evidence that I am human, and alive, for now.

So take some time to write down the positive impact you want to make by your next birthday.

To me, writing is a gift. To Isaac Asimov, it is "simply thinking through my fingers."

THE TAKEAWAY: Make a positive impact on your birthday

186   JULY 4 — Celebrate the United States' mutiny (or "independence").

"When tyranny becomes law, rebellion becomes duty."
— Thomas Jefferson

"Independence" for one is "mutiny" for another.

Assuming you are American, Happy Fourth of July!

July 4th is called Independence Day in the United States, marking the signing of the Declaration of Independence in 1776. This is similar to 1857, when the First War of Independence was fought in India. The British called it the Sepoy Mutiny.

For the British, both these events were a mutiny against the Crown, a defiance of what they considered lawful governance.

Depending on your perspective, you can interpret these events in different ways. It depends on who you ask.

Today, celebrate the independence you have, but remember that freedom stems from mutiny.

THE TAKEAWAY: Celebrate the United States' mutiny (or "independence").

JULY 5 — See your past as a foundation for future success.

"The illiterate of the 21st century will not be those who cannot read and write, but those who cannot learn, unlearn, and relearn."

— Alvin Toffler

A concert pianist goes through different training than a cybersecurity analyst. Both happen to be excellent at using their fingers. Even if a concert pianist is out of work and enrolls in Per Scholas and becomes a security analyst, the sheer finger strength comes in clutch. They can apply their minds to a new career, and in 15 weeks become much more effective in understanding technical concepts such as clients, servers, scripting, and networking.

Now they know not only how to make a song but also what happens when they upload it to servers owned by YouTube, or Spotify, or Apple Music, or Amazon Music.

A seemingly unrelated talent, like a pianist's mastery of finger dexterity and disciplined practice, can translate into success in a completely different field such as cybersecurity.

There is something to be said for having a broader perspective: understanding the digital lifecycle of creative works, like uploading songs to platforms, gives the former pianist an edge when it comes to getting their work widely distributed and a unique appreciation for the intersection of art and technology.

THE TAKEAWAY: See your past as a foundation for future success.

188   JULY 6 — Find the courage to pursue your dreams.

> *"All our dreams can come true if we have the courage to pursue them."*
> –Walt Disney

Snow White Behind the Scenes on Disney+ is incredibly informative.

Walt Disney spent over four and a half years on it. Ballooning finances. Stress on his brother.

A banker from Bank of America comes in, sees the test, it scares the shit out of Walt because it isn't done yet. However, when Walt follows the banker to his car, the banker says "oh, that thing'll make you a pile of money," drives off, and writes a check.

Snow White had a European visual style but a uniquely American voice—that of Walt Disney and his team. Gustaf Tenggren was an artist who set the mood of Snow White.

Walt knew music would follow the people out of the theater, like "Singin' in the Rain" (1952) or "Heigh-Ho!" from *Snow White*—tunes that are so catchy they stick to your brain immediately.

These tunes were catchy when they came out, and they will continue to stick in our brains for many more generations.

If you have the courage to pursue a big dream, sometimes it can pay off big time. It sure did for Disney.

THE TAKEAWAY: Find the courage to pursue your dreams.

JULY 7 — Embrace change with ambition.

"Who the hell wants to hear actors talk?"

— Harry Warner in 1927, when his brother Sam Warner said the studio was developing "talkies"

In *The Brothers Warner*, directed Harry Warner's granddaughter Cass, she painfully remembers that "Warner" isn't the real family name. The real name was erased when immigrating to America. *American Film* magazine says the surname was originally "Wonskolaser."

The brothers got into any business they could without an education. They sold papers, shined shoes, stayed out late until they earned $2 to buy the family dinner.

The Jazz Singer was a huge hit. Suddenly, all movies had to be "talkies." Tragically, Sam Warner died the night before *The Jazz Singer* premiered.

Harry was the "diversify" guy who said the brothers should go beyond movies, into publishing, music, more mediums! Jack wanted to have fun and enjoy the Hollywood machine, but Harry was the guy who wanted the work to educate, entertain, and enlighten the audience.

It was interesting when Cass met with Roy Disney Jr and observed that Harry and Jack fought like Roy and Walt, the way brothers fight. I'm sure it can be like that in any family business.

These sets of brothers navigated rapid changes in the entertainment industry, from silent films, to sound, to color, animation, and television.

Maybe at first, if silent films were everything, it is easy to be skeptical of talking films. People were skeptical of Netflix and social media at first too.

THE TAKEAWAY: Embrace change with ambition.

190 JULY 8 — To make others covet a thing, make it hard to get.

My favorite quote from Tom Sawyer is *this:*

Illustration from *Tom Sawyer*
Courtesy The Mark Twain House, Hartford

"Tom said to himself that it was not such a hollow world, after all. He had discovered a great law of human action—that in order to make a man or a boy covet a thing, it is only necessary to make the thing difficult to attain."

In this scene, Tom convinces another boy to do his fence painting chore by selling it to him as a privilege.

Kind of like how when you go to a restaurant and you get the "privilege" of cooking the food yourself.

Evil by Design by **Chris Nodder** cites this passage as a classic example of persuasion. He writes that user experience designers work hard to control the emotions and behaviors of their users.

A truly great website can even get users to perform the desired task again and again and make it seem like a privilege. Success in web design is often measured by how many users you can get to beg to be involved in creating, or sharing, or commenting, or purchasing, on your website.

THE TAKEAWAY: **To make others covet a thing, make it hard to get.**

JULY 9 — Envy and humor can help sell products.

Envy and humor can help sell products.
— Socrates

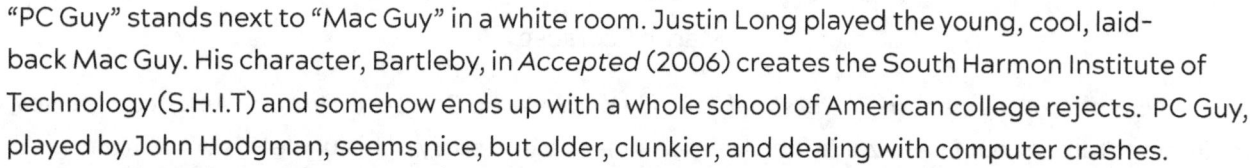

Do you remember the "Get a Mac" campaign by Apple from 2006-2009? (Wikipedia)

"PC Guy" stands next to "Mac Guy" in a white room. Justin Long played the young, cool, laid-back Mac Guy. His character, Bartleby, in *Accepted* (2006) creates the South Harmon Institute of Technology (S.H.I.T) and somehow ends up with a whole school of American college rejects. PC Guy, played by John Hodgman, seems nice, but older, clunkier, and dealing with computer crashes.

My big brother was about to go to college. You can probably guess which computer he got. It is the same kind of computer this book was created on: a Mac.

By inspiring envy, the Get a Mac campaign and "sent from my iPhone" helped cement Apple as "the creative computer" worth its high price tag.

Portraying the Mac as youthful, stylish, and capable—contrasted with the clunky, outdated PC—made owning it at a premium price seem worth it. The Mac wasn't just a computer, it was part of a modern, desirable lifestyle to which viewers would aspire.

The campaign's ability to elicit envy wasn't mean-spirited; it was lighthearted and funny. By creating a sense of "I want what they have," the campaign was effective at driving sales.

THE TAKEAWAY: Envy and humor can help sell products.

JULY 10 — Fulfill the spiritual need to share a common memory.

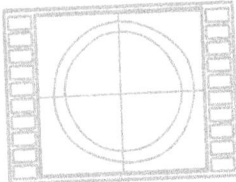

"It's as if movies answer an ancient quest for the common unconscious; they fulfill a spiritual need that people have to share a common memory."

— Martin Scorsese

In the *1995 British documentary, A Personal Journey With Martin Scorsese Through American Movies,* the director talks about Elia Kazan's film *America America*, the story of his uncle's journey from Anatolia to America.

When he was younger, he wanted to be a priest, then realized that his real calling was the movies.

Scorsese saw himself making this same journey, going from his neighborhood in New York into the land of movie making. In both places, people come together and share a common experience. He believes there is a spirituality in films, even if it does not "replace" religion. He mentions films that deal with the spiritual side of man's nature, such as DW Griffith's film *Intolerance*, or John Ford's *The Grapes of Wrath* from the Steinbeck novel, Hitchcock's *Vertigo*, to Kubrick's *2001*.

Before writing this, I came home from seeing *2001: A Space Odyssey* at the Hollywood Bowl with a live orchestra. There were *thousands* of people there to watch this movie together. People love doing stuff like that together and enjoy the opportunity to share a common memory.

Satisfying one person with your work is amazing. Satisfying thousands is even more amazing.

THE TAKEAWAY: Fulfill the spiritual need to share a common memory.

JULY 11 — Consider the role violence plays in your life.

"Art should comfort the disturbed and disturb the comfortable."
— Banksy

I woke up, had some coffee, and played *Warzone* with my brother. Also, we got a new TV, and my dad was watching a violent movie on it.

So the question arises in my mind: What role does violence play in my modern life? Violence forced a divide in India. Violence killed off Native Americans and enslaved Africans. Violence is like pledging a frat, like guys I remember from college. There are so many paddles in rooms all over the world, reminding you of the violence.

Quentin Tarantino movies have aesthetic violence. Ryan Coogler? More choreographed. Less exploding bags of fake blood. Disney's new *Black Widow* movie has a stylized violence to it too, sanitized for entertainment.

There's police brutality, school shootings, global conflicts. We see the persistent grip of violence on human existence, which raises questions about its necessity and inevitability.

Violence, like art, can be both repugnant and fascinating. We see the darker side of human nature, but also the side of self-protection and resistance.

Is violence an inescapable part of being human? Or can it be transcended through compassion, dialogue, and creativity?

THE TAKEAWAY: Consider the role violence plays in your life.

JULY 12 — Stick to the theory, not intuition.

"If you can't explain it simply, you don't understand it well enough."

—Albert Einstein

If someone asked me to explain business theory simply, I'd say it has three parts.

1. What assumptions are there about how a society is structured?
2. What's the market like?
3. What technology does the customer use?

All this helps us define what the organization is paid to do.

What results does an organization consider meaningful when pursuing its mission? How does it envision itself making a difference? What are the domains we need to succeed in to maintain or exceed our goals?

To build an organization that endures and grows long after the founder is gone, there needs to be a clear and simple theory that penetrates through the entire business. A company that was a superstar yesterday might stagnate and enter a crisis today. Did the company have a muddled, unclear set of intuitions about how the business should be run? Maybe the business needs a new theory to explain what's what.

THE TAKEAWAY: Stick to the theory, not intuition.

JULY 13 — Pay labor for their work or troubleshoot strikes.

"This is not just about us. This is about all workers."

— Fran Drescher

On July 13, 2023, **CNBC's David Faber** spoke to Disney CEO Bob Iger in Sun Valley at "billionaire summer camp." Faber asked Iger about being in the midst of a writer's strike, how it was very likely the actors would strike, and how would this impact Disney. Iger found it "very disturbing" to go on strike when the disruptive COVID-19 was still ongoing.

On Twitter (now X), Cody Ziglar tweeted about writing a very hyped Disney+ *She-Hulk* episode that featured the return of Daredevil from Netflix. Ziglar revealed that his residual check was for $396. Only **0.000015%** of the episode's $25 million budget went in a residual payment to the writer of that Disney+ TV show, but the CEO of Disney finds it disturbing that people go on strike to demand more.

Not everyone aspires to work in Hollywood, but it is interesting how that struggle mirrors the broader fight for workers' rights across many industries being changed by AI and automation.

A **full transcript** is available of the speech given by Fran Drescher, President of SAG-AFTRA and actress on the TV show *The Nanny*, saying how "the jig is up" to the Alliance of Motion Picture and Television Producers (AMPTP).

The AMPTP generates billions in profits from works such as *The Nanny*, but the workers behind a show such as *She-Hulk* do not make a reasonable share, leading to strikes that possibly could have been avoided.

THE TAKEAWAY: Pay labor fairly for their work, or you may be troubleshooting strikes.

196   JULY 14 — Take time to reflect on crazy things.

> *"When you arise in the morning, think of what a precious privilege it is to be alive—to breathe, to think, to enjoy, to love."*
>
> — Marcus Aurelius

This morning, my mind remembered some phantom images and sounds.

Days before Spotify, listening to music I pirated on my iPod.

How much fun it was to sing in my high school choir. And, of course, sneaking onto the set of *Creed* to get a selfie with Sylvester Stallone!

I admire Ryan Coogler's work. He is from the Bay Area. He has spoken about the Bay Area, its importance to him, and why the story of Oscar Grant's killing is both local and universal.

Then came *Creed*. He had this spec script written with Aaron Covington, his friend from USC. After it went into production, they decided to shoot in Philadelphia on the Temple campus. I happened to be done with a class that day, and I saw a lot of signs that said, "This way to movie set," and I followed them to TPAC on Broad Street.

I snuck on the set of this movie, got a selfie with Rocky, and posted it. It is such a privilege to be alive and remember something like this.

As today begins, take a few notes on how precious these moments are. Taking this time to reflect can reduce friction in the future hours, helping things move smoothly in your desired, strategic direction.

THE TAKEAWAY: Take time to reflect on crazy things.

JULY 15 — Find the people willing to support your vision.

"Selling your screenplay is like putting your child up for adoption."
— Dante Harper

Dante Harper, screenwriter of the movie *Edge of Tomorrow* starring Tom Cruise, said this to my class over Skype at Temple University.

He was giving tips like:
- Fall in love with the work.
- Think about structure.
- Work as an editor.

"I've learned that the moment you get the ear of a producer, you have to keep them in a dream-state long enough with your story for them to produce it," he said.

Studio execs come and go, and everyone has different tastes. Jack Warner once grumbled to Warren Beatty that "gangster movies went out with Cagney" when Beatty was arguing with Jack Warner about *Bonnie and Clyde*. *(Los Angeles Times)*

Old man Warner believed gangster movies went out with James Cagney.

But *Bonnie and Clyde* was a big hit in 1967. The film was divisive for sure. Many reviewers in the press said they did not like the film. The catchphrase, *They're young, they're beautiful, they kill people*, was cooked up by a studio man named Dick Lederer.

It caught the imagination of a young audience who was tired of the declining studio system movies. Faye Dunaway's berets even stirred a fashion trend after the premiere. Some reviewers then reconsidered the film and admitted they got it wrong.

THE TAKEAWAY: Find the people willing to support your vision.

198 JULY 16 — A pandemic can shut down the world, but not you.

"In the midst of chaos, there is also opportunity."
— Sun Tzu

So proud of all the learners in 2021-01-BOS that are graduating today. The graduation speaker is DeAndre Levarity, an IT engineer at EverQuote. He graduated in February 2020 from Per Scholas Boston.

He started Per Scholas training just before the pandemic and passed the A+ but continued studying during the pandemic and got even more certifications. I like this quote of his:

"Just because the WORLD is shut down, doesn't mean YOU have to shut down!"

It is the perfect thing to say to a graduating class during a pandemic, and it echoes what Sun Tzu writes in *The Art of War*.

The pandemic had so much chaos. Even then, a group of people committed themselves to getting a certification, and they were able to achieve it. These adults in the class were not able to control a lot of the things happening around them. There were snow days, screaming kids, jobs, coronavirus. Every person has different problems in the background of their life when they report to a class and go through it for 15 weeks.

Some people break under the pressure of something like a pandemic. Other people break records under that same pressure.

THE TAKEAWAY: A pandemic can shut down the world, but not you.

JULY 17 — Get in "good trouble."

"Never, ever be afraid to make some noise and get in good trouble, necessary trouble."

— John Lewis

US Congressman and civil rights activist John Lewis died on this date in 2020, at age 80.

Dawn Porter is the filmmaker behind the Lewis documentary, *Good Trouble*. She shared insights with CNN about Lewis's philosophy and his approach to a good life. She said Lewis remained focused on what he could do, not what he couldn't do.

He was also able to focus on the long term without losing sight of the short term.

Even today the struggle is ongoing for people of color to achieve equality. In *The Making of Asian America*, a history book written by Erika Lee, there are many stories of an international struggle for equality in America among Asian communities as well.

John Lewis talked about getting into "good trouble" on the Edmund Pettus Bridge in Selma, Alabama, on March 1, 2020, in commemoration of the tragic events of Bloody Sunday. That occurred on March 7, 1965, as peaceful protesters were beaten by law enforcement officers for crossing the bridge in Selma. This was almost two years after the March on Washington in 1963, where Martin Luther King delivered the iconic "I Have a Dream" speech.

The idea for peaceful protest stems from Gandhi, who got in "good trouble" for India.

Good trouble is often necessary trouble.

THE TAKEAWAY: Get in "good trouble."

200 JULY 18 — Act like Netflix and adopt new technology.

In early 1997, when Reed Hastings and Marc Randolph started thinking about a movie-by-mail business. Amazon was having good luck with books by mail. Why not films? Customers could rent VHS tapes from the company website, then return them via mail, $4 each way.

It was way too expensive with VHS, but a friend told Reed about a new invention called DVDs. Digital video discs were about the same size as compact discs, but for movies, not music.

Reed raced to the post office and, for 32 cents each, mailed himself several CDs. (Because DVDs were still new at the time, he could not test mail actual DVDs.) Then he went back to his home in Santa Cruz and waited. Two days later, his CDs came in the mail, completely unharmed.

In chapter 10 of his CompTIA A+ book, Mike Meyers writes that the DVD was released in 1995, developed by a consortium of electronics and entertainment firms.

On September 29, 2023, after 25 years, Netflix shipped its last DVD because streaming had become the dominant mechanism for content distribution.

It is possible that physical media like DVDs or CDs could come back because if you buy a physical copy, you own it, and a streaming service cannot pull it at their whim. But when you pay for a subscription or digital license, the media distributed by that platform can always disappear.

THE TAKEAWAY: Act like Netflix and adopt the hot new technology from every decade.

JULY 19 — Everyone is the hero in their own story.

The word *sonder* apparently comes from the *Dictionary of Obscure Sorrows*. It is a neologism (new word) by John Koenig.

> *Sonder — n. the realization that each random passerby is living a life as vivid and complex as your own—populated with their own ambitions, friends, routines, worries, and inherited craziness—an epic story that continues invisibly around you like an anthill sprawling deep underground, with elaborate passageways to thousands of other lives that you will never know exist.*

When I was walking around Temple University, I was experiencing this "sonder." I still experience it whenever I walk through a crowded public space.

Everyone around us has a story and a life that is vivid and complicated in its own way.

These people have their ambitions, friends, routines, worries, and crazy parts of life.

You might appear in someone else's story as an extra, or an NPC (a nonplaying character). You might be a blur on someone else's highway, just as someone else might be a blur in yours.

Every person is the protagonist of their own story, and realizing this can encourage compassion and deeper appreciation for the lives of others.

THE TAKEAWAY: Everyone is the hero in their own story.

JULY 20 — Learn from fall of Xerox and the rise of Canon.

"Gutenberg made everybody a reader. Xerox makes everybody a publisher."

— Marshall McLuhan

Xerox invented the copier. Wikipedia cites the Greek term *xerography*, meaning "dry writing," as the etymology. Very few products in history were as successful as the Xerox copier.

But soon, Xerox began to chase profits. It put more and more gimmicks on the machine. Each new model of the Xerox copier was developed solely to increase the company profit margin, and each update increased the price of the machine for the customer. Most importantly, each new accessory made the machine harder to troubleshoot when trying to print copies, which is annoying. The great majority of users did not need these additional features.

Pretty soon, a Japanese company named Canon entered the market. Canon developed what was not much more than a replica of the original Xerox machine. The Canon copier was simple, and cheap, and most importantly, easy to troubleshoot. Within less than a year, Canon captured the US market for copiers.

The worship of high profit margins destroyed Xerox—and companies such as Blockbuster—because they made themselves targets of disruption.

Jack Valenti once described Lew Wasserman as a man who was "non-Xeroxable." **(155. June 3)**

After 2023, calling a photocopy a *Xerox* is like calling a movie a *talkie*.

THE TAKEAWAY: Learn from fall of Xerox and the rise of Canon.

JULY 21 — Use these four parenting lessons from my grandmother.

> *"You do not really understand something unless you can explain it to your grandmother."*
> — Albert Einstein

$E = mc^2$

Today in 2021 is my grandmother's 85th birthday! My Dadi raised me, my brothers, my dad, and my aunts. So I asked her about raising kids because I sometimes feel myself "parenting" as a tech trainer.

My dad, her son, once said, "Alexander the Great led armies; Akash trains adults!"

Our conversation was in Hindi, but I translated it to English.
1. Have good character in front of your kids. They see you study, they see you write, they see you exercise, they do so. What if mom and dad fight? What will they think? Prevent this
2. When you become a parent, try to not talk about things that make kids feel bad. My son (author's dad) smokes cigarettes. It made young Akash feel bad! Avoid smoking!
3. Talk to your kids about smoking, alcohol, and sex. Be honest about these things. Try not to fight about these things. Do not get into fights involving these things.
4. If a child breaks something, try not to get mad. Just be glad the thing broke, not the child.

Bache ache aadat karenge jab ache ma baap dekthe hein.

(Good kids do good things when they see mom and dad do good things.)

There is something to be said about parallels between parenting and management practice. This very specific advice could apply to work or life in many scenarios.

THE TAKEAWAY: Use these four parenting lessons from my grandmother.

JULY 22 — You can define what "normal" is.

"Geniuses are made, not born."
— László Polgár

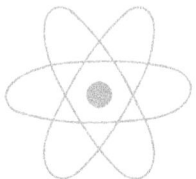

As Aristotle wrote in *Poetics*, which I wrote about on January 8, we learn by imitation. Imitation is especially important in childhood because children learn about the world by mimicking the adults, peers, and popular culture they encounter across mediums.

I wrote about the Polgar sisters on February 12 and how their family shows up in the script for the movie *Whiplash*. James Clear also mentions the Polgar family in his book *Atomic Habits*, an excellent book that I still revisit.

We usually do not choose our earliest habits. We simply imitate others until we adopt them, eventually becoming who we are pretending to be. The Polgar sisters grew up in a family that rewards good chess playing, so it is not a surprise that they became world-class chess players.

If we grew up with parents like those, playing chess would seem very normal. If we grew up around talent agents in Beverly Hills, then their behavior would also appear normal.

Human beings are social animals, and nobody wants to feel like the herd is leaving you behind.

You can leverage this knowledge in your business, when establishing its culture, or at home, if you want to become a genius at something, or raise a family of geniuses.

THE TAKEAWAY: You can define what "normal" is.

JULY 23 — **Make your boss smarter every day by overdelivering.**

"If I'm making you smarter, you're loving me more every day."
— Jack Welch, former CEO of General Electric

I recently saw Jack Welch in a LinkedIn Learning video on **overdelivering**. In the video, Jack repeatedly tells his interviewer how important it is to overdeliver.

When your boss asks you to do something, that is the bare minimum. But to do really well? Make your boss smarter every day. Whether they stay in that company, or they go to another company, keep learning and make the environment around you smarter.

Ambitious kids out of school, Jack observes, like to do the homework. The homework is what the boss was doing for 12 years of undergrad, four years of graduate school.

Doing the homework is the ticket to the game, but the game is always changing into something newer, bigger, better, and brighter.

Jack says he tells his kids every day to "overdeliver" and give the boss some fresh ideas. And the boss will love you because you make them look 10 feet tall. You become special.

THE TAKEAWAY: Make your boss smarter every day by overdelivering.

206   JULY 24 — Be prepared for someone to copy your innovations.

"Innovation distinguishes between a leader and a follower."
— Steve Jobs

When we talk about innovation, it creates excitement! But it also attracts competition.

Having competition means that the innovators have to be right the first time. There are no second chances.

Apple Computer invented the personal computer. IBM was then able to take market share from Apple through creative imitation.

On the market we also see the Microsoft Windows PC, Google Chromebook, and much more.

Nevertheless, these are all tools, and the tool does not matter. What matters is how you use it.

Some tools are ambitious inventions, others are creative imitations. It depends on who you ask. Take solace in the fact that someone out there might even want to copy you.

THE TAKEAWAY: Be prepared for someone to copy your innovations.

JULY 25 — Give the doctor within a chance to heal you.

> *"Each patient carries his own doctor inside him. We are at our best when we give the doctor who resides within each patient a chance to go to work."*
>
> — Norman Cousins, Anatomy of an Illness

For a curious person, it is interesting when a book you read cites another book.

When I was a teen, I was a big fan of David Lubar's *Dunk*, a book that mentions Norman Cousins' book *Anatomy of an Illness*. In 2018, I was a broke film school graduate intent on adapting this book for a screenplay. I even reached out to David to tell him what I was doing, and how much I loved this book he wrote. He gave me his permission to write it and shop it, and I had a lot of fun listening to him talk about the development and writing of his book. He said I should read *Anatomy of an Illness* because it could help me with the screenplay.

Norman Cousins wrote about his experience becoming severely ill and famously using "laughter therapy" to help alleviate his pain.

Cousins had evidence that negative emotions can negatively impact the biochemistry of the human body. Cousins eventually reversed this: If negative emotions produce negative chemical reactions in the body, can positive emotions produce positive chemical reactions?

He later discovered that 10 minutes of genuine belly laughter had an anesthetic effect, leading to at least two hours of pain-free sleep.

THE TAKEAWAY: Give the doctor within a chance to heal you.

208   JULY 26 — Develop effective skills for hunting.

In *Chanakya in Daily Life,* Dr. Radhakrishnan Pillai, a spiritual scientist, writes that Chanakya recommends a king have hobbies, such as listening to music, swimming, and hunting.

Dr. Pillai points out that Chanakya's *Arthashastra* does not suggest killing an animal simply to "practice on a moving target."

> *"He should go to a forest containing game, for practicing on moving targets."*

Honestly, it can be harder to capture a person or animal alive, *without* killing.

Chanakya's recommendation here reflects a practical approach to developing essential skills for a ruler who might need to lead troops in battle:
- Physical reflexes
- Hand-eye coordination
- Tracking the target
- Dynamic decision-making
- Strength
- Stamina
- Courage
- Connection with natural world

The specific activity of hunting may not really apply in modern times, but the cultivation of these skills are handy in sports, meditation, or challenges that involve a team.

THE TAKEAWAY: Develop effective skills for hunting.

JULY 27 — Support small businesses in your hometown.

"Entrepreneurs and their small enterprises are responsible for almost all the economic growth in the United States."

— Ronald Reagan

On July 27, 2010, **President Obama came to my hometown** of Edison, New Jersey, to visit Tastee Sub Shop.

Since 1963, this shop has been on Plainfield Avenue.

Since I was a teenager, I loved the sandwiches. When Obama was coming, I remember the huge crowd of people all around the block. Apparently, the shop worked with the Secret Service in preparation for the big day.

The shop owners, Carl Padovano and David Thornton, described the moment as surreal and nerve-racking because of all the attention and TV cameras.

Edison's mayor at the time, Antonia Ricigliano, says she was contacted by the White House to advise on locations for President Obama to hold a discussion about the economy and to promote a bill expanding loan programs and tax breaks for small business owners.

THE TAKEAWAY: Support small businesses in your hometown.

JULY 28 — Embrace being "crazy" and change the world.

> *"The people who are crazy enough to think they can change the world are the ones who do."*
>
> — Steve Jobs

On YouTube, you can find the Apple commercial **"Crazy Ones"** with Steve Jobs' voice. As Jobs narrates, we see Albert Einstein, Martin Luther King, Muhammad Ali, Thomas Edison, Gandhi, and many more famous figures who are like "round pegs in square holes." They see things differently and push the human race forward.

It is hard to imagine a world before Apple and Google, also known as Alphabet.

These are two firms that I cannot stop thinking about. The design of their products is crazy and awesome, just like AWS for developers. **(213. July 31)** After Clayton Christensen published *The Innovator's Dilemma*, the people running firms who read the book developed the Kindle, or Nook—products that could cannibalize the physical books business the way iTunes or Pandora or Spotify cannibalized the physical music business.

Reader, I am not married to the idea of a "book" the way I used to be. Digital media is now another way to store and deliver information.

Movies were once considered crazy to incumbents, like digital video was crazy, or podcasts.

Eventually, you realize all these mediums were once considered "crazy" at one point or another. Then someone says, "I'll show you crazy!" and they do something world-changing crazy.

It is okay if people call you crazy. Crazy has interesting company in many different fields.

THE TAKEAWAY: Embrace being "crazy" and change the world.

JULY 29 — Increase your income and reduce costs.

In *Chanakya in Daily Life*, Dr. Radhakrishnan Pillai cites ancient advice from Chanakya's *Arthashastra*:

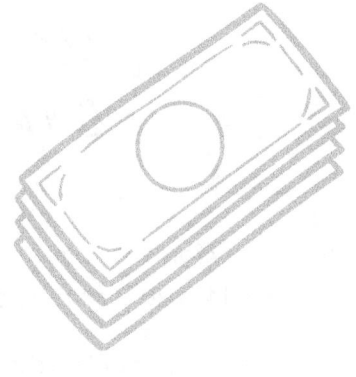

"The wise administrator should fix the revenue and show an increase in income and decrease in expenditure and should remedy the opposite of these."

It is important that any household or company has profits. The "wise administrator" naturally wants to achieve the goal, if not exceed that goal. Predictable income streams are important for governance and development.

Would anyone want to decrease the amount of money they make or save? Of course not! Nobody wishes to do great one year, and then dip over the next year. It might take some innovation to increase revenue without overburdening the working people.

Resources need to be allocated *strategically*. Efforts should be directed toward making more money sustainably, but also toward cutting wasteful spending when possible.

It is remarkable that this ancient advice, emphasizing disciplined financial planning, is still relevant today. Following principles like this can yield prosperity and stability for a household or company.

THE TAKEAWAY: **Increase your income and reduce costs.**

212   JULY 30 — Live like you die tomorrow. Learn like you will live forever

> *"Live as if you were to die tomorrow.*
> *Learn as if you were to live forever."*
>
> — Mahatma Gandhi

I met with my former student, Yovin Deonarine, who is now my teaching assistant, to prepare for the class Cycle 14 of 2021 on the Remote Training Team, with the codename 2021-14-RTT.

Who knows? This could be the last class I ever get to educate, entertain, and enlighten. By making sure the lessons and daily Canvas announcements are planned ahead of time, Yovin and I can more effectively transfer meaningful IT knowledge and skills to the students.

The Canvas announcements are our chance to make sure the learners know exactly which exam objectives we are covering and what materials and activities we are using to address those key learning objectives. There are links to tech news articles, educational videos, virtual lab scenarios, even motivational quotes, all over every announcement.

Every new announcement or lesson preparation also gives a chance to reflect on past lessons so that the next one can be better. It helps to embrace a growth mindset during lesson prep.

As Gandhi would say, it is important to prepare each lesson with passion and purpose, because who knows if I will ever get this chance again.

THE TAKEAWAY: Live like you die tomorrow. Learn like you will live forever.

JULY 31 — Provide building blocks, then get out of the way.

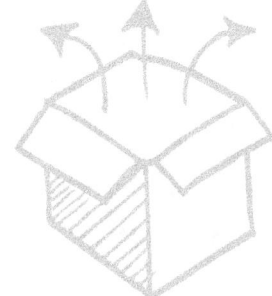

"Frugality—Accomplish more with less. Constraints breed resourcefulness, self-sufficiency, and invention. There are no extra points for growing headcount, budget size, or fixed expense."

— *Amazon leadership principles*, Jeff Bezos

In *The Everything Store*, Brad Stone writes about when Bezos became enamored with a book titled *Creation*, by Steve Grand. Grand had developed a 1990s video game called *Creatures*, where players could guide and nurture a seemingly intelligent organism on their computer screens.

Grand wrote about how his approach to creating intelligent life was to focus on designing simple computational building blocks, called primitives. Then, players sit back and watch surprising behaviors emerge. Electronics are built from basic *primitives* too, like resistors and capacitors.

Grand writes that sophisticated AI can emerge from cybernetic primitives, and then it's up to the "ratchet of evolution to change the design."

The book was dense and challenging but widely discussed in Amazon executive book clubs. Grand helped them crystallize the debate over the company's IT infrastructure problems. If Amazon wanted to stimulate creativity among developers, it shouldn't try to guess what kind of services they might want, because such guesses would be based on past patterns. Instead, Amazon should be creating primitives, the "building blocks" of computing. Then, get out of the way.

As Bezos proclaimed at the time, according to numerous employees: "Developers are alchemists, and our job is to do everything we can to get them to do their alchemy."

THE TAKEAWAY: **Provide building blocks, then get out of the way.**

AUGUST

AUGUST 1 — Is today a test, or a celebration?

> *"Every moment of your life is either a test or a celebration."*
> — David Deida

Deida writes about a woman trying to test her man, or a man she might like, to see if he is unshakeable or not. The pick-up artist community calls these "shit tests."

Urban Dictionary defines shit test as "A manufactured grievance a woman uses to test the mettle, competence, and confidence of her mate."

When a calm, confident person tries to approach you, you might try to make them fold with your questions or comments or snide remarks, to see how they respond. The 2005 movie *Hitch* has such a scene, when Eva Mendes' character, Sara, is approached by a man.

Sara asks for his name. He responds with, "They call me Chip," and she playfully says "Aw, you can't get them to stop," as if Chip is a guy with no power to change what his friends call him. When Chip laughs, he agrees to Sara's power move. He rewards her disrespect with a laugh. Chip failed the "shit test." He does not get to sit with her at the bar. We might say "Chip has no game." If he *did* have game, maybe he could have seduced her.

Women testing men who approach them is a common scenario, but anyone can "shit test" another whenever they want.

Life is either a celebration, or a test. Which will it be today?

THE TAKEAWAY: Is today a test, or a celebration?

AUGUST 2 — Find something to learn and something to teach.

"The teacher and the taught together create the teaching."

— Eckhart Tolle

I once heard Eckhart Tolle cite a concept Hindus have known for thousands of years: You do not "have" a body.

Your soul simply exists inside your current body until the body decays, then the soul moves on.

Gamers have popularized phrases such as "you get a new life" or "you respawn." This is a digital form of reincarnation, where your character dies but then gets reborn to try again. The ancient cycle of samsara, the endless cycle of birth and death, is right there in a video game.

If I learn something new and helpful about beating a video game, I can teach it to someone else, creating a teaching between us.

Today, there is something you get to learn. But there might also be something you get to teach.

THE TAKEAWAY: **Find something to learn and something to teach.**

AUGUST 3 — Empower everyone to contribute freely and easily.

"Imagine a world in which every single person on the planet is given free access to the sum of all human knowledge. That's what we're doing."

— Jimmy Wales

I learned a lot on this day from the podcast *Masters of Scale* with Reid Hoffman, when he talked to Jimmy Wales, the founder of Wikipedia.

Wikipedia wasn't even Jimmy's first online encyclopedia. In 2000, he launched Nupedia. Wales was convinced that Nupedia needed a strict peer-review process with seven stages of review. Nupedia was to be academic and rigorous, a "real encyclopedia." After two years, Nupedia had an underwhelming 24 articles. Jimmy soon realized how paralyzing it could be for a writer to submit an article and wait for a seven-stage review process. Even experts on a subject might feel paralyzed when facing seven stages of review.

Enter the wiki system for creating and organizing content on a computer screen collaboratively, which can be edited by anyone.

Developed by computer programmer Howard "Ward" Cunningham in 1994, this new wiki system generated more content at Nupedia in two weeks than had been generated in the prior two years.

Everybody was able to chip in, in the way Wikipedia is known for. Wikipedia is now the eighth-most visited website in the world, with over six million articles on its English version, and users are still contributing in nearly 300 languages to this day.

THE TAKEAWAY: Empower everyone to contribute freely and easily.

AUGUST 4 — Never stop asking questions.

"No man really becomes a fool until he stops asking questions."
— Charles Proteus Steinmetz

Charles Proteus Steinmetz earned over 200 patents and titles such as "Forger of Thunderbolts" and "Wizard of Schenectady." According to this 17-minute-long documentary, Steinmetz had a process for setting goals. First, he identified the hot new science, or problems to solve. He was obsessed with physics, chemistry, economics, medicine, math, anything that built up to electrical engineering.

There is a famous story featuring Steinmetz and automobile pioneer Henry Ford I found in *Smithsonian Magazine*. Ford and his electrical engineers were unable to solve some problem with a gigantic generator. So Ford called Steinmetz to pull up to the General Electric plant.

Steinmetz rejected all engineering assistance and asked only for a notebook, a pencil, and a cot. According to this story, Steinmetz listened to the generator and did calculations on the notepad for two straight days and nights. On the second night, he asked for a ladder. He climbed up the ladder and made a chalk mark on the side of the generator.

Then he told Ford's skeptical engineers to remove a plate at the mark, then replace 16 windings from the field coil. They did, and the generator worked.

Henry Ford was thrilled until he got a bill from Steinmetz for $10,000.

Making chalk mark: $1.
Knowing where to make the mark: $9,999.

THE TAKEAWAY: **Never stop asking questions.**

AUGUST 5 — Talk to yourself like you would to someone you love.

"Talk to yourself like you would to someone you love."
— Brené Brown

I still have vivid memories of sitting in Temple University Morgan Hall on Cecil and Broad in Philadelphia, eating dining hall food and watching Tony Robbins videos on my laptop.

Tony's burning question, in his life and career, was always "what is it that makes people do what they do?" Tony helped me notice that questions are like endless loops in my brain, a supercomputer that will find the answer to any question I might have, right or wrong! So it is very important to ask the right questions. With the right economy of words, questions that feel good to ask or important to ask. Find the answer for yourself and your team.

Your life is a collection of experiences governed by your brain trying to find pleasure and avoid pain. Do not hate your brain for being what it is now. Besides, neuroplasticity means you can re-associate pain and pleasure centers and rewire neurons, until you can realistically, without sacrificing your health or well-being, achieve goals.

Question yourself, interrogate yourself, to live and grow.

Otherwise you will decompose and die.

Tony does this work, and he and the people he serves grow through his work.

If your internal questions are not helping you grow, they are helping you die. Focus on growing and having more positive self-talk, like you would with someone you love.

THE TAKEAWAY: Talk to yourself like you would to someone you love.

219

AUGUST 6 — Problems seem smaller compared to atomic bombs.

"Now I am become Death, the destroyer of worlds."

— J. Robert Oppenheimer, quoting the Bhagavad Gita

On this day in 1945, the US dropped the first atomic bomb on Hiroshima, Japan. Three days later, another was dropped on Nagasaki.

In a scene from Christopher Nolan's *Oppenheimer*, released over 70 years after WWII ended, Oppenheimer tells President Truman he feels the blood on his hands. Truman gives Oppenheimer a look, then pulls a white handkerchief from his breast pocket and offers it to the complex, self-loathing scientist, reminding him that the people of Japan do not care who built the bomb. They only care who said to drop it.

This is such a big problem compared to the problem I had on this date in 2021, which was figuring out what to stream in order to pass the time during the COVID pandemic.

Sometimes, reminding yourself of big problems, real or fictional, makes yours seem smaller. I am not saying your problems are not valid or meaningful to you, because they are. I am simply saying it might help to once in a while put your problems into perspective and realize there are bigger problems out there compared to what you are dealing with.

THE TAKEAWAY: Problems seem smaller when compared to atomic bombs.

AUGUST 7 — Show up with love every day.

"You don't get to pick your team sometimes, but you don't get to pick your children either, and yet you show up with love everyday"

— Simon Sinek

I am not a parent, but I have been working as a manager, and I learned it is important to control your temper, as either a parent or a manager. I give my parents and the adults in my life a lot of credit for managing their temper around my younger self.

If you react with anger at your subordinate, they will probably be angry to their subordinates. If a kid gets angry abuse at home, they will probably bring it to school.

Starting a new project is like taking care of an "infant" who cannot take care of itself. A good parent should keep an infant project in the "nursery" until it is deemed ready to leave.

Consider these three American companies, which make many products but do not release experimental products until they are truly ready to leave the "nursery."
- Procter & Gamble
- Johnson & Johnson
- 3M

These three companies set up the new venture as a separate business and put a project manager in charge. This manager now has to show up with love every day to get this "infant product" ready to leave its "nursery."

THE TAKEAWAY: Show up with love every day.

221   AUGUST 8 — Figure out a way to use trends in your favor.

Akash Malik updated his status.

Like for a job I see u doing one day

Aug 8, 2011, 3:10 PM

"Fashion is what you adopt when you don't know who you are."
— Quentin Crisp

In 2011, the term "lms" (like my status) was Facebook's breakout meme, Liz Gannes writes.

In 2010 it was "hmu" (hit me up), and in 2009 it was "FML" (f*** my life).

On August 8, 2011, evidence suggests I too, was caught up in the trend. I posted this, got likes from my Facebook friends, then posted to the "walls" of whoever "lms."

I wonder if you remember this trend, Reader, or even heard of it. Will it be important in 2061? Probably not. Social media has shaped communication, social interactions, and self-expression throughout its growth. It is so unlikely that this trend or other past trends will be fashionable decades from now, but what might endure is the memory of how our communications evolved over time.

Social media often says less about the words themselves and more about our desire to share a common memory and connect with other people.

Some people are adopting the trend just because they don't know what else to say or do, but others might be more intentional about adopting it, using the trend to drive attention to other things they are doing.

THE TAKEAWAY: Figure out a way to use trends in your favor.

AUGUST 9 — Create an environment for unexpected brilliance.

On his Substack, **Ted Hope** posted "The Hierarchy of Needs of a Creative Person (or Film Professional)," based on Maslow's Hierarchy of Needs.

A producer on more than 70 films and studio executive on over 60, Ted Hope launched Amazon's entry into feature film production. By his own admission, his hierarchy of needs is not a "necessary order" but what he thinks a creative professional needs to work well.

1. Survival (food, water, shelter)
2. Experience
3. External knowledge (world, individuals, film world)
4. Grit and resilience
5. Pleasure
6. Process: organization and accomplishment
7. Curiosity
8. Self-knowledge (personal)
9. Collaboration
10. Lifestyle (how to create)
11. Purpose
12. Quality of execution (lift the good to great)
13. Impact
14. Peace and patience
15. Stamina and ferocity
16. Increased autonomy
17. Improvement overall
18. Holistic approach to life and art
19. Mastery
20. Joy

THE TAKEAWAY: Create an environment for unexpected brilliance.

AUGUST 10 — Question yesterday's logic.

"The greatest danger in times of turbulence is not the turbulence; it is to act with yesterday's logic."

— Peter Drucker

These are a few questions to bring out the hidden potential of an enterprise.
1. What restrictions make us vulnerable?
2. What is out of balance in our business or the way we run it?
3. What scary threats can become exciting opportunities?

Clinging to outdated ideas or strategies can be more detrimental than the challenges themselves.

The retail company sticking to brick-and-mortar and ignoring e-commerce is *not* going to do well. A company that insists on full-time in the office and not offering hybrid or fully remote work is also not going to be received favorably. Energy companies doubling down on fossil fuels, *despite* a global shift to renewable energy, are not doing any favors for future generations. Hospitals used to only take paper records, but thankfully now almost every hospital is using electronic health records to be more efficient.

It is important to question how the restriction of yesterday's logic can hinder your progress, which can be costly in turbulent times.

THE TAKEAWAY: **Question yesterday's logic.**

AUGUST 11 — Lead by example, it's the only way.

"Example is not the main thing in influencing others. It is the only thing."
— Albert Schweitzer

In *The Outsiders: Eight Unconventional CEOs and Their Radically Rational Blueprint for Success*, William N. Thorndike Jr. writes about unconventional CEOs such as Tom Murphy, whose Capital Cities acquired the ABC TV network.

In Murphy's time, the whole broadcasting industry had a "limousine culture." One of the cherished perks for a TV executive was taking a limo to lunch, even if it was just a few blocks away. Tom Murphy, however, showed up to all ABC meetings in cabs. Before long, this practice became the norm through the ABC executive ranks.

Murphy was once asked if this was a CEO "leading by example."

He responded, "Is there any other way?"

Murphy's seemingly small, everyday decision to take a cab instead of a limo wasn't a flashy move, but it sent a powerful message and created a ripple effect throughout the company.

The network continued to be profitable, and in 1995, Murphy sold Capital Cities/ABC to Disney, run by Michael Eisner, for $19 billion. One dollar invested with Murphy in 1966 would have been worth $204 by the time the company sold to Disney.

THE TAKEAWAY: **Lead by example, it's the only way.**

225
AUGUST 12 — If you can digitize it, do it.

"Anything that can be digitized will be digitized."
— Kara Swisher

Digital music? The iPod.
Digital books? The Kindle.
Digital video? YouTube.

You are made up of biological materials, but you might one day be digitized into an avatar.

Maybe like me, you were born and raised around both analog and digital media technology. Perhaps you are older than me and better remember a world before everything was digitized.

You used to call your friend over a landline with physical buttons. Now you can digitally message them with digital buttons. Every part of the human experience, from birth to puberty to sickness to death, is online. Over and over and over again.

What does this mean for you? It means you should lean into it.

I am not saying you should ignore physical media completely. Physical media like books, CDs, VHS tapes, and DVDs are still valuable and in use, but it is more likely the future of media will be mostly digital, and this is something to take advantage of.

Deloitte did a study on 2025 digital media trends, finding that 56 percent of Gen Zs and 43 percent of millennials believe that social media content is more relevant to them than traditional media like TV shows and movies. Roughly 50 percent of Gen Zs and millennials feel a stronger personal connection to digital media creators than they do with TV personalities or actors.

THE TAKEAWAY: If you can digitize it, do it.

AUGUST 13 — An ounce of prevention is still worth a pound of cure.

Coronavirus has made this so much more relevant than ever before.

If you were a germaphobe before the COVID-19 pandemic, you are likely a much bigger germaphobe after. I still am sometimes. There was a time I took this Ben Franklin quote way too seriously. There were also times I wished that the people who lead my country, or my portfolio of businesses, also took this quote more seriously.

Consider your "ecosystem," Reader. Of people, of devices, the content that lives in them, "viral" infections or songs within them. You want those hosts and networks and information highways encrypted, right? Ideally so no unauthorized person can come in and hack it.

When Chanakya was the Prime Minister of the Maurya Empire, he started adding small amounts of poison in Emperor Chandragupta Maurya's food so he would get used to it. By inoculating the king in this way, Chanakya prevented the emperor from being poisoned by enemies. In a sense, Chanakya "encrypted" the king's blood to prevent poisoning.

Prevent viruses in your life — technically, medically and psychologically.

This way, you can prevent viruses parentally or managerially.

Save yourself time, money, and energy trying to buy a cure later for an illness that is preventable now.

THE TAKEAWAY: An ounce of prevention is still worth a pound of cure.

227 AUGUST 14 — You are not paid to "reform" the customer, but to "satisfy."

In the 2015 film *Straight Outta Compton*, rapper Ice Cube is watching a crowd destroy NWA records.

Cube says, "Ain't that some shit? Speak a little truth and people lose their minds."

Eazy-E responds with another truth: That the people who are destroying NWA records can do whatever they want because they already bought the records. Eazy-E seems to understand what business NWA is truly in. The rap group was in the business of selling physical records to people who buy music. But even people who hate their music might buy those same records to ruin them. Either way, Eazy-E would shrug it off. Sales are sales.

NWA is not necessarily trying to "reform" the audience to their way of thinking. They simply wished to express their truths through the magical medium of music. Once the artist releases their work, the work is no longer theirs. It belongs to the listener.

Or, once a lesson is done, it is no longer the teacher's lesson, but the student's learning.

THE TAKEAWAY: You are not paid to "reform" the customer, but to "satisfy."

AUGUST 15 — Take inspiration from violence across artistic mediums.

"Violence is one of the most fun things to watch."
— Quentin Tarantino

I was about 15 years old in 2011, celebrating India's Independence Day, watching *Rise of the Planet of the Apes*, then *Call of Duty: Black Ops*, then posting on Facebook about it.

Violence across multiple mediums and realities.

For *Creed 3*, Cinematographer Kramer Morgenthau discusses for *TheWrap* how he and Michael B. Jordan created a fight sequence they called "The Void." Here Adonis and Damian grew up together. Now they are fighting in a championship fight surrounded by lots of noise. But in the void of the boxing ring, the noise fades away. It's an expressive take on boxing, like in *Raging Bull*.

Jordan also cites the manga and anime series *Dragon Ball* as inspiration. Fans of his might remember he wore a Vegeta-inspired *Saiyan armor* outfit as Killmonger in the movie *Black Panther*.

As Tarantino has often said, violence has a place in storytelling as an artistic and engaging tool.

You can find inspiration for it all over the world.

THE TAKEAWAY: Take inspiration from violence across artistic mediums.

253

229 AUGUST 16 — Broaden the scope of your "competition."

"It's 8:00 in the evening, you're next to your TV—which remote control do you pick up: PlayStation remote? TV remote? Or do you turn Netflix on?"

— Reed Hastings

Sometimes, your competition comes from an entirely different industry.

Consider two successful American industries, the coal mines and the railroads. People in both industries believed that God had given them an unshakable, unstoppable monopoly.

These proud, successful railroad owners did not consider cars to be their competition, and paid for it. Successful managers in the railroad business should have broadened their view, and identify competition from not only other railroads, but all potential forms of transportation.

Reed Hastings is getting at this idea of broadening the scope by encouraging employees to think abstractly about competitors to Netflix. Different people do different things to relax, unwind, and connect with other people over. People could choose Netflix, but they could also choose YouTube, live sports, PlayStation games, books, and more.

Do you know what Hastings called the number one competitor of Netflix? Sleep. Sleep is a far broader competitor than video games or sports.

THE TAKEAWAY: **Broaden the scope of your "competition."**

AUGUST 17 — Remember to protect your flank.

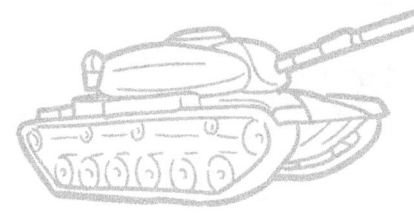

"Victory awaits him who has everything in order—luck, people call it. Defeat is certain for him who has neglected to take the necessary precautions in time."

— Roald Amundsen

"First with the most" is a strategy that comes from the Confederate general Nathan Bedford Forrest. He would often say "get there first with the most men," and relentlessly harassed Union forces during the Vicksburg Campaign in 1862 and 1863.

It is a strategy with the highest potential reward, but it is also very risky. To get there first with the most soldiers means there can be no mistakes or second chances. The leader must be right the first time, otherwise they fail.

How can you outflank this strategy? With the second strategy, "hit 'em where they ain't."

Everything has its weakness. When you are working on your plan, someone else is working on theirs. There will be blind spots to look out for. It is good to have precautions in place for areas you may have neglected.

THE TAKEAWAY: Remember to protect your flank.

231 AUGUST 18 — Hit 'em where they ain't.

"Keep your eye clear, and hit 'em where they ain't."

— Willie Keeler, Baseball Hall of Fame

When the Apple II appeared on the market in June 1977, it was an instant sensation. It was so sensational, IBM got to work to outflank Apple.

Within 18 months, IBM had a PC that did everything the Apple II did.

IBM soon became the market leader worldwide and retained that status for many years. Apple almost went under and only turned around more than 20 years later in the 1990s.

Have you heard of the Blue Ocean Strategy from a book of the same name by W. Chan Kim and Renee Mauborgne? The basic idea is to ignore the red ocean of your competition, which is likely fierce and full of blood, and instead go where the competition is not by pursuing a different route, the "blue ocean." In the blue ocean, you are now thinking about creating solutions where there aren't any.

THE TAKEAWAY: Hit 'em where they ain't.

AUGUST 19 — Become indispensable to a small niche.

"The successful warrior is the average man, with laser-like focus."

— Bruce Lee

You are trying to do something big, Reader. You are running into trouble. So you got my book to see if it has wisdom you are lacking, something that could help you out of a jam.

Even if you feel you are average, you give the best advice you can to help other human beings.

One effective way is by finding, and occupying, a specialized niche. You can't be everything for everyone, but you can be everything for someone.

For example, GoPro does well in action cameras and serves a very specific need that traditional camera makers do not. For adventurous people, self-described "adrenaline junkies," GoPro is their go-to camera when it comes to getting action-packed shots.

Another way to occupy a niche is to have an ultra-specialty skill. **William Cohen** gives the example of a chiropractor versus a "board-certified upper cervical chiropractor." The second one is so specialized and hard-to-find that people might drive hundreds of miles for an appointment, meaning this chiropractor could charge a *fortune* for their niche services.

THE TAKEAWAY: Become indispensable to a small niche.

AUGUST 20 — Create change instead of reacting to change.

"How can you make sense of the future when you only have data about the past?"
— Clayton Christensen

To achieve market leadership, Peter Drucker advocates changing the economic characteristics of a product, market, or industry. Netflix did this when they shifted from DVD rentals to streaming. Netflix saw YouTube and user-generated videos and anticipated the rise of high-speed internet capable of delivering premium movies and TV instead of DVD-by-mail.

Amazon did this with the shift into cloud computing. By transforming computing power into a scalable, pay-as-you-go service, the tradition of data centers got disrupted.

When Tesla introduced electric vehicles, they were envisioning a future of sustainability that did not rely on data from the combustion engine car market.

The challenge is to imagine something that does not exist yet. Or if it does exist, it's so small you can't see it getting big yet.

The idea is to focus on being a forward thinker. Review the historical data, but take a look at the changes happening around you as well, and try to anticipate where the puck is going before it gets there.

Getting it wrong happens, and that's ok. The important thing is becoming heroic enough to try.

THE TAKEAWAY: Create change instead of reacting to change.

AUGUST 21 — Choose your friends wisely.

"There is some self-interest behind every friendship. There is no friendship without self-interests. This is a bitter truth."

— Chanakya

The ancient Indian strategist, teacher, and philosopher Chanakya emphasized the reality of human nature in his *Arthashastra.* Chanakya called this verse about friendship a "bitter" truth, but it does not necessarily negate the value of friendship. He is simply emphasizing that friends exist because of mutual benefits, and trust should be given cautiously because friends can always betray us.

It is important to understand your intentions, and those of a potential friend, to assure your alliance fulfills your respective goals.

Avoid toxic friendships. There are people out there who are deceitful, envious, or exploitative. No matter how appealing it may seem at the outset, a relationship with such a person does not grow in the long term. It may also help to let go of relationships that were once positive but are no longer positive. People evolve over time, and relationships do as well. A true friend will be there for you in difficult times. Look for friends who stand by when you need them most and return the favor yourself.

Through careful judgment and mutual respect, emotion, and impulse, Chanakya believed that a person can be more successful when choosing friends.

THE TAKEAWAY: Choose your friends wisely.

AUGUST 22 — Be prepared for black swans in negotiation.

"Negotiation is not an act of battle; it's a process of discovery. The goal is to uncover as much information as possible."

— Chris Voss

Christopher "Chris" Voss is a former FBI hostage negotiator turned academic. He's taught a MasterClass, Harvard classes, and has written books such as *Never Split the Difference*.

In his class, he mentions **Nassim Nicholas Taleb's book**, *The Black Swan*, from 2007, and that black swans exist in Australia.

In negotiation a "black swan" means a key piece of unexpected information that changes everything.

Both sides of a negotiation have unknowns. Your party has its motivations, and the other party has their motivations, and it takes some time to uncover what the other party wants.

So do not lose your cool. Exercise tactical empathy. Mirroring body language and the speech patterns of the adversary can also help, Mr. Voss might advise.

Genuine curiosity is also useful when negotiating. Sometimes, asking the right question at the right time can get the other side to reveal some key information that changes everything.

THE TAKEAWAY: Be prepared for black swans in negotiation.

AUGUST 23 — Write a letter to yourself, then open it four years later.

"Time is the longest distance between two places."
— Tennessee Williams

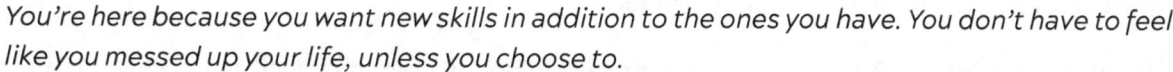

I wrote a letter to myself in 2019, in Per Scholas, Newark:

> Dear Akash,
>
> You're here because you want new skills in addition to the ones you have. You don't have to feel like you messed up your life, unless you choose to.
>
> Remember Marcus Aurelius, Book 5: "In a sense, people are our proper occupation. Our job is to do them good and put up with them. But when they obstruct our proper tasks, they become irrelevant to us — like sun, winds, animals. Our actions may be impeded by [people], but there can be no impeding our intentions or our dispositions… The impediment to action advances action. What stands in the way becomes the way."
>
> Your mind has been conditioned, externally and from within yourself, to be a liberator of minds, a filmmaker and a storyteller and a speaker. You now humbly continue your education at Per Scholas.
>
> Embrace them. See them as a way to a better life, for you and your wallet, but also for your mind and your family. Serve your family as they have served you — dutifully, lovingly. See the present as all there is, and the future as nonexistent (sort of).
>
> Don't let embarrassment or shyness stop you from achieving your dreams.
>
> Yours sincerely,
> Akash Malik

Try writing a letter to yourself, then open it years later. You might be surprised.

THE TAKEAWAY: Write a letter to yourself, then open it four years later.

237 AUGUST 24 — Be prepared to pivot if you find a better strategy.

"Taking smart risks can be very gratifying."
— Reed Hastings

In 2012, then Amazon Web Services (AWS) CEO Andy Jassy spoke to Reed Hastings at the AWS re:Invent conference.

Jassy asked Hastings about Netflix' cloud evolution.

Reed said it started in 2008, when the advent of streaming foretold that Netflix's computational resources was going to grow very rapidly. Netflix started to figure out how to build data centers. Then, Reed read Nicholas Carr's book *The Big Switch*, which pointed out that companies like Netflix used to have a VP of electricity, a real and important role because electricity is expensive and hard to manage.

Instead of that route, Netflix pivoted to building on AWS in 2009.

Jassy asked about any tech trends Hastings foresees, and Hastings points to the client side, the rise of handheld touchscreen devices like tablets or iPhones with Siri built in. Hastings used Siri as an example: You talk a bit, Siri does a bit of digital signal processing, sends it up to the cloud, and it tries to match what you're saying with a show that might interest you.

More cloud resources can only make Siri better, but Netflix still has to figure out the ranking of its movies and shows. What Netflix puts in your first two home screens dominates what you end up watching.

If it's the right stuff, then the customer is happy. If it's wrong, you might watch or do something else.

THE TAKEAWAY: Be prepared to pivot if you find a better strategy.

AUGUST 25 — Follow your moral compass with discipline.

In my copy of the English translation of *Chanakya Neeti*, Chanakya writes,

> "An industrious person can never be poor, always keeping God in mind keeps one away from sin, the silence does not let quarrels appear, and an ever-vigilant person has no cause for fear."

With consistent effort and hard work, a person can achieve success. To Chanakya, poverty is not just a lack of money, but a form of laziness. Industrious people can do well, even if they start off poor.

Keeping God in mind suggests the importance of good morals as well. When a person has a higher purpose or spiritual connection to something, they avoid temptation or envy or other behavior we might call "unethical."

In moments of anger or tension, people often say things they don't mean, and this is where silence can be handy.

A person who can stay silent, even when they are quarreling with another, can possibly negotiate their way to diffusing a situation and finding peace. And of course, being vigilant when it comes to your surroundings, anticipating danger, and avoiding potential problems whenever possible leads to less anxiety and fear.

Beliefs are simply stories you tell yourself, Reader. You can tell yourself better stories.

THE TAKEAWAY: Follow your moral compass with discipline.

239

AUGUST 26 — Remember who you were after the shipwreck.

"I made a prosperous voyage," Zeno later joked, *"when I suffered shipwreck."*

There was once a time I was a broke film school graduate, about to turn 23.

I enrolled in Per Scholas. I studied. Commuted daily to Newark by train, carrying the same MacBook Pro I had since college.

It was scary, but when I figured out how to run a virtual machine on this Mac using VMware Fusion, I got so excited because I exceeded what I thought was possible!

I thought before I could only do things like writing or directing or editing, but I found I could do tech if I set my mind to it. Since the pandemic, I even taught hundreds of other adults around the US about lots of technology, during a pandemic when the film industry largely shut down.

It all began with a shipwreck. My ship crashed, but I was able to troubleshoot and patch it up.

THE TAKEAWAY: Remember who you were after the shipwreck.

AUGUST 27 — Improve upon what is already out there.

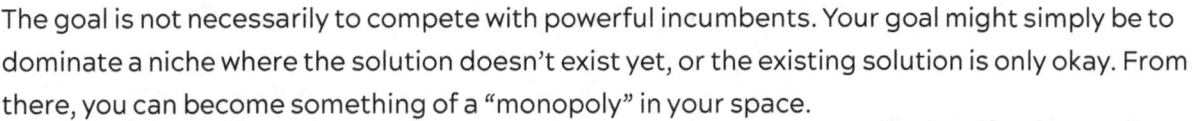

"Monopoly is the condition of every successful business."
— Peter Thiel

The goal is not necessarily to compete with powerful incumbents. Your goal might simply be to dominate a niche where the solution doesn't exist yet, or the existing solution is only okay. From there, you can become something of a "monopoly" in your space.

Employees at a company try to look for areas where existing products are not doing well.

They look for a specialized niche market that is so small, once there is a truly superior product, there is no reason for anyone else to go in and compete.

They are not trying to make new products, but to improve on "bad" ones.

It is insane how many products are still out there, being sold, that could use an improvement.

THE TAKEAWAY: Improve upon what is already out there.

241   AUGUST 28 — Figure out your advantage and use it.

"Don't find customers for your products, find products for your customers."
— Seth Godin

The **HR Exchange Network** listed four entrepreneurial strategies for someone aiming for market leadership from one of the greatest of all time, Peter Drucker.

1. **"Fustest with the Mostest."**
   Example: With the iPhone, Apple created the modern smartphone market, sparking many products that closely imitate what Apple makes, such as Samsung. A jury found that Samsung of infringeding on Apple's design and software in 2012.

2. **"Keep your eye on the ball and hit 'em where they ain't."**
   Example: Major League Baseball right fielder Willie Keeler owed this to his success in baseball. Tesla is doing this with electric vehicles. While traditional automakers prioritize internal combustion engines, Tesla focuses on electric vehicles. Now automakers are catching up.

3. **Find and occupy a specialized "ecological niche."**
   Example: GoPro does well in action cameras, carving out a niche distinct from traditional camera makers. Another example is Or Nerd Fitness, which specializes in the niche of making fitness accessible to underdogs, misfits, and all types of nerds.

4. **Changing the economic characteristics of a product, market, or an industry.**
   Example: Hulu and Netflix, which changed media consumption by shifting from DVD rentals to streaming after seeing the success YouTube was having. Legacy media companies like Disney are now catching up.

Becoming indispensable and dominant in your market is a great place to be in

THE TAKEAWAY: Figure out your advantage and use it.

AUGUST 29 — Take care of the people who cared for you.

"In youth we learn; in age we understand."
— Marie von Ebner-Eschenbach

Today in 2021 I was escorting my elderly grandfather to the bathroom. My family kept saying "use the cane," but he stubbornly tried to walk with his two legs. I was even holding his arm the way he used to hold mine when I was young.

The whole experience was vivid and vulnerable. It is hard to use the bathroom at 88 years old. Walking there, waiting for him to go, wash his hands, dry his hands, exit. I saw many other men, of all ages, walk in and out freely before he was finished.

As we grow up, we receive years of support from our elders. But as we age, we find ourselves becoming the ones providing the support to them. The dynamics of these relationships shift over time.

By caring for someone in their later years, and reflecting on the process of aging, we gain a new perspective on the wisdom and struggles of our beloved elders. It is a spiritual, rewarding, and peaceful experience.

THE TAKEAWAY: Take care of the people who cared for you.

AUGUST 30 — Embrace the unexpected surprises of meditation.

"When there are thoughts, it is distraction: when there are no thoughts, it is meditation."

— Ramana Maharshi

In his book, *Chanakya in Daily Life*, author and spiritual guide Dr. Radhakrishnan Pillai writes how meditation is not just something you "do."

Meditation is a state of mind. The practice of meditating is something a person can develop throughout a lifetime.

One thing I learned about myself while meditating is this: I am much more than my thoughts or my feelings.

If you are curious like me, you think a lot, and you start searching for a really fast answer to a question online. It is cool that you can type almost any question, big or small, into a search engine and get an authoritative answer.

But some answers are better found within yourself instead of searching online. No matter your background, I believe meditation can surprise you with some insights. LSD can too, but it's not for everyone.

THE TAKEAWAY: Embrace the unexpected surprises of meditation.

AUGUST 31 — Combat ignorance with knowledge.

"There is only one good, knowledge, and one evil, ignorance."

— Socrates

To Socrates, the pursuit of wisdom and understanding was the ultimate virtue, while ignorance was the root of all wrongdoing and misjudgment.

His philosophy emphasizes the importance of self-awareness and continuous questioning, now called the Socratic method, because he believed that a lack of knowledge often leads to misguided actions.

People do commit evil out of hatred, or selfishness, but those attributes also stem from ignorance—a lack of knowledge.

Do you remember all the times you did bad things out of curiosity, just to see what would happen? Maybe you were rude as a kid, tried shoplifting candy as a teen, or acted on bad information and got caught, then punished.

This is why lifelong learning is so important. You can learn from books, articles, videos, and classes to try and understand the "why" and "how" of the world. Then, you identify how you can grow yourself within it.

There are learning opportunities out there, opportunities to show off your virtues—chances to flex your skills and knowledge in front of others and get paid for it.

THE TAKEAWAY: Combat ignorance with knowledge.

Part Three:
ENLIGHTENMENT

SEPTEMBER

SEPTEMBER 1 — Be transparent with people to build trust.

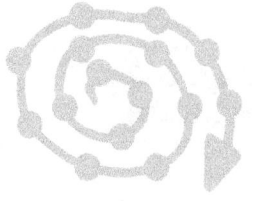

"You can't connect the dots looking forward; you can only connect them looking backward."

— Steve Jobs

In February 2012, the US government released an FBI file on Steve Jobs, per *Wired* magazine, with notes from a Federal agent who was investigating a bomb-threat extortion attempt against Jobs in 1985.

There is also explanation from Jobs on his LSD usage from 1972 through 1974. Jobs said he used LSD approximately 10 to 15 times, usually on a sugar cube or in a hard gelatin. He said it was a positive, life-changing experience, and he was glad he did it.

According to my diary, I tried LSD on this day in 2014 when I went to college. I remember it was on a piece of paper, and I wanted to better understand what Jobs was talking about. It was a positive experience for me.

It is important to be transparent about things like this among the people you count as friends or with whom you work. Harnessing these sorts of insights can fuel innovation and build trust.

In general, honesty is the best policy about most things, if not all.

THE TAKEAWAY: **Be transparent with people to build trust.**

246   **SEPTEMBER 2 — Use a time log to maximize daily productivity.**

"Dost thou love life? Then do not squander time, for that's the stuff life is made of."

— Benjamin Franklin

Executives often keep a continuous log of their days. *Business Insider* shared the daily routines of Tim Cook, Mark Zuckerberg, and other executives. I tried following some of those schedules to try and maximize my productivity, but I realized I had to find what works for me, not someone else.

A *nalika* system is what Chanakya used, writes Dr. Radhakrishnan Pillai in his book, *Chanakya in Daily Life*.

What works for me is having a bunch of smartphone alarms. Some hotels offer wake up calls if you request one from the concierge, which could be helpful.

Whatever your schedule is, the most important thing is documentation. Documenting how much time a task takes can help you manage your daily schedule so you don't waste any time.

An instructor day for me at Per Scholas looks like a 90-minute session, a fifteen-minute break, another 90-minute session, lunch, 90-minute session15-minute break, 90-minute session, and done. Movies tend to be 90 minutes to two hours long on average for that same reason. Human attention span starts to dwindle after about 90 minutes to two hours.

With a noisy world full of social media, kids, a job, friends who want to play video games, it is easier than ever to lose track of the day. This is where a logging practice comes in handy.

THE TAKEAWAY: Use a time log to maximize daily productivity.

SEPTEMBER 3 — Embrace responsibility in your relationships.

In *Chanakya in Daily Life*, Dr. Radhakrishnan Pillai writes about Chanakya being a family man.

> *"As between a father and son, husband and wife, brother and sister, maternal uncle and nephew, or teacher and pupil, for the one abandoning the other and going away, the fine for violence shall be the punishment."*

Every relationship has responsibilities. One cannot take another person for granted or run away from responsibilities when the time comes to be responsible. In those tough moments, it helps to take a break and walk away, perhaps into another room.

Do not make any decisions out of anger, or frustration, or to shove it in a person's face. Sometimes, the best decision is no decision. Let some time pass, cool down, then respond. Abandoning such responsibility is a personal failure, and it could even be a punishable offense.

Relationships are important to nurture, and people need to be accountable to their parents, siblings, friends, classmates, and mentors.

A well-governed society starts with strong relationships between people who trust each other, not only at work but also within the home.

THE TAKEAWAY: Embrace responsibility in your relationships.

248   SEPTEMBER 4 — Review all the assets available daily.

Dr. Radhakrishnan Pillai writes in *Chanakya in Daily Life* of advice Chanakya had for the king in *Arthashastra*:

"During the seventh part of the day, he should review elephants, horses, chariots, and troops."

In cybersecurity, business, or personal life, it is good to spend a part of the day vigilantly reviewing your defenses. Leaders need to be connected to the details that drive the company by assessing available resources, plans, and teams that are essential to success.

Asset review can be for your personal finances, professional development, or preparing for any ongoing or upcoming crisis, such as a flood or fire.

Misfortune is destined, so while there is time to prepare, it is good to prepare.

It is also good for a leader to personally review all the assets and not delegate oversight to someone else. There might be many automated or AI tools available to do that, but even so, a leader should do the final review to catch any potential mistakes.

THE TAKEAWAY: Review all the assets available daily.

SEPTEMBER 5 — Walk the talk.

On August 9, 2023, Made in America 2023 was canceled, per **CBS.**

The event was scheduled to be headlined by Lizzo. A lot has happened since then.

Like Lizzo and the August 2023 allegations against her (*Vox*).

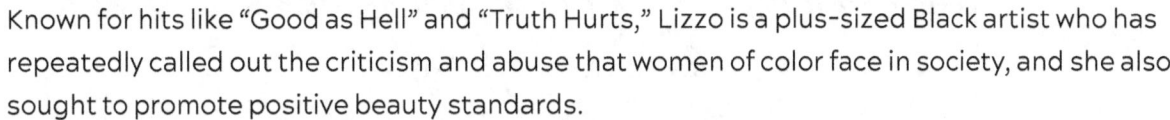

Known for hits like "Good as Hell" and "Truth Hurts," Lizzo is a plus-sized Black artist who has repeatedly called out the criticism and abuse that women of color face in society, and she also sought to promote positive beauty standards.

But two of the plaintiffs, Arianna Davis and Crystal Williams, appeared on her show alleging harassment by Lizzo in a hostile work environment. The potential harassment in the lawsuit, called Lizzo's message and image into question.

Lizzo and her management team were accused of treating their performers in the opposite way that was advocated by her music.

It was shocking to me to read this because Lizzo represents body positivity publicly, but privately she was weight shaming her dancers and demeaning them.

Whatever your message, hypocrisy of any degree will undermine it.

THE TAKEAWAY: Walk the talk.

SEPTEMBER 6 — Learn to avoid mistakes you see others making.

In my Manoj Publications copy of *Chanakya Neeti*, there is this Chanakya quote:

> *"A born blind can't see, so does a man blinded with passion of love. A drunkard can't see what is good or what is bad. And a selfish man is also blind to the evil of his actions done to achieve the selfish goal."*

There are many movies or books with characters blinded by alcohol, lust, or bloodlust. Or a mix of all three. They make for amazing writing or performances in film and TV!

Censorship, like the **Hays Code** in 20th-century America, is long gone in 2023. Movies and TV often take us behind closed doors, showing more intimate aspects of humanity.

Thanks to YouTube, Google, and the world wide web of the Internet, we can see more. We can see blind people get their sight back. Or see crimes of passion, or what a man does when he is blinded by love. Or see drunk people do stupid drunk things. Or see selfish, violent people do evil things to achieve their goals with no regard for the victims.

It has become apparent to me that a big part of troubleshooting life is avoiding such problems. Sometimes you foresee them and prepare for them. Or perhaps those foreseen never occur. Other times you have to adjust on the fly.

THE TAKEAWAY: Learn to avoid mistakes you see others making.

SEPTEMBER 7 — Find fuels that work today, not yesterday.

In the book *When Hollywood Had a King*, author Connie Bruck writes about movie distributors who were unhappy with the gross revenues they were negotiating from pay TV, especially HBO, as compared to movie theaters.

Eventually, most of the major movie studios had talks about creating a pay TV network of their own. MCA/Universal, Paramount, Columbia, Fox, and the Getty Oil Company, formed a joint venture called Premiere.

For nine months, Premiere would exclusively get certain films by the partners before other pay TV services like HBO. Michael Fuchs, who became HBO CEO in 1984, negotiated with MCA/Universal and described them as "hostile" to HBO from the start.

Fuchs said that MCA/Universal was infused with the idea that they were leaders of the industry. They were the most arrogant studio to deal with, by far. And they were so rooted in the past.

Fuchs recalled going to visit MCA's Black Tower and seeing co-founder Jules Stein's antique furniture. To him, that always symbolized where the MCA heads were at.

Reader, you can learn lessons or traditions from people in the past, or other firms you admire. But at some point you must recognize when a powerful dinosaur becomes a fossil.

Strategies or fuels of the past may not work as strategies or fuel for younger generations.

THE TAKEAWAY: **Find fuels that work today, not yesterday.**

252   SEPTEMBER 8 — Know your "why."

"Efforts and courage are not enough without purpose and direction."
— John F. Kennedy

In Tim Burton and John August's adaptation of *Charlie and the Chocolate Factory* (2005), Mr. Bucket lost his job at the toothpaste factory but studied his way to getting technician work, repairing the same robot that took his job at factory.

That is sort of why I find working at Per Scholas so interesting. Mr. Bucket, like many Per Scholians, learned technology while unemployed, and got himself a new job. Then his son got a chocolate factory, but it still worked out well for Mr. Bucket with his new skills. He was very motivated to support his family no matter what it took.

Life is short. You can learn a remarkable number of things in a short amount of time.

Losing your job can give you the drive to gain new skills, try new things, and find a mission that you can put your effort and courage toward.

THE TAKEAWAY: **Know your "why."**

SEPTEMBER 9 — **Look for the business behind the business.**

"Amateurs study tactics; professionals study logistics."
— General Omar N. Bradley

In the *Masters of Scale* podcast, Reid Hoffman cites the example of Rent the Runway's founder, Jenn Hyman.

Jenn tells Reid how she started Rent the Runway with a single dress for a special occasion and pivoted from there. For their customers, Rent the Runway offers access to glamour. But underneath? It is the largest dry-cleaning operation in the world. With a deep well of data. As Reid points out, the back-end business of dry cleaning looks very different from the front end.

What about Amazon? Not just an online retailer, but massive warehouse operations. Apple? Beautiful iPhones, but also massive worldwide assembly lines.

A restaurant has a nice ambiance with smiling waitstaff and gorgeously plated courses, but behind that it's like *The Bear*, with a furious kitchen trying to fulfill orders with fire, ice, and steam. Fresh vegetables come in the morning, followed by fish; at the end of the night, the trash is tossed.

The front end looks very different from the back end. The staff up front use a different set of skills than the ones in the back, but all the people and logistics are important to running a good shop.

THE TAKEAWAY: Look for the business behind the business.

SEPTEMBER 10 — Document performance over time.

"The discipline of writing something down is the first step toward making it happen

— Lee Iacocca

This photo is from this morning in 2021. It looks almost the same years later. I am at my desk, writing this on my iPhone, while my work laptop is running Zoom, and my personal MacBook has a PDF or iBooks or a word processor file open.

I wrote about what technologies I was studying, ways to improve my writing, and ways to do better at personal tasks such as working out and eating healthy.

The discipline of consistently writing and learning over long periods of time helps me become better. I have failed many practice tests on the way to earning more certifications. I wrote a lot of bad pages before writing good ones. Seeing the documentation grow over time is a reminder that I am constantly in a state of growth.

THE TAKEAWAY: Use technology to document performance over time.

SEPTEMBER 11 — Eliminate the "widow-maker" positions at your firm.

"If you always do what you've always done, you'll always get what you've always got."

— Henry Ford

"Widow-maker" is a term used by 19th-century New England shipbuilders. It describes a well-built new ship that still managed to have two fatal accidents in a row. Instead of attempting to fix the problems, they immediately destroyed the ship to prevent another accident from occurring.

In organizations, a "widow-maker" job defeats two competent people in a row. It will almost certainly defeat a third person, no matter how competent.

Sometimes we need to recognize when a job is too much, no matter how good it looks on paper. Instead of trying to put people into a doomed situation, it might be better to break up the job for two or three people, or just remove it entirely to avoid further harm.

Imagine trying to advocate for diversity, equity, and inclusion in an organization with systemic racism, gender inequities, and a toxic culture. Even with the best intentions, a highly competent person in this role may face constant resistance, sabotage, or inadequate resources, making it extremely hard to achieve success at the job.

The only action left is to abolish and restructure the widow-maker position.

THE TAKEAWAY: Eliminate the "widow-maker" positions at your firm.

SEPTEMBER 12 — Exert effort sustainably.

"The miracle isn't that I finished. The miracle is that I had the courage to start."

— John Bingham, runner and author

This day in 490 BCE is the traditionally accepted date for the Battle of Marathon, an epic fight between the Greeks and the Persians. It was a watershed victory at the time, because the Greeks started to believe that the Persians could actually lose.

The most interesting legend that comes from Marathon is the runner Pheidippides.

Before the battle, Pheidippides reportedly ran from Athens to Sparta in two days to request military aid against the invading Persians, then after the victory, ran from the battlefield to Athens to deliver news of the victory. He got to Athens, said "We won!" and then died.

Whether it is fact or fiction, the modern marathon in the Olympics stems from this legend. People work hard to build endurance and stamina and sacrifice a lot of time training for marathons.

There is something to be said for balancing effort with sustainability. After all, the original marathon runner did not run another marathon. It would be nice to avoid that for now.

THE TAKEAWAY: **Exert effort sustainably.**

SEPTEMBER 13 — Get a decent day job while pursuing your passion.

"Do what you have to do until you can do what you want to do."

— Oprah Winfrey

The Computing Technology Industry Association (CompTIA) is an organization that provides certifications and training in information technology. CompTIA certifications are valuable for people looking to start or advance their careers in IT.

In 2019, a CompTIA A+ certified technician could make $40,000 a year or more. A Network+ certified technician could earn more than $85,000 a year in an administrator role. When I was in film school, I was motivated by art and music; I was not so much motivated by money until I had to start paying bills.

Wikipedia states that Ang Lee struggled for six years after he graduated from Tisch. Although signed to William Morris, he was an unemployed, full-time, stay-at-home dad for six years. His wife, a molecular biologist, was the breadwinner.

When Michael Ovitz left William Morris with Ron Meyer, Bill Haber, Rowland Perkins, and Mike Rosenfeld to start their own agency, Creative Artists Agency, their wives were also paying the bills.

It's a struggle to move to a big city to work in music or movies or any artistic career. Teaching an IT class or working in IT at least pays the bills while a person can pursue artistic crafts.

THE TAKEAWAY: Get a decent day job while pursuing your passion.

258

SEPTEMBER 14 — Balance ambition with enjoying life.

"In the name of art and everything art stands for, remember this: art is only the search. It's not the final form."

— Gary Busey, Entourage

In the episode of *Entourage* "Busey and the Beach," the Hollywood super-agent Ari Gold tells his assistant Emily to "storm the beach like it's Normandy" as part of his plan to get Vincent Chase his next acting project, and to avoid his client getting poached by an agent who was once Ari's assistant.

It is hilarious that he compares getting Vince's attention to a military invasion, and a bit dark, but that is why we love Ari Gold. The Normandy reference captures it so well: Ari is such a bombastic person, with military-level enthusiasm, and Vince is just laid back and going with the flow, which is a recurring and funny juxtaposition in the show.

Similarly, there is something to be said about finding a balance between being ambitious and enjoying life for the journey that it is.

THE TAKEAWAY: Balance ambition with enjoying life.

SEPTEMBER 15 — Talk about one painting in three different ways.

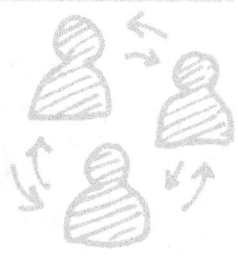

In the first chapter of his memoir, *Who Is Michael Ovitz?*, the author writes about first impressions at Creative Artists Agency (CAA).

CAA's focus on first impressions won the firm many new clients before the agents even spoke.

One striking example is when Michael gave visitors a tour of the CAA office. He would stop the tour by the prints of the art on the wall and talk with actors about composition and mood. He would talk with directors about the power of the images.

With executives, he talked about being well rounded and having a life outside the office.

This is a lesson I recently shared with an Amazon Web Services (AWS) re/Start class when talking about networking. Human networking, not computer networking. It takes skill and practice to talk about art. Music, paintings, literature, movies, television, even computer engineers and smartphone manufactures might feel their work can be "art," inspired by past forms and content.

To a parent, Fortnite might be a waste of time, or a free babysitter so they can focus on dinner.

To a child, it is socializing with friends. To the developer, it is a way to pay rent while they work on their screenplay. To the world? Fortnite could be played in stadiums, competitively, with millions in cash prizes.

Fortnite is not a painting, but a person can talk about it in several different ways.

THE TAKEAWAY: **Talk about one painting in three different ways.**

260

SEPTEMBER 16 — Fame, "the clacking of tongues," is a worthless prize.

In the *Meditations of Marcus Aurelius*, the Gregory Hayes translation, Marcus writes about what we should prize as humans.

Not transpiration, because plants also do that. Not respiration, because beasts and wild animals breathe too. Not being struck by passing thoughts. Not being jerked like a puppet by your inner, primal impulses. Not moving in herds or organizing into herds like armies of birds. Not eating or relieving yourself afterwards. Not the clapping of an audience the "clacking of their tongues," he writes of public praise.

What's left for us? To Marcus Aurelius, it is simply doing what we were designed for. Like the nurseryman who cares for the vines or the horse trainer or the dog breeder. Or educators. Or entertainers. Or pundits, priests, or rabbis, who share enlightenment.

Reader, this man was the Emperor of Rome, considered an embodiment of God by many, yet he also struggled with the same issues we do. I once sought fame, power, money, and respect of my family, my peers, women, and a godlike status.

Now, I could care less if people remember me or forget about me.

Soon they will move on and discuss another Spectacular Person. There is a never-ending fascination of humans who are famous, accomplished, and/or attractive. I find comfort in the fact that ultimately I will die. Death is what gives life meaning.

THE TAKEAWAY: **Fame, "the clacking of tongues," is a worthless prize.**

SEPTEMBER 17 — Show respect toward animals, nature, and people.

In *Chanakya in Daily Life*, Dr. Radhakrishnan Pillai writes about daily rituals, citing Chanakya:

"And, after going around a cow with her calf and a bull, he should proceed to the assembly hall."

Chanakya tells the king to visit the cow, calf, and bull before going to work at the assembly hall, or *durbar*, where official and administrative activities of the kingdom took place.

Even before one's official workday begins, Chanakya advises a king to connect with nature.

Indian culture has always shown respect toward animals and nature. Many Indians choose to be vegetarian as a result of this respect toward living beings. An underlying respect for nature is especially important for people who live in cities. A city may be cut off from nature, but a ritual such as tending a garden is helpful.

As Aristotle writes in *Poetics*, it is fun imitating animals. Humans enjoy imitation. They learn by imitation as well. Kids and adults might imitate a king.

Imagine imitating a tyrant who burns plants versus imitating a gracious leader who cares for trees, birds, and cows.

There was once a child who collected insects and dead animals to study. Indeed, Charles Darwin had a great appreciation for nature. **(163. June 11)**

THE TAKEAWAY: Show respect toward animals, nature, and people.

SEPTEMBER 18 — Learn about art from the great artists.

"The purpose of art is to lay bare the questions that have been hidden by the answers."

— James Baldwin

In his memoir, Michael Ovitz writes about reading all the great books of Hollywood history. He saw every Oscar-winning film going back to 1929. But he admits that he didn't "get" movies until he started watching them with Martin Scorsese.

In the late 1980s, he recalls renting a one-bedroom apartment in a Manhattan building on West 57 Street. Ovitz would fly in from LA at 1:00 am, drop his bags, and knock on Marty's door. He got a plate of food, then sat in front of whatever was playing that night on Marty's projector.

If you've ever listened to an interview of Martin Scorsese, you know he is a human film encyclopedia.

He loved the work of Michael Powell, the husband of his editor, Thelma Schoonmaker, especially *The Red Shoes*. Wikipedia cites Brian De Palma, Francis Ford Coppola, and Steven Spielberg as fans of the movie as well.

I remember watching YouTube as a teenager in Edison, NJ, feeling the same way as Ovitz did when he visited Scorsese. I only "got" movies—becoming addicted to them and ultimately learning the art of filmmaking—because of watching Marty on YouTube, talking about how important visual literacy is, and that pictures and sound can tell stories just like words.

THE TAKEAWAY: Learn about art from the great artists.

SEPTEMBER 19 — Patiently teach yourself, then educate others.

"He who opens a school door, closes a prison."
— Victor Hugo

It is important to spend time cultivating a deep love of art or sports or something. It builds a fortress for the soul.

The work we do causes the soul to adapt and change.

The soul recognizes the importance of self-education, patience, restraint from giving into human flaws, and reflecting on the lessons learned through life, art, sport, and more.

You need to first be patient with teaching the person in the mirror before you can teach others. As Norman Cousins wrote, there is a doctor within you as well as a patient.

Education can help people become responsible citizens and better human beings. People can educate themselves and provide a better future for themselves and their families than can a life of crime.

THE TAKEAWAY: Patiently teach yourself, then educate others.

264
SEPTEMBER 20 — Be willing to take a risk.

"It is not the mountain we conquer but ourselves."
— Edmund Hillary

Quinn Shephard is writing and directing her second feature film, *Not Okay*. She didn't go to film school. *Variety* writes that she lost an investor then put her own college fund into her feature film, titled *Blame.*

I remember meeting Quinn in the 2010s, in Neal Bennett's classroom at Arts High School in NJ, when she was trying to make Blame. I later took an Avid Media Composer certification class with Neal, who later became a media professor at Rutgers.

Quinn's first acting role was Abigail in *The Crucible* in high school. My first acting role in high school was *The Wedding Singer*, a play based on the Adam Sandler movie. I played Mookie/Fake Mr. T/Loser Guy/Suit #4, and I was asked to do an offensive Indian accent.

I ended up writing and directing my own South Asian play with some classmates at my very crowded high school.

It is a lot of fun doing creative stuff and showing your work at exhibitions and screenings. Having a good producer helps. It also helps to write a lot and have parents who trust you, as Quinn says in an interview for the website *No Film School*.

Losing an investor could have been a major setback, but instead of giving up, she chose to risk her own college fund, and it paid off, a rare combination of bravery and commitment.

THE TAKEAWAY: Be willing to take a risk.

SEPTEMBER 21 — Do not let your ambition make you foolish.

In *Chanakya in Daily Life,* interpreting the wisdom of the ancient philosopher, jurist, and royal advisor, Dr. Radhakrishnan Pillai writes about the eldest son. Traditionally, the eldest son will become the head of the family and head of the family business.

If the king has only one son, he is going to want that boy to become king, even if the spoiled prince would *not* make a good king. But even if the king has 100 sons, the king can be blind to their faults.

In the Indian epic *Mahabharata*, Dhritarashtra was literally and metaphorically blind, because he loved his sons, despite all his sons being cruel and deceitful.

His sense of judgement was flawed. He gave Duryodhana, his cruel son, the throne. Wise elders such as Bhishma and Vidura warned against giving Duryodhana the throne, but he refused.

We all know what ends up happening. The Mahabharata war took place. The family was destroyed. All 100 sons of Dhritarashtra were killed in the great war by their cousins.

It is foolish to hope that the cruel prince will suddenly become virtuous when given the kingdom.

In today's world, I would advise avoiding working at companies run by dishonest people. There are many examples as to why that won't go well.

THE TAKEAWAY: Do not let your ambition make you foolish.

266

SEPTEMBER 22 — Embrace thinking and acting like an Olympian god.

"It is difficulties that show what men are. For the future, in case of any difficulty, remember that God, like a gymnastic trainer, has pitted you against a rough antagonist. For what end? That you may be an Olympic conqueror; and this cannot be without toil."

— Epictetus

On this day in 2019, I was writing to myself about how shitty the year had been.

Now, after a pandemic and continuous training of new technologists, I have advanced as a thinker and troubleshooter of life, and I feel like I grew from facing those difficulties. My bosses had me build furniture, make coffee, and slice tomatoes and avocado, which I began to do better and better as I practiced.

These tasks are "work," as in achieving "results." Put in your boss' mind that you can achieve results from the moment you walk in the door to conduct your business.

Have confidence. You are not "worthless." After all, you are still alive.

You have more to learn and do. Emphasize your strengths, not your weakness.

The path to greatness is not avoiding the obstacles when they push against you, but facing them, flipping them, turning them into fuel to push you from behind.

THE TAKEAWAY: Embrace thinking and acting like an Olympian God.

SEPTEMBER 23 — Try Chanakya's plan for an organized life.

"For a well-planned and organized life, one must live religiously, earn money, and save, store food grains, keep life-saving and first-aid medicine in domestic stock, and act upon the advice of the teacher."

— Chanakya Neeti

When I think of teachers, I think of my in-person school experiences. Then, the pandemic Zoom school experiences. Per Scholas remote training.

Now, I see teachers everywhere. In schools, in YouTube videos, Zoom screen sharing, blogs.

Once all these people are able to live religiously, save up money, and stock up on food and medicine, they can learn from a teacher anywhere in the world through the Internet.

There are really three things that sustain life.
- Food
- Water
- Learning

If you are not growing, you are dying. A person marooned on an island with no means of growing their supply of food, water, or helpful knowledge is not making it off the island.

Try writing a letter to yourself, then open it years later. You might be surprised.

THE TAKEAWAY: Try Chanakya's plan for an organized life.

SEPTEMBER 24 — Spend time being curious, not bored.

"The cure to boredom is curiosity. There is no cure for curiosity."

— Dorothy Parker

I could dive deep into this day and likely uncover lots of crazy events.

When I dug through my Facebook data, I found that on this day in 2009, I was watching George Lopez on Nick at Nite and trying to go to sleep. I saw George Lopez in the movie *Blue Beetle,* and seeing his performance reminded me of how fondly I watched him and his TV family.

I may have been envious they were on TV, but now with YouTube, it is not hard to get on TV.

What is actually hard? Finding something worthwhile to say, repeating it, and saying more good things.

Time spent in boredom or jealousy is time misspent. It is better to spend time being curious.

THE TAKEAWAY: Spend time being curious, not bored.

SEPTEMBER 25 — **Harmonize your immediate and long-term futures.**

"Individually, we are one drop. Together, we are an ocean."

— Ryunosuke Satoro

Ever since my aunt moved from India to Edison, New Jersey, in the 1970s, my family members have attended Edison High School, which experienced its ups and downs over decades.

The district hired Charles K. Ross, aka "Boss Ross," in 2010 to turn the school around. At that time, it was a bit of a "zoo," to quote another student who went there with me.

When I met this new principal, I shared my longstanding connection to the school, that the school was a zoo when my big brother graduated from it, and I hoped he could turn it around.

One of the first things Boss Ross did when he took over was "no iPods in study hall." That very quickly changed from 2010 to 2014, when technology became commonplace. Someone who was absent could still keep up with the lessons they missed.

Soon, the whole school had better WiFi. Now every student gets a Mac.

Maybe Boss Ross saw iPods as a distraction in the school's immediate future, but over time digital technology became important in the long-term success of the school. When he saw that, he reversed his decision about being strict on technology use in school.

THE TAKEAWAY: Harmonize your immediate and long-term futures.

270

SEPTEMBER 26 — Understand that stories are a sacred responsibility.

"Everybody in Hollywood is standing in a field full of haystacks, trying to find a bunch of needles. They don't know which needle they're going to use when they find them, but they have to start with a needle. We invented a metal detector."

— Franklin Leonard, *The Black List*

As a Black kid from the deep South, film and TV was Franklin Leonard's portal to other worlds. Leonard describes himself as Steve Urkel, who was on TV when Leonard applied to Harvard and got in.

Leonard was aware of how Hollywood film and television defined the conversation around how people themselves and other people, not only in the U.S. but around the world.

He cites some numbers on *Masters of Scale,* like 66 percent of gang members in film over the last 10 years are Black, but according to the FBI, only 33 percent of gang members are Black.

Fifty percent of Latinx immigrants shown on television over the past 10 years were shown as criminals. The people who chant "build the wall" may not know any Latinx criminal immigrants, but they saw Latinx criminals on TV, so it must be true, when most studies Leonard saw show Latinx immigrant communities are safer than American communities.

Working in Hollywood is a sacred responsibility, and Leonard cares about creating a sustainable culture for storytellers. The Black List brought us movies such as *Slumdog Millionaire, Juno,* and *The King's Speech*. I hope it will bring us many more.

THE TAKEAWAY: Understand that stories are a sacred responsibility.

SEPTEMBER 27 — Find your method to discipline yourself.

In his book, *Chanakya in Daily Life*, Dr. Radhakrishnan Pillai cites Chanakya's method to discipline a king in *Arthashastra*:

"He (king) should set the preceptors or ministers as the bounds of proper conduct (for himself), who should restrain him from occasions of harm, or when he is erring in private, should prick him with the goad in the form of indication of time for the performance of his regular duties by means of the shadow of the water clock."

When one is not sure if one can follow discipline on one's own, appoint a trusted teacher. This teacher, or any other trusted advisor, can set a proper boundary and be empowered to stop the king from doing harmful things to themselves or their kingdom.

A parent, a spouse, a friend—even in a roomful of people—this teacher can stop the king from making a mistake. The king, Dr. Radhakrishnan Pillai writes, might also have many meetings with people of high positions.

There is a tendency for one meeting to spill over into the next meeting.

A soft reminder from the teacher, a minister, or in today's world an executive assistant, can get the king to politely end a meeting to prepare for the next meeting.

A person who does whatever pleases his mind does not achieve anything on time. This is where self-discipline, or the teacher, comes in, to help decide what to achieve today.

THE TAKEAWAY: Find your method to discipline yourself.

272

SEPTEMBER 28 — Start at the end of your comfort zone.

"Life begins at the end of your comfort zone."
— Neale Donald Walsch

The main problem executives have is that they are insulated from the outside world. Some might say these executives are in their "ivory tower."

These executives need to get out of their comfort zones and collect critical information on unknown environments.

These could look like polls on customer satisfaction or buying habits, tech developments, the competitors, and government policies connected to their industry.

And they should consider their underpaid, college-educated, overworked assistants. These hardworking executives-in-training are out there with magnifying glasses, to find clues for their bosses.

They love the keyboard shortcut "Cmd + F" or "Ctrl + F" to find information, or they use search engines, and they are always trying to work outside of their comfort zones, unlike their bosses, who usually really like their comforts.

THE TAKEAWAY: **Start at the end of your comfort zone.**

SEPTEMBER 29 — The saddest thing in life is wasted talent.

"The saddest thing in life is wasted talent, and the choices that you make will shape your life forever."

— Calogero, *A Bronx Tale*

One summer in the 2000s, like many families in New Jersey, my family took a vacation to Atlantic City.

On one of these trips, my parents got tickets for *A Bronx Tale*, the one-man show by Chazz Palminteri. It was a vivid experience I remember from my boyhood.

After the amazing show, a nice lady in the audience told me this is a movie as well! The 1993 film was Robert De Niro's directorial debut, and Chazz even plays Sonny in the film.

I watched that movie as a young man. When I went to film school, I found the screenplay PDF and downloaded it from the Internet. Reading it felt very special to me. It reminded me of sitting in the audience with my family, seeing the one-man show.

My current company, Per Scholas, started in the Bronx and expanded to Per Scholas Newark. I imagine my nonprofit also agrees with this idea from the film: that wasted talent is a tragedy.

We should try to avoid it.

THE TAKEAWAY: The saddest thing in life is wasted talent.

SEPTEMBER 30 — Change yourself to change your world's tendencies.

"We but mirror the world. All the tendencies present in the outer world are to be found in the world of our body. If we could change ourselves, the tendencies in the world would also change. As a man changes his own nature, so does the attitude of the world change towards him. This is the divine mystery supreme. A wonderful thing it is and the source of our happiness. We need not wait to see what others do."

— Mohandas Karamchand Gandhi

In 1982, Ben Kingsley played Gandhi the movie of the same name, a Creative Artists Agency package.

Almost 30 years after *Gandhi*, Ben Kingsley played George Melies in the movie *Hugo* (2011).

I saw *Hugo* before I saw *Gandhi*. Both feature great performances from Kingsley.

You learn a lot about a person, or character, from the objects they surround themselves with. In cinema, this is called *mise-en-scène*, everything that appears in front of the camera. It includes shot composition, the sets, props, actors blocking, movement, costumes, and lighting.

With computer-generated imagery, generative AI might one day do *mise-en-scène*. AI is yet another tool a filmmaker can use, like the automaton in *Hugo*.

All the tools and visual vocabulary that Melies and filmmakers of that era were discovering can now be done with a computer.

But as Gandhi says, we but mirror the world around us. Computers, or movies, cannot change any man's nature, unless that man decides he wants to change himself and his tendencies.

THE TAKEAWAY: **Change yourself to change your world's tendencies.**

OCTOBER 1 — Honor Jimmy Carter by serving those who need help.

"You can do what you have to do, and sometimes you can do it even better than you think you can."
— Jimmy Carter

Born October 1, 1924, Jimmy Carter served as the 39th President of the United States from 1977 to 1981. Formerly a peanut farmer and naval officer, Carter brought a down-to-earth approach to the presidency.

His administration focused on human rights, energy conservation, and global peace, including the Camp David Accords, which advanced peace between Egypt and Israel. The administration also had little to no corruption, saw no wars, brought awareness to climate change, required seatbelts in cars, and returned the Panama Canal to Panama.

After leaving office, Carter founded The Carter Center and became a tireless advocate for humanitarian causes, earning the Nobel Peace Prize in 2002 for his work fighting disease, promoting democracy, and monitoring elections worldwide. His efforts with Habitat for Humanity also underscored his commitment to improving lives through service.

Despite health challenges in his later years, he remained a symbol of integrity and hope.

Carter enjoyed 77 years of marriage with his wife and wrote numerous books about different subjects. On December 29, 2024, Carter passed away at 100 years old, the longest-living president in American history.

THE TAKEAWAY: Honor Jimmy Carter by serving those who need help.

276 OCTOBER 2 — Celebrate Gandhi and commit to nonviolence.

"First they ignore you, then they laugh at you, then they fight you, then you win."

— Mahatma Gandhi

On October 2, 1869, Mohandas Karamchand Gandhi was born. A lawyer by training, Gandhi promoted *satyagraha*, a philosophy of truth and nonviolence that was instrumental to India achieving independence from the British.

Gandhi led iconic movements such as the Dandi March (Salt March) in 1930 and the Quit India Movement in 1942.

He talked about simplicity, self-reliance, and tolerance, inspiring leaders such as Martin Luther King Jr. and Nelson Mandela.

October 2 is a national holiday in India, Gandhi Jayanti, and it is also the International Day of Nonviolence, promoting his vision of peace in a world full of never-ending violent conflicts.

On January 30, 1948, Nathuram Vinayak Godse assassinated Gandhi. Despite this assassination, Gandhi's principles remain timeless, reminding us that there are ways to achieve justice without resorting to violence.

THE TAKEAWAY: Celebrate Gandhi and commit to nonviolence.

OCTOBER 3 — Fight for freedom like Bhagat Singh Thind.

"The human mind is where everyone has to live and find his only opportunity for peace, happiness, and wholeness. Only the unified mind can see things whole."

–Bhagat S. Thind

Bhagat Singh Thind was born on this day in 1892.

Erika Lee in her excellent history book *The Making of Asian America* cited this primary source, "Hindus Too Brunette to Vote Here," an article from a 1923 issue of *The Literary Digest*. It details how Thind was a high-caste Hindu born in Punjab who entered the US in 1913, was drafted in WWI, and served for six months before being honorably discharged.

He applied for naturalization papers, and the judge decided in his favor. The case was appealed to the Circuit Court of Appeals, and then the Supreme Court, where it was rejected.

Ashwin Ramaswami, who ran for the senate in Georgia in 2024, writes for *Indiaspora* that he learned from Thind's son, David, that Dr. Thind's legacy goes beyond that single court case. He also cites many more South Asians in American history, such as Aaron Burr's mistress Mary Emmons, the 1920s-era Bengali Harlem, and the 1956 election of Dalip Singh Saund.

Long story short, Dr. Bhagat Singh Thind, and many more Indian-Americans, struggled for American citizenship, which was intricately linked with the Indian independence movement.

I wrote about making good trouble on the entry for July 17 (199).

THE TAKEAWAY: Fight for freedom like Bhagat Singh Thind.

278 OCTOBER 4 — Storyboard the entire user journey for your product.

"Build something 100 people love, not something 1 million people kind of like."

— Brian Chesky, Airbnb CEO

In an **interview** with Bloomberg's Emily Chang, Brian Chesky repeats an insight he also shared with Reid Hoffman on his podcast *Masters of Scale*. He talks about an early project he did called Snow White. Walt Disney was one of his heroes, Disney storyboarded the whole film before animating, and Brian also uses storyboards.

One approach is doing two storyboards, a "big picture" storyboard and a "close up." Let's say you want to help a pet owner in a small town who needs to find and schedule a dog walker. She is busy studying at night and cannot walk her dog. The user could be at work, picturing their sad dog at home, when they open the app and see smiling faces of dog walkers!

Now the user opens the app and books an appointment. The next morning, before taking the drive to work, a dog walker appears! Now the user sets the appointment as recurring daily.

That's big picture, focusing on "how" and "why" this dog walking app should exist.

The second storyboard is close up on the "what," such as:
1. Open the app from home screen.
2. Enter username and password.
3. Tap calendar.
4. Pick a day and time that works.
5. Repeat this weekly, yes or no?
6. Checkout confirmation window.
7. Done! Show more happy dogs and walkers.
8. User is emailed confirmation and receipt.

THE TAKEAWAY: Storyboard the entire user journey for your product.

OCTOBER 5 — Be compassionate with others but strict with yourself.

In 2021, Facebook, Instagram, and WhatsApp all went down for six hours. How did that make you feel? Disconnected? Insecure? Is Meta your "social cloud" of sorts?

According to Chris Nodder's book *Evil by Design*, Mark Zuckerberg runs an evil firm, exploiting his platform's user data to cause conflict, or engagement, and of course, there was the Cambridge-Analytica scandal. **(10. January 10)**

Reader, I am compassionate with others about social media, as I am for those who smoke and drink.

But I am strict with myself. I have been so much happier as a result of my self-imposed limits on using it.

THE TAKEAWAY: Be compassionate with others but strict with yourself.

OCTOBER 6 — Make sure your smartphone is secure.

"We become what we behold. We shape our tools, and thereafter our tools shape us."

— Marshall McLuhan

The smartphone does a number of things, replacing at least 10 or 20 different devices people once used. For example:

- camera
- alarm clock
- calendar
- stream video
- mobile games
- train tickets, subway cards, boarding passes
- credit cards
- MP3 players, podcasts
- books
- calls and texts
- GPS
- notebook and planner
- newspapers and magazines
- flashlight
- TV remote
- word processor
- morning weather
- and much more

Even now I am dictating this document to my iPhone 6 using Google Docs. Voice recorders used to be dedicated devices. I remember my Armitron electronic watch. G Shock watches were a thing for a while, but now smartwatches are a second phone screen.

Smartphones now shape a lot of our personal and professional lives.

This means it is all the more important to use two-factor authentication, strong passwords, and limit app permissions on personal information to maintain security and privacy on the Internet. Because of this, we must now make sure these devices are physically and technically secure. Bad things could happen if your personal phone fell into the wrong hands.

THE TAKEAWAY: **Make sure your smartphone is secure.**

OCTOBER 7 — Embrace the social part of your nature.

"Man is by nature a social animal; an individual who is unsocial naturally and not accidentally is either beneath our notice or more than human."

— Aristotle, *Politics*

On this day a few years back, I enjoyed walking and talking with my father all morning. I then headed to The Players in New York. I used to work there, but now I am a member.

Although we were still in a pandemic at that point, The Players club was still open, with members living their nature. Interacting, moving from the library to The Grill to The Booth Room, to the bar, and so on. I really do like being a member, it's a cool place.

The pandemic made it hard to connect with people in person, which is a problem because humans are social creatures who want to be around other people.

In the past I sometimes chose to ignore seeing friends in person and instead would go home to play video games, read books, or watch TV, most of which I did by myself.

I made this choice because I found pleasure in those activities, but I also went against my own human nature. Socializing is part of being human.

THE TAKEAWAY: Embrace the social part of your nature.

OCTOBER 8 — Make your country enforce international ecological law.

"I want you to act as if the house is on fire, because it is."

— Greta Thunberg

Protecting the environment today would basically involve international ecological laws.

We can quarantine polluters and forbid shipments internationally if the goods are produced under conditions that pollute or damage the natural places where humans and animals live.

I love Coca-Cola. But I hate destroying the planet when I open a bottle to drink it.

According to Reuters, in February 2022, eight in ten American adults support government policies to reduce single-use plastic. Coca-Cola, PepsiCo, and other international brands also called for a global pact to cut plastic production, a key growth area for the oil industry.

The human body is about 70 percent water, and it's not like people can control their thirst. That means it is up to beverage makers to take responsibility for the waste they produce when they sell drinks.

In June 2023, Forbes estimated wealthy countries owe $192 trillion for CO2 emission to poor countries; $80 trillion is how much the US specifically could be liable to pay over 25 years.

If the US, Canada, Europe, Australia, Saudi Arabia, and UAE are filling the atmosphere with dangerous gases, humans cannot breathe, and these countries owe something to me, you, and many other nations.

As a global citizen, I demand compensation for my future being stolen. A world full of trash is not good.

THE TAKEAWAY: **Make your country enforce international ecological law.**

OCTOBER 9 — Embrace the disease of film.

"Film is a disease," Frank Capra said. "When it infects your bloodstream... when it takes over as the number-one hormone, it plays Iago to your psyche. The antidote to film is more film."

— Martin Scorsese

The *Taxi Driver* script, written by Paul Schrader, quotes Thomas Wolfe's essay "God's Lonely Man" before going into a description of Travis Bickle.

"The whole conviction of my life now rests upon the belief that loneliness, far from being a rare and curious phenomenon, is the central and inevitable fact of human existence."

Hugo, written by John Logan, based on the book by Brian Selznick, was written decades later and describes how great the movies are. The character cites Tom Mix, Lon Chaney, and Douglas Fairbanks. *Hugo* even imitates movie sword fighting when he is with his friend Isabelle. Seeing a movie is like seeing dreams in the middle of the day.

To paraphrase Oh Dae-su in Park Chan-wook's *Oldboy* (2003), a man can see the TV as his:
- church,
- friend,
- teacher,
- lover, and more.

In high school, I saw *Taxi Driver* on my laptop in my parent's basement. Little did I know, I would catch "film disease." **Deadline** quoted Scorsese as saying he considers himself a teacher more than a filmmaker.

He feels pride that he has influenced people not only with his work but also with his recommendations of past films or film artists that inspire new works of art.

THE TAKEAWAY: Embrace the disease of film.

OCTOBER 10 — Diagnose the problem correctly; then you can cure it.

"A wrong answer to the right problem can be repaired and salvaged. But the right answer to the wrong problem, that's very difficult to fix, if only because it's so difficult to diagnose."

— Peter Drucker

In ancient times, information and education was only for rich or high-caste people, but now, with digital technology, information is about almost *anything* and is freely available on the Internet.

So, it is likely there is someone out there who is willing to say yes to you, *if* you present the right answer to the right problem.

To get to the right answer, the first step is to establish a theory, then test the theory. Once the theory can define the problem correctly, the correct solution can be found.

If you misunderstand or misidentify the problem, even the "perfect" solution may fail because it addresses something irrelevant to the problem.

On the other hand, a wrong solution to the correctly identified problem can often be adjusted, refined, or rebuilt because the core understanding is sound.

Diagnosing the problem correctly is a critical skill. It sometimes requires taking a few tries to get it right.

THE TAKEAWAY: Diagnose the problem correctly; then you can cure it.

OCTOBER 11 — **Once the problem is clearly defined, the decision is easy.**

> *"If I had an hour to solve a problem I'd spend 55 minutes thinking about the problem and 5 minutes thinking about solutions."*
>
> — Albert Einstein

Effective decision-making often involves asking questions such as:
1. What do I focus on?
2. What meaning do I assign to what I see?
3. Now that I know all that, what do I do moving forward?

If someone was rushed to the hospital, in the time before diagnosis, the symptoms can be overwhelming, painful and confusing. But once the problem is named — say, appendicitis — the decision to go to surgery becomes straightforward.

If a person is torn about whether to stay in a relationship or not, they might consider trying to clearly identify the problem. Perhaps they realize they don't feel respected, and so the decision to leave, or seek serious change in the relationship, becomes much more obvious.

Design people like to say, "Fall in love with the problem, not the solution." It might take 55 minutes to define the problem — like "users can't find the checkout button" — but the design fix takes five minutes.

When a problem is fuzzy, you're wrestling more with uncertainty than with an actual choice. Once the issue is defined, it's like shining a light in a dark room and seeing the obvious path.

THE TAKEAWAY: Once the problem is clearly defined, the decision is easy.

OCTOBER 12 — Document the details of your travels.

"When you are rich, people treat you with respect."

— Anthony Horowitz

INT. LUFTHANSA LOUNGE (IAD) WASHINGTON, DC, 3:37 PM EST

My brother Aman and I ate in the lounge and waited for the flight to Egypt via Frankfurt.

INT. LUFTHANSA LOUNGE (FRA) FRANKFURT, GERMANY 8:47 AM CEST

I say, "The Lufthansa lounge in Frankfurt has better food than DC." Aman agrees.

INT. CAIRO AIRPORT (CAI) CAIRO, EGYPT, 2:30 PM EEST

Aman mentioned his Mexico trip from 10 days prior when we landed in Cairo, causing Egyptian airport staff to force him into tests for disease. They were afraid of COVID-19 and South American diseases.

It ended up working out. Aman told the English-speaking guy, Usama, that we were staying at the Sheraton, then Kempinski, two high-end hotels in Cairo.

Whenever Usama moved Aman around the airport to get tested or talk to someone, I loyally followed. Aman thinks Usama liked that.

Usama started treating us well. He linked us with this Egyptologist named Adam, who planned to meet us at our hotel and present us with private tour packages to Imhotep's Djoser Pyramid, Sphinx, Giza, Saqqara, Alexandria, and more, at a discount!

EXT. RESTAURANT ALONG NILE RIVER, CAIRO, EGYPT, 8:43 PM EEST

Aman and I bought dinner at a place by the Nile near our hotel. We talked a lot about how wealthy travelers tend to get treated better.

THE TAKEAWAY: Document the details of your travels.

OCTOBER 13 — **Understand The Ankh, Egyptian key of eternal life.**

"The ankh symbol—sometimes referred to as the key of life or the key of the Nile—is representative of eternal life in Ancient Egypt. Created by Africans long ago, the ankh is said to be the first—or original—cross."

— National Park Service

The "Ankh," or key of eternal life, hung around Adam's neck when we were in Egypt on this date. I shared with Adam that I saw it as Monster Reborn in Yu-Gi-Oh, and that in Hindi, "ankh" is "eye." He said Ankh is often referred to as "the original cross." Round female aspects, with pointed male aspects.

We did a lot of exploration on this date. Sakkara. Giza. Camels. Sphinx. I took many pictures and videos. Being in Egypt, I felt like a "monster reborn" to be honest, exploring these tombs with my brother and Adam.

THE TAKEAWAY: **Understand The Ankh, Egyptian key of eternal life.**

OCTOBER 14 — You cannot think well on an empty stomach.

"One cannot think well, love well, sleep well, if one has not dined well."

— Virginia Woolf

Adam and Shareef, our driver, took Aman and me to Alexandria, Egypt, on this date.

I was having negative thoughts about:
- How gray my hair was at 25.
- One day writing a book about lessons I had learned so far.
- All my screenplay drafts going nowhere.
- Envy of people getting married, becoming parents, buying homes.
- Going back to work when I got back from Egypt.

If you ever have thoughts like this consuming you, try to focus on something else around you.

Life is not a tragedy, or a comedy. It is a gift.

Envy is simply telling you the areas of life you need to work on. Like dating. Or exercise. Or traveling and seeing more of the world. You might also just be hungry. Adam and Shareef went to get us local Namoura Cake, aka "Harissa," a Middle Eastern sweet made with flour and sweet syrup. But first, SHAWARMA! It resembled a very thin burrito, and it was delicious.

Aman said something important I felt I had to write down when I shared what thoughts I was having. He said, *"The only person putting pressure on you to do more is you. The world is not on your shoulders. It is indifferent. People think mostly about themselves, not about you."*

Maybe it's what he said, or the food, but I felt better afterwards.

THE TAKEAWAY: You cannot think well on an empty stomach.

OCTOBER 15 — Give others a tour of something you love.

"Denial ain't just a river in Egypt."
— Mark Twain

I had two incredible tour guides when I went to Egypt: Randa Abdel Wahab, who is incredibly knowledgeable about Egypt, and Adam (**@adamzetours**), who liked The Undertaker, the WWE wrestler.

Adam said that Egyptians are obsessed with death. It makes sense—many pharaohs, many tombs. Like cotton, tourism is a big part of the Egyptian economy. People want to see the beautiful Nile River, like they read about in books. They want to touch the fragile, translucent rock called alabaster.

Randa and Adam design their work, their tours, to their love of Egyptology. Randa said she was in med school, hated it, then shifted to her passion of Egyptology. Her daughter is also interested in Egyptology. Randa and Adam have been doing these tours for a very long time and they love it.

My brother Aman and I really enjoyed having such passionate, fun-loving tour guides on our trip to Egypt. Wherever I go next, I have to get a passionate tour guide. A good guide makes a big difference on any tour you take in the world.

You can learn a lot on the Internet, sure. But it is one thing to read about Egypt, and another to go there and experience it from people who truly love Egypt and want others to love it too.

THE TAKEAWAY: Give others a tour of something you love.

290 OCTOBER 16 — Treat your team better than Hollywood treats assistants.

"There are a thousand Evelyns out there who are being terribly underpaid and all of them can destroy every secret we have in Hollywood."

— Craig Mazin, Scriptnotes episode 422

An agency assistant like Evelyn takes home about $1,900 a month, or about $22,800 a year.

When Craig Mazin moved to LA in 1992, his first job paid $20,000 a year. Evelyn is getting about what Craig was making in 1992. But in 2019, that salary is far less survivable.

Executive assistants play an important part in the American entertainment industry, and beyond. These underpaid assistants know phone numbers, addresses, credit card numbers, Social Security numbers, the gate code to the house, the code to the door alarm.

They see financial statements. They handle confidential documents and scripts. Why are they overworked and underpaid? They could ruin careers by revealing every secret they know.

Entertainment company CEOs make a lot of money, as do SVPs. Assistants should get more.

Listening to this podcast reminded me of interviews I had at companies such as United Talent Agency, or Gersh, and how I am sort of happy I did not end up like Evelyn. Working in a place where you resent how little you get paid, and how much more the bosses get paid, does not sound like fun.

From the 2021 #PayUpHollywood Survey, which was to support staffers hit by the pandemic, to the 2023 strikes, Hollywood seems to be in desperate need of troubleshooting.

THE TAKEAWAY: **Treat your team better than Hollywood treats assistants.**

OCTOBER 17 — Try following the four broad stages of Vedic life.

> *"The law laid down in the Vedic lore (tradition) is beneficial, as it prescribes the respective duties of the four stages of life."*
>
> — Chanakya, ancient philosopher, jurist, and royal advisor.

In his book *Chanakya in Daily Life*, Dr. Radhakrishnan Pillai points out how the Indian Vedas had "a broad vision for life."

From birth until death, the Vedas gave humanity a systematic way to lead a good life.
1. *Student life (Brahmacharya-ashram)*
2. *Householder's life (Grihasta-ashram)*
3. *Retired (Vanaprastha-ashram)*
4. *Monk (Sannyasa—ashram)*

In the *Arthashatra*, Chanakya divided life into these four phases so people alive today can troubleshoot life, with clear guidelines for a fulfilling life.

Imagine the life of a raging, ambitious Hollywood agent. It could be profitable, but short.

Now imagine the life of a peaceful hermit, which could be long, but not very profitable.

The Indian tradition derived its wisdom from experiments carried out across generations so the future generations can make informed choices.

It can help to study the Vedas, its four stages, when trying to lead a life of prosperity.

THE TAKEAWAY: Try following the four broad stages of Vedic life.

OCTOBER 18 — Practice exercise and work routines, and find your legs.

"Take the day. Put together your personal things. Talk to your co-workers. Tomorrow, go out and get some exercise. Go for a jog. Give yourself routines and pretty soon you'll find your legs."

— Ryan Bingham

In Jason Reitman's *Up in the Air*, Ryan Bingham (George Clooney) speaks to Steve (Zach Galifinakis) after he gets laid off:

Ryan acts quite friendly to Steve to his face. But we soon discover this is his job as a professional "downsizer." Ryan is nice to Steve as he talks to him, and takes his keycard, and nice as Steve walks out. But Ryan knows he will never speak to Steve again after this.

When I got laid off, like Steve I felt like the world had just ended.

I am sure the hundreds of thousands of people who were laid off in 2023 and 2024 found it hard to get out of bed, let alone out of the house, to exercise or see friends or find a new job, especially if you were laid off from a job you really liked and your coworkers felt like family.

It is hard to let all that go and then look toward upward spirals instead of downward spirals. **(362. December 27)** But it is possible. There is still another team out there who does not yet know they need you.

There are more exercise or work routines out there, waiting for you to discover them.

THE TAKEAWAY: Practice your exercise routines and work routines, and you'll find your legs.

OCTOBER 19 — Have good habits when caring for yourself and others.

"And since strong habit leads, and we are accustomed to employ desire and aversion only to things which are not within the power of our will, we ought to oppose to this habit a contrary habit, and where there is great slipperiness in the appearances, there to oppose the habit of exercise."

–Epictetus' Discourses (Book 3 Chapter 12)

It's interesting how this ancient wisdom from Epictetus connects to taking care of family members. In *Chanakya in Daily Life*, Dr. Radhakrishnan Pillai cites Chanakya:

"The duties of a householder are: making gifts to dependents and eating what is left over (after the others have eaten)."

In a family, those who are capable of earning should take care of the rest who are not earning. There are members who earn money, and members who are too young or too old to be earning.

Those "dependents" are the elders whose working life is behind them, or children who are still in school. There could also be family members who have physical or mental disabilities.

It is easy to see taking care of family members as a burdensome habit. But it is better to take pride in taking care of your dependents.

Prioritizing your family members is a very good habit, as is prioritizing your party guests, roommates, and friends, before you partake of something desirable.

THE TAKEAWAY: Have good habits when caring for yourself and others.

294 OCTOBER 20 — Acknowledge when you got the prediction wrong.

"Apple flexing so hard about how they gave back ports that they took away is just poetry."

— Marques Brownlee Tweet Oct 18, 2021

Apple Support Tech Specs — MacBook Pro (Retina, 15-inch, Mid 2015)

Apple unveils MacBook Pro featuring M2 Pro and M2 Max — January 17, 2023 (image)

Reader, on October 18, 2021, even the mighty Apple admitted it was wrong. They also validated my choice back in January 2017 to buy the Mid 2015 MacBook Pro with all the beautiful ports, instead of the 2016 USB-C model that Apple called "the future."

Future of what? Dongles? USB-C is technically superior, yes. The EU forced the iPhone 15 and onward to support the now widely used port.

But ports such as HDMI, SD, and MagSafe are very useful. It is ridiculous, as Brownlee wrote, that Apple took away ports, sold a lot of dongles, then gave the ports back, and somehow people are happy with Apple about all of it.

THE TAKEAWAY: Acknowledge when you got the prediction wrong.

OCTOBER 21 — Build your own brand, not just "the platform."

"I made The Farewell for me, for my family, and for other immigrant children, or children of immigrants, who feel caught in between two worlds."

— Lulu Wang

In a Director's Roundtable by *The Hollywood Reporter,* Lulu Wang talks about getting an offer at Sundance from A24 for *The Farewell*, and a much larger offer from a large streaming platform. Her financier and producers really wanted the streaming deal. But she says taking that deal is more about building the platform brand, not Wang's brand.

> **An established filmmaker before digital already has a brand, and new streamers will want those older movies to build their brand. But newer filmmakers don't have a brand yet.**

Todd Phillips and Martin Scorsese agreed, a film such as *The Farewell* would get lost on streaming among a sea of other titles.

Wang likens her situation to the music business: an independent musician can put their music on iTunes or Spotify, but it is the established artists who get the lion's share of attention.

As an independent, aspiring artist, how can you build your own brand, not just the platform's brand? Perhaps you can use powerful platforms such as YouTube, Spotify, Meta, or LinkedIn, but at some point you probably need a website or brand that you own to drive your fans to, where you can sell your products without being beholden to any large platform.

THE TAKEAWAY: Build your own brand, not just "the platform."

OCTOBER 22 — Live in connection with your inner, deeper self.

"The past has no power over the present moment."
— Eckhart Tolle

On YouTube, **Eckhart Tolle** does an Inner-Body Awareness Practice:

He says without awareness, you have no choice. You "run on auto," pre-programming with conditioning that your mind has had since childhood. In a way, you are a walking program "asleep" to what is around you.

So as you become "aware," the element of choice comes in. It is good to believe that you have freedom to make your own choices. But Tolle says to look more deeply. It is not you, but your *conscious mind* that is making the choice. There is an intelligence even greater than the knowledge in your conscious mind.

Waking up from this "asleep walking program" is part of the process you are going through.

Perhaps once you face daily life again, you give in to the demands of those around you. In other words, you lose yourself to this asleep walking program once again.

This is something to avoid. To access the present moment, it is good to emphasize conscious breathing and sensory perception, to break free from compulsive thinking and connect with a deeper sense of self. By redirecting your attention from your negative thoughts to the present moment, you can cultivate a deeper sense of presence and universal intelligence.

THE TAKEAWAY: Live in connection with your inner, deeper self.

OCTOBER 23 — Cultivate the inner qualities money cannot buy.

In the *Meditations of Marcus Aurelius* translated by Gregory Hayes, he writes:

"Practice the virtues you can show: honesty, gravity, endurance, austerity, resignation, abstinence, patience, sincerity, moderation, seriousness, high-mindedness. Don't you see how much you have to offer—beyond excuses such as 'can't'?"

Which reminds me of wisdom from Chanakya in *Chanakya Neeti*, from Manoj Publications:

"The wise person should groom their children carefully to make them persons of high qualities and see them employed in productive work. Only the persons of learning and qualities find respect in the society."

Reader, there are so many things you have to offer this world that no amount of money can afford. It is so easy to blame our problems on our parents or friends or the place we grew up. But ultimately, before we go to sleep, we answer to ourselves and hope that God is listening.

I studied show business. Nobody is always truthful. Or dignified.

Sometimes, you scream, "I can't take it anymore" and you lash out verbally or violently, or both.

But you have more than rage within. There is honesty, curiosity, patience, sincerity, and more.

It is important to cultivate these qualities within yourself, and perhaps in your children.

THE TAKEAWAY: Cultivate the inner qualities money cannot buy.

OCTOBER 24 — Feel pride in your accomplishments, then move on.

"A man must not become vain upon doing charity, penance, gaining knowledge, cultivating politeness and on becoming worldly wise. Because this world is full of gems who excel in these fields and are far more accomplished. There is always one better."

— Chanakya Neeti

It has been nine weeks since I passed both CompTIA A+ exams, and I feel proud of myself, of course I do, but I am careful not to become vain and suddenly think I am master of the universe.

When I went to Temple University, I saw tech companies and cloud computing rise, but I was mostly focused on digital filmmaking. Sometimes movies are also called "flicks."

I spent four years in the "flix," now I am deeper in the "net." NET-flix. Netflix.

I started seeing terms in the news like "cord-cutting," and "cord never," and I noticed people spending many hours diving down "the information superhighway," owned by cellular networks such as AT&T, Comcast, Optimum, or Spectrum.

We now watch what we want on demand, and the Internet algorithms can serve us whatever it thinks we like with amazing accuracy. The CompTIA A+ only scratches the surface! There is still networking, cybersecurity, compliance, penetration testing, cloud computing, and artificial intelligence.

There is still much out there to learn and implement when building your empire. Now is not the time to get hung up on winning one battle in the war.

THE TAKEAWAY: Feel pride in your accomplishments, then move on.

OCTOBER 25 — Worry about necessary choices, not unnecessary ones.

"You have power over your mind—not outside events. Realize this, and you will find strength."

— Marcus Aurelius, *Meditations*

I do not drink alcohol often. I prefer Coca-Cola because it is delicious. Whatever drink you prefer, hard or soft, pleasure feels good. Comfort feels good.

Dopamine, Oxytocin, Serotonin, Endorphins—the whole DOSE feels good flowing in your body.

Unless you aim to impress another, or you have a medical condition, you should order whatever you like. Because at the end of the day, your drink choice is an unnecessary decision.

Does a surgeon make any unnecessary decisions? Of course not! Every choice a surgeon makes has a purpose. There is no need to waste movement or make unnecessary cuts that could put a patient's life at risk.

This principle applies to life and work as well: minimize your decision fatigue by focusing on your mind, which is in your control, and not the outside events.

> **THE TAKEAWAY: Worry about necessary choices, not unnecessary ones.**

300

OCTOBER 26 — Study the greats, especially those you do not know yet.

"There is more treasure in books than in all the pirates' loot on Treasure Island, and best of all, you can enjoy these riches every day of your life."

— Walt Disney

On this day in 2018, I purchased my very first book on Audible, *Who Is Michael Ovitz?* by Michael Ovitz.

I have a lot of memories of being dirt-poor in Los Angeles, but now I am feeling wealthy because I possess valuable knowledge in my book collection.

I love Ovitz's memoir of a real-life Ari Gold who did, among many things:

- Told Earvin "Magic" Johnson to read *The Wall Street Journal* every day and help him transform into a business mogul.
- Created *Rain Man,* which the lead actors privately called "two schmucks in a car," *Ghostbusters, Goodfellas, Jurassic Park,* the list of CAA movies goes on.
- In a town built on fantasy, always presented the image of wealth and success:
- Created talent agency powerhouse CAA (2016): Adam Fields tells a story about calling in a bomb scare when he was Marty Baum's assistant, to delay a plane for a producer on his way to Paris.
- Wrote the CAA creed: "You don't have one agent, you have five"—and, later, "ten," "fifty," "one hundred." But, as he put it, "signing clients and steering the agency really came down to the three of us, and, often, to me."

THE TAKEAWAY: Study the greats, especially those you do not know yet.

OCTOBER 27 — Look for conflicts to find something of interest.

"No conflict, no interest."

— John Doerr

As human beings, we seek conflict every day. Especially when we are bored and need something to do.

We seek stories filled with conflict in music, movies, and art.

In life, one might "wake up and choose violence." Because no conflict, no interest.

Ken Auletta talks to GaryVee, citing Michael Kassan for his "no conflict, no interest mentality."

Kassan is a power broker in the advertising industry. If there is a negotiation between a client, platform, and agency, Kassan is at that table, at times representing all three. You might ask, "Is that a conflict of interest?" but Kassan would say, "No conflict, no interest."

Michael Ovitz also describes this philosophy of "no conflict, no interest" in his memoir. If CAA poached a client, the client's old agency hated CAA. If a CAA movie went to Universal, the other movie studios hated CAA.

Ovitz describes "Agenting 101" as not representing two similar stars, because it is a conflict of interest, but instead he too preached, "No conflict, no interest." He mentions he had to unsign Arnold Schwarzenegger because Sylvester Stallone felt threatened, one of the few CAA clients who didn't buy the "no conflict, no interest" theory.

Conflict can be incredibly lucrative if you are on the right side of it.

THE TAKEAWAY: Look for conflicts to find something of interest.

302

OCTOBER 28 — Note how the mind and the tongue want different things.

"As Howard Moskowitz loves to say, 'The mind knows not what the tongue wants'."

— *Malcolm Gladwell*

On NPR, Gladwell described Howard Moskowitz as a psychophysicist. Howard's job is to measure things and find truths about human decision-making.

One of Howard's first clients was Pepsi. Pepsi wanted to discuss a new sweetener, aspartame, for Diet Pepsi. They wanted Howard to figure out the right amount per can.

Pepsi had a sweetness band between 8 and 12 percent. Anything below 8 percent is not sweet enough, anything above 12 percent is too sweet. Howard made experimental batches of Pepsi and had thousands of people drink the batches, while plotting their reactions on a curve. Then, Howard realized the data made no sense.

What Howard discovered when doing this for Pepsi was there is no one best Diet Pepsi. Some people want a very sweet Diet Pepsi, some don't like sweet. Pepsi didn't buy it, but Howard talked about this experiment obsessively and had a breakthrough with Prego.

In the 1980s, Prego was behind Ragu, the dominant spaghetti sauce. So they came to Howard, who made 45 varieties of spaghetti sauce: sweetness, level of garlic, tartness, sourness, "tomatoeyness," visible solids. Americans fall into one of three groups.
- plain
- spicy
- chunky

The third one was significant. In the 1980s, chunky spaghetti sauce did not exist. Howard fulfilled a need for chunky tomato sauce nobody in America knew their tongue wanted!

THE TAKEAWAY: Note how the mind and the tongue want different things.

OCTOBER 29 — Fleas can jump many times higher than elephants.

"Fleas can jump many times their own height, but not an elephant."

— Peter Drucker

Large firms have a hard time adapting quickly to change compared to smaller firms.

Airbnb CEO Brian Chesky spoke to this idea on the podcast *Masters of Scale*. In 2008, Barack Obama was running against John McCain. Chesky was at the Democratic National Convention with his co-founder, Joe Gebbia, testing out a PR campaign for Airbnb.

Brian and Joe saw the campaign coming up. They were thousands of dollars in credit card debt. Airbnb ("Air Bed and Breakfast") was not selling beds. So, they tried to sell breakfast.

They decided to create a Barack Obama-themed breakfast cereal: Obama O's, "The breakfast of change." John McCain was a captain in the Navy, and so they came up with Cap'n McCain's, like Cap'n Crunch: "A maverick in every bite."

They ended up making a thousand boxes of cereal and sold them for $40 a box.

$40,000 is great! But they had to physically make every cereal box. This meant printed poster board, folding it into shape, and applying hot glue. Brian says he burned himself a lot when making 1,000 boxes of cereal.

A large cereal company might not have jumped so fast to make 2008 campaign cereal boxes. Two co-founders can move much faster than multiple departments of a giant corporation.

THE TAKEAWAY: Fleas can jump many times higher than elephants.

OCTOBER 30 — Whether you think you can or can't, you're right.

"Whether you think you can, or you think you can't—you're right."

— Henry Ford

On this day in 2012 on Facebook, I posted goodbye spring break, hello all day trick or treating.

On this day in 2019, I worked a cashier gig at The Players.

In 2020, it was Per Scholas Staff Retreat Day, and I was missing The Players. This club in New York City founded by Edwin Booth has existed for over a hundred years. They built web traffic in a pandemic by digitizing the building and set up an Augmented or Virtual Reality tour. It could be members-only, like Kumospace, which does immersive virtual events.

I miss going and seeing people at The Players, but it is nice to see that someone made an immersive experience that is virtual. This person probably thought "meeting" people was impossible, until they overcame such "limiting beliefs" to create something like Kumospace.

As the Henry Ford quote implies, you are right whether you think you can or you can't do something. It is usually better to believe something is possible, even during an insane time like a pandemic.

THE TAKEAWAY: Whether you think you can or can't, you're right.

OCTOBER 31 — Be elusive among celebrities to grow your mystique.

"The more you leave out, the more you highlight what you leave in."

— Henry Green

In Connie Bruck's *When Hollywood Had a King*, Bruck writes about Jules Stein, the physician and businessman who co-founded Music Corporation of America (MCA). As a teenager he enrolled in summer school to finish school fast and get out of South Bend, Indiana.

While in summer school, he decided to promote Saturday night dances for the students of Winona Lake and the Indiana University summer school. He soon "negotiated" with colleges, saying that he would play in the college band in exchange for free tuition. Eventually, the University of West Virginia said yes. Stein got free tuition, books, and a job playing in the Swisher Theatre.

He saw a problem in college too: the students had trouble locating one another. So he bought ads and put out a student guide, with "Jules Caesar Stein" in huge letters. He later called that a mistake, and he never did anything "vulgar" like that again.

His anonymity would become a distinct feature of his business life.

After working and studying his way through medical school in Chicago, Stein was working for a well-regarded Chicago ophthalmologist when he realized he would not make enough money in medicine. So in 1924, Stein started MCA as a band-booking agency and hired Lew Wasserman, who also tended to be extremely secretive.

This story reminded me of a Naval Ravikant quote: "You want to be rich and anonymous, not poor and famous."

THE TAKEAWAY: Be elusive among celebrities to grow your mystique.

NOVEMBER

NOVEMBER 1 — Know what to sell, who to sell to, and when to sell it.

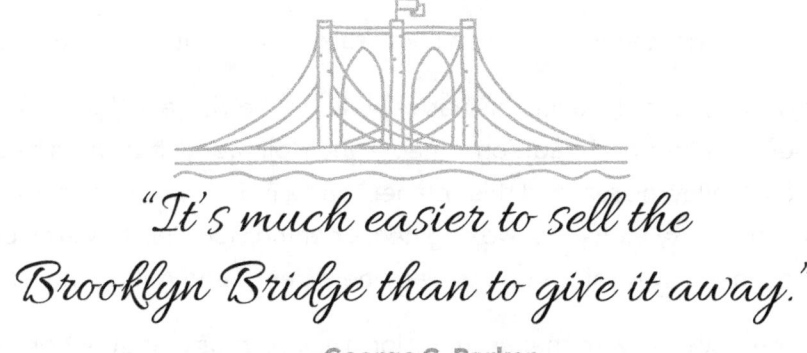

"It's much easier to sell the Brooklyn Bridge than to give it away."
— George C. Parker

In other words, giving a thing away for free is harder than selling the thing.

Nonprofits want the end user to be not only a user but also a doer who takes action. Per Scholas, for example, uses its training services to get people to either enroll or donate to the cause of changing human beings through technical training.

Nonprofits used to think they didn't need marketing either, but you do need to market a free service without giving it away. Nobody trusts what they can get for free.

You have to know what to sell, who to sell it to, and when to sell it, because a potential learner is a different client than a potential donor.

I can sell a nonprofit like Per Scholas in at least four different ways.
1. To the learners and alumni, it can be sold as a place to get free technical training.
2. To Per Scholas staff members, it can be sold as a place where you can make an impact.
3. To an enterprise partner, it can be sold as a place to up-skill and re-skill existing staff.
4. To philanthropic partners, it can be sold as a way to help people from underserved communities who did not have the same educational opportunities as others have had in life.

THE TAKEAWAY: **Know what to sell, who to sell it to, and when to sell it.**

NOVEMBER 2 — Start by asking "why" and then keep going.

In a C-SPAN interview, journalist Brian Lamb talks to the writer Ken Auletta.

Lamb asks Auletta about leaving his native New York to visit another "planet," Silicon Valley. Auletta understood traditional media and Hollywood, but when he started spending time in Silicon Valley, he realized this "planet" had a much different set of values. He met Sergey Brin and Larry Page, the two engineers behind Google. They started from the assumption that "most of the way things operate are inefficient," and Auletta agreed.

When an engineer is empowered with that assumption, they start asking questions such as "Why can't we have free phone service? Why can't we digitize all 20 million books in print? Why can we put TV for free on YouTube? Why can't we sell ads much more cheaply?"

They could even make ads more efficient by only charging for clicks, which was untraditional.

These questions, Auletta points out, start to invade other people's business. Innovations such as AdSense or Google News certainly do invade advertising and the news business.

Auletta soon began to realize that at Google, the engineer is the content creator—the equivalent of a screenwriter or director because they create content for a screen such as Google search, or Google Maps, and so on.

It all starts by asking "why."

THE TAKEAWAY: Start by asking "why" and then keep going.

NOVEMBER 3 — Have helpful knowledge available at home and at work. 308

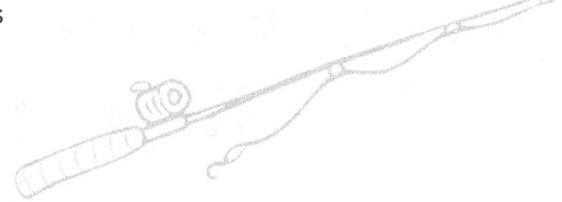

In *Chanakya in Daily Life*, Dr. Radhakrishnan Pillai writes about having knowledge handy at work and at home. Citing Chanakya Neeti, Dr. Pillai states, *"Knowledge is like a holy Kamadhenu cow. It bears fruit in all seasons. In foreign lands it protects and rewards."*

As the saying goes, give a man a fish, he eats for a day. Teach a man to fish, he eats for a lifetime.

Kamadhenu is a sacred cow mentioned in the Indian scriptures that can grant wishes and bring prosperity. Anyone who has such a cow might consider it a built-in secret treasure, or a gift that keeps on giving.

Knowledge can do the same. A person who has gathered lots of useful knowledge at home or at work will find that their knowledge can also bear fruit in all seasons. Perhaps it is your physical book collection, your digital library, your web browser bookmarks. A strong knowledge base you can refer to, especially when you really need it, can be so helpful.

Dr. Radhakrishnan Pillai says his collection of 5,000 books has grown over time. How big is your collection?

THE TAKEAWAY: Have helpful knowledge available at home and at work.

NOVEMBER 4 — Make a future budget to fund the money makers.

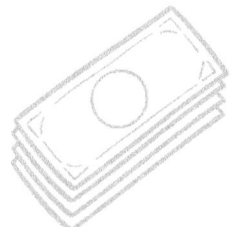

*"If you want creativity, take a zero off your budget.
If you want sustainability, take off two zeros."*

— Jaime Lerner, former mayor of Curitiba, Brazil

In good times, the future budget is high, and expenses go up across the board. In bad times, the future budget is low, and expenses are cut across the board.

The first budget is an operating budget with variable operating expenses and fixed capital expenses, to maintain the present business. That budget should be, at minimum, what needs to be spent to keep operations going. In lean times, this budget should be cut.

There should also be a second, separate budget for experimental money makers, the maximum funding that these new activities need to produce meaningful results.

This principle can also apply to your budget of time. Spending time on activities you need to do to keep operations going is important, but setting aside time to experiment is also important.

When Google went public in 2004, they famously encouraged employees to spend 20% of their time working on other projects outside their regular projects. Significant innovations such as AdSense and Google News came out of this 20% time in which Googlers were experimenting.

THE TAKEAWAY: Make a future budget to fund the money makers.

NOVEMBER 5 — Turn a mountain of data into useful information.

"Data is not information, information is not knowledge, knowledge is not understanding, understanding is not wisdom."

— Clifford Stoll, writer and astronomer

Raw data, by itself, is often overwhelming and lacks meaning until we get to process it and reflect on it.

Consider cybersecurity. In that field, gathering and processing threat intelligence comes in the form of raw data, and narrative reports from security companies such as McAfee, Mandiant (now a subsidiary of Google), Cloudflare, and more.

You have to turn the many sources of "data" into useful "information."

Perhaps you do not work or study cybersecurity, but you do have lots of data at your fingertips that you need to analyze to make more informed decisions.

Oftentimes, you need to decide what "data" to ignore and what "information" to use.

THE TAKEAWAY: Turn a mountain of data into useful information.

311   NOVEMBER 6 — Your technology must support your love story.

James Cameron did an interview with **Charlie Rose in 1997** about the making of *Titanic*.

Rose asked Cameron to explain the overwhelming challenge of making a movie about a giant ship that is sinking into the ocean.

Cameron says the ship was indeed huge, and it took a long time just to deal with making it measure up accordingly to movie audiences. Months and months of engineering. Figuring out angles of the sets. How and when to use visual effects. Safety requirements and protocols. Making sure thousands of amps of electricity do not go into a salt water set, and keeping hundreds of people around it safe while working.

But when Rose asks what the toughest challenge was, Cameron says it is the chemistry of the love story. All the other stuff doesn't count if Jack and Rose, the leads, have no chemistry.

The love story is good. But to me, the real love story behind the love story is James Cameron's love of diving and shipwrecks. He said he went down 12 times to see the actual Titanic ship, and he put Jack and Rose on the ship to make the audience care about the tragedy.

And believe me, we did.

The technology of the ship, the story of the budget ballooning—that is all secondary. What really matters are the characters, their choices, and the chemistry of the love story.

THE TAKEAWAY: **Your technology must support your love story.**

NOVEMBER 7 — Find your leverage.

"Give me a lever long enough and a place to stand, and I will move the earth"

— Archimedes

According to Archimedes, with a big enough lever and a stable fulcrum, even the impossible can become possible.

In life, leverage is all about using limited resources efficiently to make a job easier and get better results. You can leverage time by focusing on important tasks first. By spending time on tasks that yield the biggest results, you can get more done with less time spent. You can also leverage time by batching tasks, such as sending all your emails in one go as opposed to throughout the day, saving time and energy by not repeatedly starting and stopping.

Financial leverage could be a company taking out a loan to expand into a new market, or expecting the new revenue to be greater than the interest paid on the loan.

Businesses with higher fixed costs and lower variable costs, such as software companies, can achieve operational leverage. Revenue and profits can scale up significantly, and since many of the costs are fixed and do not scale up, the company gets a higher margin of profit for each additional unit sold.

You can leverage intelligence as well. Businesses often hire consultants or experts instead of learning everything in-house, leveraging external expertise and not reinventing the wheel. You can often solve problems more efficiently by relying on another person's expertise instead of using resources to build up that expertise yourself.

THE TAKEAWAY: **Find your leverage.**

NOVEMBER 8 — Play your part.

"Remember that you are an actor in a drama, of such a kind as the author pleases to make it. If short, of a short one; if long, of a long one. If it is his pleasure you should act a poor man, a cripple, a governor, or a private person, see that you act it naturally. For this is your business, to act well the character assigned you; to choose it is another's."

–From *The Enchiridion*, by Epictetus, *The Internet Classics Archive*

We are all actors in a divine play. You get a role assigned to you, then you play it until you are assigned a new role. You play a role with your family, your friends, and your colleagues.

If it pleases the author, your role may be short or long. Perhaps you will act poor, or crippled, or just act normally. Whatever your character is, Epictetus says you should act it out naturally.

You also should not resent others for playing their parts. A mother plays her part. A father plays his part. A sibling plays their part, and so on. Any time you are being challenged by another human being, remind yourself that they are trying to do their job, as you are trying to do yours.

THE TAKEAWAY: Play your part.

NOVEMBER 9 — Set goals, discuss with team, review, and repeat.

In *Chanakya in Daily Life*, Dr. Radhakrishnan Pillai writes about goal setting, citing a formula used by Chanakya that is still being used by organizations today: *"He should check the accounts for each day, group of five days (weekly), fortnight, month, four months, and a year."*

Productive people do tend to set goals for the day, the week, the month, the quarter, and the year. It is important to review these goals regularly and keep track of any progress or setbacks.

As a Per Scholas instructor, I deliver curriculums of 15 weeks, such as AWS or CompTIA A+.

Each day I set a daily goal of completing a few lessons and lab scenarios. Eventually, perhaps after a week or two, a module is completed.

After one module ends, another begins, and I guide the class into the next part, until all the modules are complete. When the time comes and all lessons are complete, students prep for the certification exam. Along the way, I work with my teammates to set goals, discuss progress, and repeat.

Sometimes this process feels automatic, and goal setting feels very natural in the flow of working with my teammates. Other times, it can be a drag, but the process is still important.

THE TAKEAWAY: **Set goals, discuss with team, review, and repeat.**

NOVEMBER 10 — Prepare for the future by investigating the past.

"Those who cannot remember the past are condemned to repeat it."

— George Santayana

The products, services, markets, and technologies that we saw in the past will probably not be the same products, services, markets, and technologies of tomorrow.

For example, the film industry of 1923 is very different from the film industry of 2023. The same can be said for music or books.

It is a bit of a balancing act, studying the past, living in the present, and building for the future.

But the rewards are there for those who can do it. People who understand history can avoid the mistakes of their predecessors, which is especially important in fields like politics or business, or even in personal growth.

It is a gift to have a good memory, or someone in your life who has a good memory, so you can do better in the present day.

THE TAKEAWAY: Prepare for the future by investigating the past.

NOVEMBER 11 — Practice digital discipline.

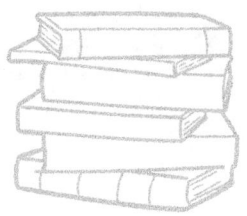

In *Chanakya in Daily Life*, Dr. Radhakrishnan Pillai writes, "A family that prays together, stays together."

When religion was a daily evening practice, it strengthened the bonds among family members. Unfortunately, evenings are now phone-scrolling time or TV time, not family time.

This is not all bad. Technology connects us with friends and family around the world. It used to be expensive to connect with people across the world, but not anymore, thanks to the Internet.

Abundance, however, creates a new problem. In an interconnected world where so much is at your fingertips, digital discipline is required to stop watching TV or using smartphones.

Digital discipline can be built simply by reading some wisdom. There is wisdom found in philosophy, in religious texts such as *The Bible* or *Bhagwad Gita*, and of course, on the Internet.

Studies have found Millennials to be the least religious generation in American history, but without being religious or dogmatic, a person can still find wisdom in religious texts the way Chanakya did.

Even one small page of wisdom a day can compound over a lifetime, but it does require some digital discipline to find wisdom and actually follow it.

THE TAKEAWAY: Practice digital discipline.

NOVEMBER 12 — Do not let the house divide against itself.

"If a house is divided against itself, that house cannot stand."

— Mark 3:25, *The Bible*

An organization is effective because it concentrates on one task, whether it is related to society, community, or family. The entire organization has to deal with whatever problem arises that affects it.

If any of these organizations start to splinter into too many branches, the root of the tree may suffer and be destroyed. This is true of businesses, unions, schools, hospitals, churches, and so on.

An organization must be single-minded in their pursuit to be truly effective.

THE TAKEAWAY: Do not let the house divide against itself.

NOVEMBER 13 — Get busy living, or get busy dying.

"Sometimes even to live is an act of courage."

— Lucius Annaeus Seneca, Letters to Lucilius

On the Google Chrome store, there is an extension called "Death Clock," which sounds morbid but is supposed to be motivational. You put in your age and it counts down to your death based on average life expectancy.

I first used it when I was 23. It was a good reminder to not spend my remaining 50 years of life entertaining myself pointlessly on the Internet.

As Seneca wrote in his essay *On the Shortness of Life*, "The life we receive is not short, but we make it so by being wasteful, and not controlling what we do with the time we have left."

We are very good at guarding our physical bodies against threats, but we are not as good at guarding our time from outside forces that seek to waste it for us.

THE TAKEAWAY: **Get busy living, or get busy dying.**

319

NOVEMBER 14 — Pay penance to acquire divine weapons.

The *Mahabharata* is an ancient Hindu epic narrated by Vyasa and transcribed by Ganesha, the god of wisdom.

The epic centers around the Kurukshetra War between two groups of cousins and is full of philosophy and devotional material that scholars have been studying for many years, notably the section known as the *Bhagavad Gita*.

For me, one of the most interesting sections is the quest for divine weapons. During exile, Arjuna performs intense penance (*tapasya*) to acquire weapons from gods. There is even a real-world connection between Arjuna's penance and J. Robert Oppenheimer, the father of the atomic bomb. Oppenheimer was deeply influenced by the *Bhagavad Gita* and the dilemma Arjuna faces in using his divine weapons in the war on his own family.

Just as Arjuna performed spiritual *tapasya* in pursuit of celestial weapons, Oppenheimer pursued scientific knowledge in pursuit of the atomic bomb, a "divine" weapon with unprecedented power that completely changed the outcome of World War II. Both of these men knew that these weapons, if achieved, would lead to immense destruction.

After the bomb's successful test, Oppenheimer famously quoted a line from the Bhagavad Gita: "Now I am become Death, the destroyer of worlds," reflecting Arjuna's own moral conflict about using the weapons.

In both these cases, we see a journey that involves acquiring divine power through dedicated pursuit and facing ethical questions about using this power to end a war and fulfill a duty.

THE TAKEAWAY: **Pay penance to acquire divine weapons.**

NOVEMBER 15 — Trust, but verify.

"Trust, but verify."

—English translation of Russian proverb

In *Lies My Teacher Told Me*, James Loewen writes about bad US history textbooks. He wrote about how textbooks failed to blame the US government for its opposition to the civil rights movement. He says many textbooks actually give credit to the federal government for the advances made during this period. He calls it "the Hollywood approach" to civil rights.

Loewen cites Alan Parker's Mississippi Burning (1988), which concocts two fictional white FBI agents who play "good cop/bad cop" to solve a murder in 1964.

The real story involved supporters of the civil rights movement, Michael Schwerner's widow Rita, and every white northern friend available, to pressure Congress and the executive branch of the federal government to force the FBI to open a Mississippi office and make bringing the murderers to justice a priority.

A similar story is found with David Grann's *Killers of the Flower Moon: The Osage Murders and the Birth of the FBI*. The book largely follows FBI agent Tom White's perspective, to offer readers more insight into the investigation and the FBI's origins. It was later adapted into a film directed by Martin Scorsese.

The takeaway here is to research the past yourself using primary historical sources. Using reprinted textbooks with a "Hollywood approach" may not always yield accurate results, at least for "factivists."

Trust your teachers and textbook, but also verify for yourself.

THE TAKEAWAY: Trust, but verify.

321
NOVEMBER 16 — Actively learn from those you deeply admire.

James Cameron is incredibly fascinating to me because he explores unknown aspects of oceans outside of filmmaking. He cites explorers Lewis and Clark in an interview he gave to PopMech;—perhaps they inspired him.

From New York, Martin Scorsese and Spike Lee are also interesting filmmakers. Lee and Scorsese made *Clockers* (1995) together a few years after *Goodfellas* was released. The film originally entered production with Martin Scorsese attached to direct, after having collaborated with Price on The Color of Money (1986), but he dropped out to make *Casino* (1995). Spike Lee stepped in to rewrite and direct the Price script. Scorsese remained a co-producer.

As Mark T. Conrad writes in *The Philosophy of Spike Lee* about *Clockers*, "Headlines in newspapers report murders committed by children with guns, video games in which violence is carried out in electronic landscapes, and graffiti whose cartooning quality is emphasized.

> **Conrad points out how the title credits resemble a cartoon, and so does the movie poster. "Clockers" comes from right to left across the screen in childish red and yellow letters.**

The movie poster itself resembles an old Flash game called "Beat Me Up" that I used to play online. The film raises the tragic question of how, and why, red blood from black bodies stains streets. (65. March 5)

It is a question we are still dealing with, unfortunately, that must be solved. It is cool that a director I admire, Spike, learned from Marty, another artist I admire.

THE TAKEAWAY: **Actively learn from those you deeply admire.**

NOVEMBER 17 — Communicate simply.

> *"There's no such thing as simple. Simple is hard."*
> — Martin Scorsese

People often think simple is quick or easy, but it is actually a lengthy process to get down to the most refined, essential version of something.

Simple can actually be incredibly difficult to achieve. Especially when it comes to creative endeavors such as filmmaking, writing, design, or problem-solving.

Achieving simplicity often requires a deep understanding of a subject, an iterative process of getting better over years, and the ability to strip away the unnecessary without losing the core.

If you can explain something to someone else in a simple way, it demonstrates mastery of a subject. It is not about cutting corners or dumbing things down, but about working to reveal the best of what matters most.

THE TAKEAWAY: **Communicate simply.**

323   NOVEMBER 18 — Make your thoughts solid.

"Prayer is only another name for good, clean, direct thinking. When you pray, think well what you are saying, and make your thoughts into things that are solid. In that manner, your prayer will have strength, and that strength shall become part of you, mind, body, and spirit."

— *How Green Was My Valley*, directed by John Ford (1941), based on the Richard Llewellyn novel

People pray for all sorts of things, such as:
- Doing well in school
- Doing well at work
- Saving money to buy things
- Divine weapons

The passage at the top of this page has a profound perspective on praying. It suggests prayer is not simply about words or rituals, but having strong clarity and intent in one's thoughts.

Focused, purposeful thoughts can shape one's inner and outer realities. Thoughts can be envisioned as "solid" entities, capable of strength that one can find within to face the struggles that come with being alive.

This line resonates in context of the film and novel by telling the story of the Morgans, a hardworking Welsh mining family whose lives are shaped by faith, community, and resilience in the face of change.

THE TAKEAWAY: **Make your thoughts solid.**

NOVEMBER 19 — Manage yourself before managing others.

"The first and best victory is to conquer self. To be conquered by self is, of all things, the most shameful and vile."

— Plato

After a manager conquers themself, their first step is to set objectives, determine goals toward the objectives, and how to reach both the goals and the objectives. They can then organize the activities, decisions, and relationships needed to divide up jobs and get them done.

From there you can motivate and communicate, turning a group of strangers into a team. This team eventually establishes yardsticks to measure performance for the individual teammates and the team as a whole.

This manager is one I wouldn't mind reporting to. Nobody is perfect, but this person is able to manage themselves well enough to lead a team, and that is priceless.

We all have something to conquer within ourselves before we can better manage ourselves, let alone other people.

THE TAKEAWAY: Manage yourself before managing others.

NOVEMBER 20 — Use data-driven decision-making.

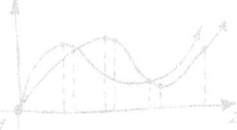

Advertising is here to stay, whether you like it or not. Even Netflix pivoted from being ad-free to embracing ad-supported, realizing their ad tier users make $8.50 more a month or more versus their ad-free users.

People are willing to pay less for streaming services and sit through a few ads. These ads may even be compelling, because the data can identify demographics, interests, behaviors, purchase history, and watch history.

If an ad is underperforming, advertisers can quickly change their targets, modify the message, or reallocate budgets for higher performing campaigns.

Basically, digital advertisers know a lot about you, what you like and don't like, and serve you product recommendations, personalized discounts, or custom messages accordingly. Which is upsetting for consumers who do not like ads and might even be using ad blockers.

But as a person running a business and trying to make decisions to market their products to potential customers, using data to drive those decisions can be very effective.

THE TAKEAWAY: **Use data-driven decision-making.**

NOVEMBER 21 — Stick to your circle of competence.

"I'm no genius. I'm smart in spots— but I stay around those spots."

— Thomas J Watson Sr., Founder of IBM

The investor Warren Buffett frequently emphasized sticking to your *circle of competence*, which is about only focusing on tasks or topics you genuinely know best.

Through life experience, study, or both, every human being has built up a knowledge base about *something* in the world. Some areas are easily understood by many. Other areas are not so easy to comprehend in a short period of time.

Shane Parrish, who wrote for *BusinessInsider* about this topic, mentions a restaurant as an easy business to understand: you get a space, set it up as a restaurant, hire employees, then serve food and drinks. From there, you just need to get enough customers to pay an appropriate price to cover all the operating expenses, then the rest is profit.

But microchips? Biotech? Far fewer people can understand, let alone explain those subjects, because they fall outside of their circle of competence.

The takeaway here is sticking to what you know and separating that from what you *think* you know. Doing that will greatly improve the odds of being successful in life and business.

THE TAKEAWAY: Stick to your circle of competence.

327

NOVEMBER 22 — Be ready to improvise.

"What's interesting about this scene to me is it's entirely different than what we had scripted."

— Todd Phillips

Sometimes you go to work with something you wrote and prepared, but then you have to toss it out the day of shooting.

In *The New York Times* video, **"Anatomy of a Scene,"** Todd Phillips describes the script he wrote: Arthur Fleck goes into a bathroom to hide his gun, wash off his makeup, and stare at himself like "what have I done." But when they got to set, Joaquin Phoenix and Todd were not feeling the scene anymore. They realized Arthur would not care to hide his gun just after having an intense, life-defining moment.

An hour of tossing around ideas went by before Todd pulled out his phone to play some music he just got from Hildur Gudnadottir, the composer of *Joker*. Joaquin started to dance to the music, as 250 people on the crew waited outside.

This was an amazing dance that defined the film, and it was all improvised.

THE TAKEAWAY: Be ready to improvise.

NOVEMBER 23 — Remember how the tortoise beat the hare.

Do you remember how the tortoise beat the hare in **Aesop's fable**?

This arrogant hare thought he was so fast that he took the turtle's challenge. Confident he would win, he took a nap halfway through the race. Then the tortoise, slow and steady, won the race.

Like the tortoise, a person can make progress slowly. With consistency and patience, they can eventually find success. Persistence and determination can make even impossible goals possible, regardless of what others say or do.

The hare underestimated the tortoise in the same way people may underestimate others based on appearance, skills, or past performance. Relying solely on talent does not always guarantee success.

THE TAKEAWAY: Remember how the tortoise beat the hare.

329

NOVEMBER 24 — Practice charity with a good heart.

There is a lesser-known story in the *Mahabharata*, one of the two major Sanskrit epics of ancient India that takes place after the Kurukshetra War.

King Yudhishthira performs a grand *yagna* (sacrifice) to atone for the war's toll on his family and kingdom, giving everyone riches beyond belief. During the ceremony, a half-golden mongoose appears, rolls around in the leftover offerings, then mocks Yudhishthira's charity, saying it pales in comparison to a true act of sacrifice he witnessed.

The mongoose tells of a poor family—husband, wife, son, and daughter-in-law—who found a little flour during a famine. As they prepared to eat, a starving stranger begged for food. Each family member gave up their portion to feed the stranger and died that very night.

The stranger, the god Dharma in disguise, blessed the family and took them to heaven. The mongoose then rolled in the crumbs of their bread, and half of his body turned to gold. Since then, the mongoose has searched for another act of charity as selfless as that of the family, hoping to turn fully golden. But King Yudhishthira's offerings were not it.

Around this time of year, people in the US and Canada celebrate Thanksgiving, a holiday focused on gratitude, family, feasting, and charity.

The mongoose story emphasizes the idea that true charity is not about how much you give to charity, but about how profound acts kindness and giving can be when done with sincerity and compassion, no matter the size of the charity.

THE TAKEAWAY: **Practice charity with a good heart.**

NOVEMBER 25 — Overnight success takes years.

"It doesn't matter how many times you fail. You only have to be right once and then everyone can tell you that you are an overnight success."

— Mark Cuban

As the quote illustrates, calling someone an "overnight success" usually overshadows the years of hard work, sacrifice, and persistence that precedes that person's success. When someone is recognized for their success it may seem sudden, but a lot of hard work that happened before that moment goes unseen.

Here is some of the hard work that goes unseen:
1. Skill development — Artists, athletes, or entrepreneurs spend years refining their craft before their big break.
2. Building relationships — It takes time to build trust, find the right mentors, or form partnerships that open doors.
3. Failure and lessons — Years spent trying and failing teach resilience, adaptability, and can yield innovations.
4. Incremental progress — Writing every day, pitching hundreds of ideas, rehearsing for hours, testing countless product versions until one clicks.
5. Compound interest — 77. March 17 — It is better to earn compound interest instead of paying it.

THE TAKEAWAY: Overnight success takes years.

331

NOVEMBER 26 — Consider different perspectives on "manliness."

"Nancy Lee, who received her PhD in Gender and Cultural Studies, wrote a paper titled "'Let's Hug It Out, Bitch!' The Negotiation of Hegemony and Homosociality Through Speech in HBO's *Entourage*."

In season 5, episode 5, "Tree Trippers" (2008), washed up Hollywood movie star Vincent Chase is hallucinating on magic mushrooms in Joshua Tree National Park with his entourage friends E, Drama, and Turtle. Vince is trying to decide whether he should risk his career comeback on a G-rated family film, *Benji*, or if he should pursue a more "credible" role as a fire fighter in *Smoke Jumpers*. At one point, Vince's brother Drama asks why Vince is so attached to *Smoke Jumpers*. Vince responds that it is because his best friend and manager, E, found the good script.

Vince wants to be good. He wants the entourage to be good. And he wants everyone to know that E makes Vince good.

Turtle sighs. "You and E really have something special, Vin." Vince looks directly at E and smiles. E smiles fondly back.

Nancy points out how none of the guys in this HBO show want to seem "gay" or "whipped."

But if you and I read this comedy scene, I would not fault you for thinking Vince has romantic feelings for E. After all, "manliness" has changed significantly since this episode aired on HBO.

I found Nancy's work to be interesting. I had no idea TV shows could be studied this way.

THE TAKEAWAY: Consider different perspectives on "manliness."

NOVEMBER 27 — "Writing" goes far beyond pen and paper.

Thanks to my iPhone's dictation feature, writing for me is now "talking to the page."

There is your basic page that you always start with, in Apple Pages, Google Docs, or Microsoft Word, the "default" for most people. There is the lawyer's favorite paper, yellow legal pads. There's doctor prescription paper, napkins in restaurants, marble notebooks, spiral notebooks.

Everyone can "choose their weapon," so to speak.

With smartphones and social networks like YouTube, Meta, and TikTok, speech is now as powerful as writing.

It is amazing how technology enables me and billions of others to create so much, so fast. There will never be an end to the production of digital media technology, which could be text or code or video or photos.

Of course, there is the challenge of copyright with artificial intelligence.

Sarah Silverman and other big-name authors are waging war against OpenAI and various other firms because the authors did not consent to the use of their copyrighted books as training material for the companies' AI large language models, or LLMs. We will see what happens.

THE TAKEAWAY: **"Writing" goes far beyond pen and paper.**

NOVEMBER 28 — Be regular in your life to create violently original work.

> *"Be regular and orderly in your life, so that you may be violent and original in your work."*
>
> — *Gustave Flaubert*

According to Mason Currey's book Daily Rituals: How Artists Work, Gustave Flaubert began writing Madame Bovary shortly after he returned to his mother's house in Croisset, France. Then approaching his 30th birthday, it took Flaubert from September 1851 to June 1856 to submit his manuscript, nearly five years after he started.

This quote from Flaubert is profound, suggesting that maintaining a regular routine in life provides a stable foundation for the mind to unleash its full creative potential.

"Violence" could mean actual violence, like hurting or killing another person, but it could also mean the strength of an emotion or the intense passion that creativity demands.

THE TAKEAWAY: **Be regular in your life to create violently original work.**

NOVEMBER 29 — Can you snap to attention at a moment's notice?

334

Perhaps you were inspired by writers you read, and now you are a writer as well.

What does it mean to be a "writer" anyway? It's like asking, What does it mean to think?

People are full of ideas, but only a few will try to catch an idea, put it on paper, and show it to the world so other people can read them.

Validation is what you seek? Fame? Yes, it seems it is. It is what you seek. But the truth is, I can't think of anything else I'd rather be doing right now than reading or writing. Perhaps watching a movie, a show, or YouTube.

I used to be moody, obsessive, kind of a loner. Now I talk a lot more and I can't stop.

A man can be so many different men. He simply needs to don a different mask. The mask itself changes like day turns to night.

At first light there is peace. As the day goes on, the peace descends into madness. Dr. Jekyll becomes Mr. Hyde. A Zero becomes a Hero. A Wimp becomes a Vigilante.

We've seen, or perhaps have experienced, this sort of polar change. Maybe it's when you see an American black bear outside your Tony Soprano house.

THE TAKEAWAY: Can you snap to attention at a moment's notice?

NOVEMBER 30 — Build the future, don't predict it.

"The best way to predict the future is to invent it."

— Alan Kay, American computer scientist and winner of the A.M. Turing Award

It is easier, and more fun, to invent the future than to predict it.

Nobody knows the future. It is not your job to know the future. Your only job is this: to follow the guiding reason known as logos.

Logos is a word with many meanings.
1. From a Stoic perspective, logos refers to "God" or "the way things are."
2. To Aristotle, Logos is appealing to a person's logic, one of the three modes of persuasion along with ethos and pathos. An example of logos would be saying "According to the data, this method reduces errors by 60%."
3. In Christianity, Logos is used to describe Jesus as the Word of God: "In the beginning was the Word (Logos)…" (John 1:1), the idea of divine reason from Jesus Christ.

Marcus Aurelius wrote in his *Meditations*, "The person who follows reason in all things will have both leisure and a readiness to act—they are at once both cheerful and self-composed."

There is finite time to think today, as is the case every day. Wouldn't it be better to be cheerfully doing what you can to build a better future, rather than lose your composure stressing over a future that may not even happen?

THE TAKEAWAY: Build the future, don't predict it.

DECEMBER

DECEMBER 1 — Study your competitor's strengths and weaknesses.

"If you cannot measure it, you cannot improve it."
— Lord Kelvin

Benchmarking assumes that what one company does, another can do as well, if not better, in a competitive global market.

These top performers can be found inside the company, in a direct competitor, or organizations in another industry entirely.

In the Google User Experience (UX) Design Course, they call this a "competitive audit." This might look like interviews with users of a product, surveys, or focus groups to try and find user problems to solve with design principles.

Perhaps you are doing an audit of two pizza apps, direct competitors, comparing their visual layout, payment process, and delivery service, to see the pros and cons of both apps.

Then you could do an audit of indirect competitors, which have similar offerings for different audience, or different offerings for the same audience. Perhaps you are studying a Chinese food app, which has different offerings but the same audience of hungry people who are trying to decide between pizza or Chinese, or maybe even tacos (another possible audit).

Then you can gather your findings in a report, talk it over with your team, and brainstorm new ideas to improve your product and the overall customer experience.

THE TAKEAWAY: Study your competitor's strengths and weaknesses.

337   DECEMBER 2 — Time spent writing is more precious than money.

In Chanakya Neeti, *Chanakya writes, "A poor man desires for money. The animals desire power of speech, humans desire for heaven, and angels desire for Nirvana."*

There's nothing like remembering you will die *(memento mori)* to light a fire under your ass.

You might ask, "Where did all the time go?" Well, it went toward solving problems. You earned money, you bought stuff, you met people, you ate food, you did all sorts of things this past year.

On this day in 2021, the COVID-19 pandemic was raging. Thousands of people were still dying. There were insane news headlines about American politics. A random song started playing in your head from over 10 years ago.

In turbulent times like this, what helps me is writing down literally everything going on in my life, or in my head.

Once it is all on paper, it is easier to prioritize what I need to do for my job, my health, my family and friends, and any projects I am working on.

As Chanakya writes, animals desire for power of speech, which humans already have. The ability to write and use language to troubleshoot problems is a gift that should be used.

THE TAKEAWAY: **Time spent writing is more precious than money.**

DECEMBER 3 — Do simple things well.

> *"I understand there's a guy inside me who wants to lay in bed, smoke weed all day, and watch cartoons and old movies. My whole life is a series of stratagems to avoid, and outwit, that guy."*
>
> — Anthony Bourdain

Tragically, in June 2018, Bourdain was **found dead** in his hotel room, where he had hung himself. He was 61.

Bourdain was someone people wanted to be. To think someone so social, so adventurous, would do something like this was shocking.

In his book *Atomic Habits*, James Clear writes about how bad habits feed themselves. Anthony Bourdain says his life is a series of stratagems to outwit the guy in his head who wants to smoke weed and lay in bed watching TV. It only gets worse from there.

It is better to try and avoid tragedies like that, along with the slippery slopes leading up to them, by doing well at the opposite of everything "that guy" does. Simple things done well, like getting out of bed and waiting until the end of the workday to smoke weed and watch cartoons, can go a long way in improving performance.

THE TAKEAWAY: Do simple things well.

DECEMBER 4 — Take complete ownership of your life and choices.

"To be idle is a short road to death, and to be diligent is a way of life; foolish people are idle, wise people are diligent."

—Buddha

I used to hate leaving the comforts of home to go to school. But of course, a person cannot stay at home all the time.

Siddhartha Gautama's father shielded him with luxuries, making sure his son never knew pain or misery. But eventually, Siddhartha became curious and left the palace with his chariot driver. This is when Siddhartha sees old age, sickness, and death, ultimately becoming the ascetic known as The Buddha.

Even the most affluent, powerful, and influential people cannot defeat these forces of old age, sickness, and death. Life is surprisingly short, and it is important to be wise and diligent with it.

THE TAKEAWAY: **Take complete ownership of your life and choices.**

DECEMBER 5 — Watch old cowboy, gangster, and musical movies.

In the book *A Personal Journey With Martin Scorsese Through American Movies*, Scorsese talks about three genres of movies that American audiences would watch in theaters:
1. Western
2. Gangster
3. Musical

He cites three John Ford westerns in three decades, all starring John Wayne as the lead: *Stage Coach* (1939), *She Wore a Yellow Ribbon* (1949), and *The Searchers* (1956). John Wayne's cowboy characters grew darker over three decades to reflect an American psyche that was also growing darker.

DW Griffith is another director who came out of the literary tradition of Dickens, Tolstoy, and Whitman. With *Musketeers of Pig Alley* (1912) or the films of his disciple Raoul Walsh, these films dealt with outlaws and gangsters that the public sympathized with.

The western and gangster genres are very different genre from the musical. During the Great Depression, the musical became the most escapist of all film genres. With director Busby Berkeley, Scorsese says the genre came into its own. A former dance instructor, Berkeley was the first to realize that a movie musical was totally different from a staged musical. A staged musical is seen with two eyes, but on film everything is seen through one eye: the camera.

In designing his production numbers, Berkeley would rely on unusual camera movements and angles. The camera became a part of the choreography.

His ballets were pure cinema creations, pure entertainment. But sometimes he applied his wizardry to the grim realities of American life in the depression.

THE TAKEAWAY: Watch old cowboy, gangster, and musical movies.

DECEMBER 6 — Cultivate the inner king, warrior, magician, and lover.

King, Warrior, Magician, Lover is a bestselling Jungian psychology book that tries to redefine ancient concepts of masculinity.

They claim that masculinity is not abusive or domineering, but generative, creative, and empowering to the self and others.

This framework is also not limited to men; the Jungian concepts are universal and apply to any gender, but the authors believe that modern men in particular could benefit.

The *King* represents order, wisdom, and leadership. He represents a vision for the world and makes decisions for the greater good while maintaining balance and fairness. The *Warrior* is about strength, discipline, courage, and focus. The warrior is committed, persistent, and skilled at facing obstacles head on to achieve his goals, without losing control or becoming overly aggressive. The *Magician* is about knowledge, intuition, and insight. This archetype is about using wisdom and skills to solve problems and understand deeper truths about the universe. A person who thinks critically, enjoys learning and teaching, and finds hidden potential within themselves and others embodies the Magician archetype. The *Lover* is about passion, empathy, and sensuality. This man connects deeply with art, nature, and all forms of beauty found in life. A balanced Lover can nurture meaningful relationships and experience life in a rich and fulfilling way.

Every person has a bit of each archetype in them. Cultivating these archetypes through leading others, disciplined exercise, learning new things, or nurturing relationships are all good for personal growth.

THE TAKEAWAY: Cultivate the inner king, warrior, magician, and lover.

DECEMBER 7 — What is the operating system of an Apple store?

On the *Masters of Scale* podcast, Reid Hoffman and Angela Ahrendts talk about a couple of different programs that were created by Ahrendts when she was Retail Vice President at Apple.

They discuss the free in-store learning program **Today at Apple**. Ahrendts told Hoffman she would talk about how the store architecture was "hardware," and the human experience inside was "software."

Her question was, "What is the operating system of an Apple store?" If you go to **apple.com**, you get this incredible 2D experience and deep product knowledge. If you go into a store, she says, humans should have the most incredible 3D experience.

If you can buy it faster or cheaper online, what is the point of this box called a store?

Ahrendts told the teams that "you are the beating heart in your community," and managers are the "mayors" of their community. They had Teachers Tuesdays, where educators could come in and learn about great apps they could use in classrooms. They started building boardrooms in all the new stores so entrepreneurs had a place to gather and where Apple business leaders could teach entrepreneurs things they need to know.

So there are entrepreneurs in this store community, there are educators. And of course, there are adults and teenagers and kids.

Angela would even encourage adults by saying, "Instead of kids watching cartoons on Saturday mornings, bring them into the stores and do an hour of code."

THE TAKEAWAY: What is the operating system of an Apple store?

343 DECEMBER 8 — Avoid "Walter Mitty" syndrome.

I am reading the story *Walter Mitty*, written by James Thurber in 1939.

"Full strength in No. 3 turret!" shouted the Commander. "Full strength in No. 3 turret!" The crew, bending to their various tasks in the huge, hurtling eight-engined Navy hydroplane, looked at each other and grinned. "The Old Man'll get us through," they said to one another. "The Old Man ain't afraid of Hell!"

Not so fast! You're driving too fast!" said Mrs. Mitty. "What are you driving so fast for?"

This story of an ordinary, bored office worker diving into an adventure fantastical and heroic in nature, but I'm left guessing whether or not the narrator, Mitty, is describing fantasy or reality.

The eponymous hero of this story was adapted into a film once in 1947. However, it is the second adaptation with Ben Stiller in 2013, for me, that is more famous.

The word "Mittyesque" has entered the lexicon of American life since 1939. It refers to a person who spends more time in heroic daydreams than being present. Or a person who misleads others into believing they are someone other than who they are.

Reader, if this sounds like you, please stop day-dreaming heroics.

You are making a mess, crashing cars, and worst of all, not being present in your real life. You are missing all the beautiful things not asking for your attention.

You can be a hero today by simply taking out the trash. Or walking and talking with your family or friends.

THE TAKEAWAY: **Avoid "Walter Mitty" syndrome.**

DECEMBER 9 — Capitalize on your knowledge work.

Signed into law by President Franklin D. Roosevelt in 1944, the Servicemen's Readjustment Act, also called the GI Bill, gave every returning war veteran the right to attend college with the government paying the bill, along with housing and unemployment insurance.

This was an unprecedented development. It soon became clear to Peter Drucker that "knowledge workers" now exist in the society that was coming out of WWII.

By the late 1950s, Drucker had coined the term "knowledge worker" and noted that when people do work they are good at, and which fits their abilities, they can have more career success and bring more value to their customers and organization.

Many of the jobs considered "knowledge workers," such as teachers or pharmacists, existed far before Drucker coined the term.

But other jobs that emerged out of the information age, such as computer programmer or IT consultant or cybersecurity analyst, are jobs that are attainable to people who did not go to college but who are self-taught or who completed tech bootcamps such as Per Scholas.

THE TAKEAWAY: Capitalize on your knowledge work.

345 DECEMBER 10 — Get the words right. Leverage language in leadership.

At a company town hall, the leadership team asked, "what words do you never want to hear again at Per Scholas?" The word that came up the most was "overlooked," but other words people never wanted to hear again were "poverty" or "underserved" or "low income."

Per Scholas' old boilerplate:
For over 25 years, Per Scholas has prepared **motivated and curious adults** who are **unemployed or underemployed** with the technical and business skills to launch successful careers in technology, creating **onramps to businesses** in need of their talents.

Per Scholas' new boilerplate:
For over 25 years, Per Scholas has **advanced economic mobility** through **rigorous training and professional development tailored for tech**, then connecting our diverse and skilled alumni to leading businesses. With campuses in 14 cities and over 12,000 individuals already trained and placed, Per Scholas looks forward to another 25 years of building bridges for companies, ranging from innovative startups, to various Fortune 500 firms.

Why the change?

The organization noticed the disproportionate impact the COVID-19 pandemic had on the lives and livelihoods of communities of color. At the same time, a shocking wave of police brutality against Black populations added a renewed sense of urgency for building an anti-racist world.

We must engage more thoughtfully in the words we use to describe ourselves, frame our communities, and describe the world.

THE TAKEAWAY: **Get the words right. Leverage language in leadership.**

DECEMBER 11 — How many "negative costs" to get to "negative cost?"

On this date, about a year into the pandemic, I listened to the *ScriptNotes* podcast, focusing on the topic "How Movie Money Works."

John August, the screenwriter and host, explained that every movie is considered a "venture," with its own profit and loss. For example, *The Hangover 2* is its own venture, meant to produce a movie called *The Hangover 2*, and all accounting for this movie exists in this bubble for this one movie.

There is money in the venture to make the movie, to market the movie, and sell the movie.

Say you are making a film about a book, so you buy the rights to the book, then hire a writer to adapt the book into a script. Say it is $100,000 for rights, and the same cost for adaptation, that is $200,000 out of the budget.

Then there are the producers and the director. Then there are the actors. Additional salaries. This is all "above the line" cost. Rights to material, writer, producer, director, and actors. "Below the line" costs include the cinematographers, editors, technicians—the technical costs of making it.

When you add both above and below the line, you get the "negative cost" of the film.

> **THE TAKEAWAY: For any venture, consider your "negative costs."**

DECEMBER 12 — Steal from the best like Billy Wilder.

In the book *Conversations With Wilder* by Cameron Crowe, Billy Wilder reveals a secret from the Marx Brothers.

What was the secret? The brothers tried out all their comedy bits in the theater before doing them on film. Wilder also cites the producer Irving Thalberg, who would give the Marx Brothers three routines to do, and then send them on a tour of live vaudeville acts all around the vaudeville places of America before doing movies like *A Day at the Races* (1937) or *A Night at the Opera* (1935).

Thalberg tested the laughs. Was the joke a 10, or a 3?

Wilder tells Crowe that Thalberg even timed the bits with a clock. Wilder later said that he stole that timing method for movies he did, such as *Some Like It Hot* (1959). This way, no jokes got lost or laughed over by the audience.

In silent pictures, of course, that is different. For stars like Charlie Chaplin and Buster Keaton, the more laughs they got, the better.

THE TAKEAWAY: **Steal from the best like Billy Wilder.**

DECEMBER 13 — Have fun while making a movie with your friends.

Around this time in 2017, some friends and I produced a short film, *Our Nightly Fling*, I learned at least five lessons when serving as producer of this student film, which is now on **YouTube**.

1. Do or delegate tasks to enable the writer, director, cast, and crew deliver their best work.
2. Work backwards from the envisioned final edit and explain that well. Storyboards help.
3. Getting extras can be hard: people have class, jobs, family, or other schedule conflicts.
4. Be friendly and clear about what needs to be executed at that moment on set.
5. Above all, have fun. Making student films is about learning and building relationships.

THE TAKEAWAY: Have fun while making a movie with your friends.

349

DECEMBER 14 — Relate the concept of reincarnation to online life.

The term *avatar* is usually used to refer to the 10 avatars of Vishnu, a Hindu deity who is the preserver and protector of the universe.

1. Matsya (Fish)
2. Kurma (Turtle)
3. Varaha (Boar)
4. Narasimha (Man-Lion)
5. Vamana (Dwarf)
6. Parashurama (Warrior)
7. Rama (Valmiki's Ramayana)
8. Krishna (Mahabharata)
9. Buddha (formerly Siddhartha Gautama)
10. Kalki (warrior on white horse)

Every time you create a new account or digital profile, you sort of "reincarnate." You could portray the same person across multiple platforms or embrace your different alter egos.

It can be an invigorating process, feeling like you are reborn as a different person.

THE TAKEAWAY: **Relate the concept of reincarnation to online life.**

DECEMBER 15 — Eliminate all the wrong answers to find the right one.

On July 20, 1996, Charlie Munger gave an informal talk titled "Practical Thought on Practical Thought."

He described five helpful notions for solving problems on the way to turning $2 million into $2 trillion.

- First notion, Munger says, is to simplify problems by deciding big "no-brainer" questions.
- Second, he cites Galileo: Scientific reality is revealed by math, the language of God. Walt Disney similarly cited Galileo.
- Third, work through the problem forward and also backwards. One example he gives is from his time as a weather forecaster in the Air Corps, making weather forecasts for pilots. In that job, instead of thinking about how to save pilots, he thought about how to kill pilots and avoided fatal hazards, such as ice that the plane can't handle, or running out of gas before landing.
- Fourth is to use the best and most practical wisdom from the university freshman course in every academic subject. Problem solving in "a multidisciplinary manner."
- Fifth is the amazing "lollapalooza" effect, which comes from a fortuitous combination of factors.

I use **the OSI model** at Per Scholas, a common thought model in network troubleshooting. Munger might appreciate that Layer 8 (The Human Layer) is where most problems are.

I have more trouble teaching humans troubleshooting than I do the technology. Understanding technology is easy. What is hard is getting adults to work together and troubleshoot methodically with confidence, eliminating wrong answers until finding the right one.

THE TAKEAWAY: Eliminate all the wrong answers to find the right one.

351 — DECEMBER 16 — Dump everything on the page, then edit it down.

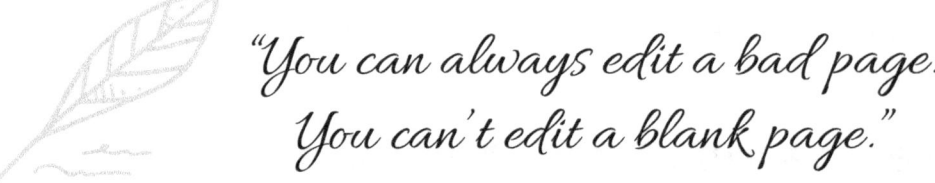

"You can always edit a bad page. You can't edit a blank page."

— Jodi Picoult

Troubleshooting Life was born this day in the pages of my digital diary.

I went to college, worked in a dying legacy media industry being disrupted by digital technology, and eventually got humbled enough to change careers and enroll in Per Scholas. I have since helped hundreds of others do the same at Per Scholas throughout my mid-20s.

Those hard times lead me to keep a journal so I could process my thoughts and feelings.

Dumping everything on a page helped me find my "reasoned choice," or *prohairesis* as the Greeks would say.

I thought I was a loser whose best work was behind him. But I was wrong! Somehow, in the hundreds of pages of my diary and notes, I found bits and pieces of writing that I thought could be helpful to others.

THE TAKEAWAY: Dump everything on the page, then edit it down.

DECEMBER 17 — Build the future like Jason Kilar of Hulu.

In his TED Talk How to Build the Future in Four Steps, Jason Kilar shares his love of the TV show *Speed Racer*.

Throughout his childhood and college, he asked deep burning questions about TV:
- Where did TV come from?
- Who are the people making TV?
- How do TV business models work?

Young Jason got to his bus stop at 3:34 pm. Then he would sprint home, but not arrive until 3:38 pm. *Speed Racer* started at 3:30pm, so he always missed the beginning. Big negative!

If a tenured television executive had to solve this problem, Kilar asserts they might try launching a 24-hour *Speed Racer* channel. Every half-hour they would play another episode, so if you miss the 3:30, show you wouldn't have to worry. You could watch again in a few hours.

But what if the executives ignored everything they knew and instead figured out a way for people to watch any show "on demand?"

That's what Jason Kilar and the "Hulugans" did. They leveraged this new technology, the Internet, to stream movies and TV. Michael Arrington had a blog called *TechCrunch*, a "bible" in Silicon Valley, and they said Hulu was absolutely insane. Jason remembers another blogger, Om Malik, created the Hulu Deathwatch, and every day he would put another day until Hulu crashed and failed.

When you try to do something that nobody has done before, it is natural to think it won't work.

THE TAKEAWAY: Build the future like Jason Kilar of Hulu.

353

DECEMBER 18 — Bad news sells faster than good news.

In 1925, Kentucky cave explorer Floyd Collins got trapped underground in Sand Cave when trying to search for new caverns. Eventually, neighbors began to worry, and then word got out around the entire country that this man was stuck.

One reporter, William Burke Miller, even camped out at the site and provided daily updates on Collins. This became sensational journalism that eventually won Miller a Pulitzer Prize.

This story became the basis of the 1951 movie *Ace in the Hole*, directed by Billy Wilder. Kirk Douglas plays Chuck Tatum, a once-famous New York reporter turned has-been who is plotting his return to greatness.

> **When he learns of a man trapped in a Native American cave dwelling, Chuck milks the story over time, to the point that more media and more people arrive at the cave entrance, creating a giant media circus.**

Bad news circulates far faster in the digital age than it did in 1925 or 1951 due to technological changes, but what did not change is people being wired to pay attention to potential threats or negative events. Scandal, disaster, and crime generally dominate the headlines for this reason, rather than positive stories. As people in news often say, "If it bleeds, it leads."

In 2017, *Ace in the Hole* was inducted into the American National Film Registry, and it is well worth a watch (or rewatch).

THE TAKEAWAY: Bad news sells faster than good news.

DECEMBER 19 — Prepare your next generation of leaders.

DuPont was controlled and managed by family for 170 years since its founding in 1802, until professional management took over in the mid-1970s.

Mayer Amschel Rothschild was an obscure coin dealer who began sending out his five sons to establish banks in Europe's capitals. Today, financial firms bearing the Rothschild name, run by Rothschilds, still do business.

In July 2023, **the Rothschild Family take-private plan of a Paris listed investment bank was executed.** French President Emmanuel Macron used to work at a Rothschild deal-making division before politics.

It's remarkable to see family-run businesses last so long. Less than 30 percent of family-owned companies make it to the second generation, and only 10 percent make it to the third. Some speculation as to why that is:
- Lack of proper succession planning.
- Conflicting family dynamics.
- Emotional decision-making.
- Poor estate planning and tax issues.
- Lack of vision after founding family members pass away.

With clear planning, professional development for future leaders, and conflict resolution strategies, family businesses can increase their chances of thriving across generations.

People do dream of handing off their empire to their kids, or proteges, when they approach retirement. This is about going a step beyond that: making sure the next generation can *thrive* by learning how other companies or empires withstood the tests of time and succession.

THE TAKEAWAY: Prepare your next generation of leaders.

355

DECEMBER 20 — Wear your metaphorical and literal seatbelt.

This day last year, I randomly remembered former New Jersey Governor **Jon Corzine** when he gave a "I Should Be Dead" public service announcement in April 2007. This was after Corzine was seriously injured in a high-speed auto accident while not wearing his seatbelt.

Funny how memory works. I must have been putting on a seatbelt. Suddenly, I remembered his face and voice on TV.

This is from *The New York Times* the day after that happened:

"After delivering a speech to the New Jersey Conference of Mayors at the Trump Taj Mahal casino in Atlantic City, Mr. Corzine was on his way to Drumthwacket, the governor's mansion in Princeton, for a meeting between the Rutgers women's basketball team and Don Imus, the talk-show host who was fired on Thursday for making a racist and sexist remark about the players."

As a child I knew to put on my seatbelt. Adults tell kids to do so. And yet, the governor of my state ignored the practice and almost died.

First a room of mayors, then off to the governor's mansion for a media-heavy meeting. Governor Corzine was in motion, in power, then in critical condition. It's a reminder that even on our busiest days, we are still flesh and blood who need to practice safety in cars.

THE TAKEAWAY: **The spotlight won't save you.**

DECEMBER 21 — Let go of the dreams rendered obsolete.

Imagine aspiring to be a silent film star right when "talkies" came out, redefining cinema and forcing an entire industry to now include *sound*, not just moving pictures.

Or imagine wanting to have a hit song on the radio, but there's this new thing called Spotify that everyone uses for music instead of the radio, and so now you want to be a hit on Spotify.

Not to mention your own personal growth from child to adult! To quote *Mad Men's* Marie Calvet, "Not every little girl gets to do what they want. The world cannot support that many ballerinas."

It is a bit scary, but it is very common for new technology and aging to rapidly transform dreams.

But the goal is the same: To keep moving forward and adapt to times that are in constant flux.

THE TAKEAWAY: Let go of the dreams rendered obsolete.

357 DECEMBER 22 — Create media that destroys minstrelsy.

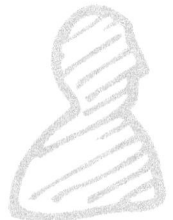

"When American people want something, they want it now... Who could ever forget those lovable pet rocks, beanie babies, Pokémon? Now the latest, hottest, newest sensation across the nation was blackface!"

— Pierre Delacroix in *Bamboozled* (2000) (Spike Lee)

While I was at Temple for film school, I learned what minstrelsy was. Our teacher screened and discussed Spike Lee's *Bamboozled*.

"Minstrelsy" means American minstrel shows, which feature songs, dances, and comedy routines based on African American stereotypes, typically by white actors with blackface.

In 2017, Hari Kondabolu interviewed many South Asians in *The Problem With Apu*. Apu is South Asian, but it is **also minstrelsy**. As Whoopi Goldberg said, "He has all the qualifications."

Minstrelsy has a long, painful legacy, and Delacroix (Damon Wayans) *knows* that making something this blatantly offensive *should* get him fired. But the network gives him a 12-episode order, and the show becomes an ironic hit. The TV executives, of many races and backgrounds, bamboozle themselves into making this show in the quest for high TV ratings.

That is the irony with satire: You could glamorize the very thing you satirize, and now everyone is in blackface because it becomes as popular as Pokémon.

Spike Lee said Elia Kazan's *A Face in the Crowd* (1957) was a direct inspiration for this movie. With the right creative talent, a similar story could get made yet again.

THE TAKEAWAY: **Create media that destroys minstrelsy.**

DECEMBER 23 — Question the narratives you are taught to believe.

In high school, I took AP US History and scored a 4 on the AP test, which means I earned college credit. But I felt like the version of history I put effort into learning was sanitized. Of course, I could not blame my teacher for this—it was the curriculum.

One day, I found the book *Lies My Teacher Told Me*, in which the historian James W. Loewen examines 12 American high school history textbooks. He concludes that the textbook authors propagate Eurocentric, mythologized views of American history. Loewen's work confirmed my suspicion that history is often shaped to fit the interests of those in power.

Loewen told NPR that his first full-time teaching job was at the HBCU Tougaloo College in Mississippi, a class of 17 students. Sixteen of those said that Reconstruction was the period after the Civil War when blacks took over the government of the Southern states, but they were too soon out of slavery and screwed up, and white folks had to take control again.

Loewen identified at least three lies in that response and got interested in the idea that history was a weapon being used against students.

As George Orwell wrote in 1944, "History is written by the winners." Those in power not only influence the present and the future, but the way society perceives the past.

THE TAKEAWAY: Question the narratives you are taught to believe.

DECEMBER 24 — Embrace individuality, which is not entirely your own.

> *"We might acknowledge that our individuality, which we so, so revere, is not entirely our own."*
>
> — Anthony Hopkins as John Quincy Adams, quote from Amistad, 1997

Americans deeply believe in individualism, and that "the good society" is one in which individuals are free to pursue their private goals independently of others. But as the Spielberg movie *Amistad* alludes to, individuality is not shaped entirely by you. It is shaped by factors beyond your control, like your personal history, society, culture, and other people with whom you associate.

We are not as independent in shaping ourselves as we might think.

External events, such as the COVID pandemic, or being captured and sold into slavery, as depicted in *Amistad*, shape your personality and behavior in unexpected ways. You might be an American citizen and pledge allegiance to the United States, but your parents are from another country, and so you feel allegiance to your ancestral home country as well. Or you live in a big city now, but you still miss your hometown in another US state.

You exist in this place between your inner self, and the world outside of you, both of which shape each other.

THE TAKEAWAY: Embrace individuality, which is not entirely your own.

DECEMBER 25 — Do not flinch in the face of the story you are telling.

360

The Searchers (1956), directed by John Ford for Warner Bros., has a **famous "doorway shot."**

The Huffington Post writes how simple this concept is: frame your subject in the middle of a doorway. In fact, simply searching for "doorway shot" on the Internet results in hundreds of pictures of John Wayne from the film.

For 1970s American filmmakers such as George Lucas or Martin Scorsese, *The Searchers* was an important touchstone. There are specific shots in *Star Wars*, or plot lines in *Taxi Driver*, that stem from *The Searchers* and pay homage to this film.

John Wayne plays Ethan Edwards, a middle-aged Confederate Civil War veteran, who spends years looking for his niece, played by Natalie Wood, who was abducted by Comanches. His relentless pursuit is a strong depiction of obsession and morality.

In 2013, Vince Gilligan said the *Breaking Bad* finale, widely considered the greatest TV finale of all time, was also inspired by *The Searchers*.

None of those storytellers flinched in the face of the narratives they had in front of them, even if they were dealing with complex characters with questionable morals.

THE TAKEAWAY: **Do not flinch in the face of the story you are telling.**

361

DECEMBER 26 — Focus on simple living, not penance living.

"Philosophy calls for simple living, not for doing penance, and the simple way of life need not be a crude one."

— Letters From a Stoic, Seneca

Philosophy may demand a simple living, not necessarily a penance living.

There might be some philosophies or religions that say you must have an ascetic life of study, fasting, manual labor, and prayer, and avoid indulging in things such as sex, drugs, or junk food.

Stoicism is not about this ascetic lifestyle of penance living. Instead, it is about "everything in moderation." It is better to live life in a disciplined way, in a home with items that fulfill their function, and not in a home full of meaningless luxuries.

People who live a life to get more decorations are never satisfied. They never find "enough."

In a modern world, full of internet connected devices such as smartphones, TVs, computers, and gaming consoles, it is popular to own these items. If you can afford them, why not buy them?

But then, you run the risk of using these devices so much, you no longer have control of yourself. This is no good.

People can admire or be impressed with you or your way of life, but they should not be impressed by your furniture. A great person can treat their ceramic plate like a priceless iPhone, but a great person can also treat their priceless iPhone like a ceramic plate. They are in control without the object controlling them.

THE TAKEAWAY: Focus on simple living, not penance living.

DECEMBER 27 — Focus on upward spirals, not downward spirals.

James Clear, in his book *How to Start New Habits*, points out how you do not crave smoking a cigarette, but the relief it provides.

You are not motivated by brushing your teeth, but by the feeling of a clean mouth. You do not want to turn on the television, but you crave information, or entertainment. Every craving is linked to a desire to change your internal state.

In theory, any bit of information could trigger either craving or repulsion.

For a smoker, the sight or smell of cigarettes cause cravings. For a nonsmoker, cigarettes are repulsive. The cue of cigarettes is meaningless, until it is interpreted by the senses.

Imagine a nonsmoker sees a smoker. They may think the smoker is nowhere close to quitting. But what if quitting was never the goal? Maybe the smoker set a goal to smoke and does not care what nonsmokers think.

One person sees a downward spiral. Another sees an upward spiral. The same goes for video games—it depends on how you look at it. The point is, whether people brand your goals healthy or unhealthy, focus on achieving them.

> THE TAKEAWAY: **Focus on upward spirals, not downward spirals.**

DECEMBER 28 — Follow these rules for successful alliances.

"In the long history of humankind (and animal kind, too) those who learned to collaborate and improvise most effectively have prevailed."

— Charles Darwin

It is so important to be adaptable and collaborate to survive and succeed, in the human workplace or in the animal kingdom.

All parties need to think through their objectives, and the objectives of the "child" partnership. All parties agree in advance on how the joint enterprise should be run, and they thought through carefully about who will manage the alliance.

Each party internally manages the relationship of the joint enterprise, and in a large firm, these "dangerous" liaisons should be handled by one senior executive.

Of course, every partnership has disagreements, and there should be a third party who all sides know and respect and whose verdict can be taken as final by all when the parties are arguing.

Above all, avoid getting into alliances out of envy, because those often end in tragedy.

THE TAKEAWAY: **Follow these rules for successful alliances.**

DECEMBER 29 — Prepare for the "heaven interview" after your death.

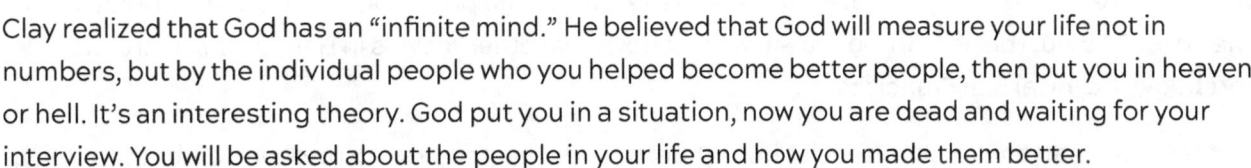

Professor Clayton Christensen developed many theories at Harvard Business School.

Such as jobs-to-be-done, or how God does not employ accountants.

The *Wall Street Journal* published an article about how Clay "turned his life into a case study."

Clay realized that God has an "infinite mind." He believed that God will measure your life not in numbers, but by the individual people who you helped become better people, then put you in heaven or hell. It's an interesting theory. God put you in a situation, now you are dead and waiting for your interview. You will be asked about the people in your life and how you made them better.

This was a driving insight for Professor Christensen. In his lifetime he knew people who celebrated great jobs at McKinsey or Goldman Sachs or other iconic companies.

Reunion after reunion, they would come back to Harvard and celebrate. But by the tenth reunion, some were not coming back.

In *How Will You Measure Your Life?* he writes, "Behind the facade of professional success, there were numerous stories of divorces or unhappy marriages… one classmate hadn't talked to his children in years. Another was on her third marriage."

Death is an assignment of life, but no one knows the due date. Your interview as to whether you go to heaven or not could be tomorrow, or in 50 years.

Whenever it is, did you prepare for the interview by helping people become better?

THE TAKEAWAY: Prepare for the "heaven interview" after your death.

DECEMBER 30 — Put your money where your mouth is.

In 1941, Warner Bros released *The Maltese Falcon*.

This was the studio's third attempt with the Dashiell Hammett novel, after *Dangerous Female (1931)* and *Satan Met a Lady (1936)*.

The Huston-Bogart version in 1941 was the best iteration. I recommend it, even in 2023. Hammett's character, Sam Spade, was who he and other detectives he knew aspired to be like: "hardboiled," born to solve murders, bag femme fatales, and talk tough. The protagonist survives to the end of the novel. The Huston-Bogart portrayal overshadows two other movies in Hammett's distrustful, foreboding, cynical San Francisco.

Fun fact: Manhattan Project physicist Robert Serber, who helped develop atomic bomb technology, was also a fan of Dashiell Hammett. He dubbed one bomb "Thin Man" for a Hammett protagonist, a second bomb "Fat Man," from *The Maltese Falcon*, and a third "Little Boy," as world-weary Sam Spade calls a hoodlum.

Considering the *Oppenheimer* and *Barbie* memes that circulated in 2023, this fact is even more fun.

One of my favorite lines in the Dashiell Hammett book is said by Gutman to Spade after shortchanging Spade: "With a dollar of this you can buy more than with 10 dollars of talk," which feels like a more cynical take on "put your money where your mouth is."

The same rings true of people today: their mouths speak of values and priorities, but it's actually their spending habits that reveal more truth about their values.

THE TAKEAWAY: Put your money where your mouth is.

DECEMBER 31 — You are a human "being," not a human "doing."

High-achieving, ambitious people often overwork themselves and sacrifice their happiness.

In Chapter 6 of his memoir *Who Is Michael Ovitz?* the author recalls getting advice from Ted Ashley, chairman of the Warner Bros. film studio from 1969 to 1980.

Ted said that Michael could have worked 10 percent less, and it wouldn't have made a difference. But Michael would have been a whole lot happier.

Ted knew the workaholic agent would most likely not take the advice, but it is solid nonetheless!

Humans have finite life spans to solve problems such as:
- Getting yourself and your family out of poverty.
- Nurturing meaningful relationships.
- Overcoming boredom.

As this year "dies," and a new year is "born," tell Death in private about your choices.

Perhaps you need to make the choice to relax. Relaxing even 10 percent can make a difference to your happiness.

> **THE TAKEAWAY: You are a human "being," not a human "doing."**

About the Author

Akash Malik is a writer, educator, and media storyteller who helps people troubleshoot their lives through tech, creativity, and timeless wisdom. A graduate of Temple University with a degree in Film and Media Arts, he has worked across classrooms, startups, movie sets, editing bays and soundstages. He currently manages a team of technology instructors at Per Scholas, a nonprofit founded in 1995 that has over 30,000 alumni at all levels of business. Born in the 1990s and raised in New Jersey, Akash writes with the heart of a teacher, the eye of a filmmaker, and the mind of a modern philosopher. *Troubleshooting Life* is his debut book: part diary, part playbook, and part daily reboot.